EMP

Law

Colin Thomas, LLB(Hons.), Dip. Ed., is a Barrister and Senior Lecturer in Law at Wolverhampton Polytechnic. He specialises in company law and employment law, and is the author of *Company Law*, also published in the Teach Yourself series.

TEACH YOURSELF

EMPLOYMENT

Law

Colin Thomas

Hodder & Stoughton

LONDON SYDNEY AUCKLAND

To Charlotte

British Library Cataloguing in Publication Data
Thomas, Colin
  Teach yourself employment law. – 2nd ed.
  I. Title
  344.42

  ISBN 0-340-55939-X

First published 1984
Second edition 1992
Second impression 1993

Typeset in Linotron Century Old Style by
Rowland Phototypesetting Ltd, Bury St Edmunds, Suffolk.
Printed in Great Britain for the educational publishing
division of Hodder & Stoughton Ltd, Mill Road, Dunton Green,
Sevenoaks, Kent by Clays Ltd, St Ives plc.

—— CONTENTS ——

Abbreviations

EA 1988	Employment Act 1988
EA 1989	Employment Act 1989
EA 1990	Employment Act 1990
EPA 1975	Employment Protection Act 1975
EPCA	Employment Protection (Consolidation) Act 1978
HSWA	Health and Safety at Work Act 1974
RRA	Race Relations Act 1976
SDA	Sex Discrimination Act 1975
SSA	Social Security Act 1975
TUA 1984	Trade Union Act 1984
TULRA	Trade Union and Labour Relations Act 1974
EAT	Employment Appeal Tribunal

PREFACE

This book provides an outline of the basic rights and duties of the parties to a contract of employment. As such, it will appeal to students, trade unionists, personnel managers, and anyone concerned with the fields of employment and industrial relations.

All information contained in this book is believed to have been correct at the time of going to press. The main difficulty in writing the book was in deciding which cases to include from the ever-changing mass of case law decided by the courts and tribunals. Employment law has changed significantly since the publication of the previous edition. New legislation has been passed, important cases and issues have been decided and there has been the significant influence of decisions of the European Court of Justice.

References in the text to male employees apply equally to female employees, with a few specified exceptions.

Colin Thomas
1992

1

THE CONTRACT OF EMPLOYMENT

Employment legislation has, in the last two decades, dealt comprehensively with the rights and obligations of the parties to contracts of employment. Employees' rights have been the subject of a number of Acts, and the Employment Protection (Consolidation) Act 1978 consolidates 'certain enactments relating to the rights of employees arising out of their employment'.

It is therefore important to determine whether a person is an employee for the following reasons:

1 only employees and apprentices are entitled to the various benefits conferred by the EPCA, for example, redundancy payments, compensation for unfair dismissal, and so on;
2 there are different rates of national insurance contributions for employees and for self-employed persons. The benefits also differ: for example, self-employed persons are not entitled to industrial injury or unemployment benefits;
3 income tax is generally deducted from an employee's wages under the PAYE system. Self-employed persons are subject to direct tax assessments under a different schedule of the Income Tax Acts;
4 an employer owes a greater duty of care to his employee than to other individuals. Although he owes a common duty of care (under

the Occupiers Liability Act) to any visitor who enters his property, he owes a particular duty under both the common law and the Health and Safety at Work Act to provide for the safety and welfare of his employees;

5 an employer is vicariously liable for the torts (civil wrongs) committed by his employees in the course of employment;

6 there are various obligations owed by the employer to the employees, and vice versa, which do not arise unless there is a contract of employment. These rights and obligations are dealt with in detail in Chapters 3 and 4.

Although various Acts refer to the contract of employment, they do not attempt to define such a contract. The courts have therefore formulated various tests and guidelines to determine whether a contract of employment (otherwise known as a *contract of service*) exists in a given situation.

As Lord Denning once remarked: 'It is often easy to recognise a *contract of service* when you see it, but difficult to say wherein the difference lies'.

There are other contractual relationships in which one party renders service to another which are not contracts of service. The most common example is that of a person who enters into a contract with another to undertake a specific task, e.g. if I ask an electrician to fit an additional power socket in my garage. A contract comes into existence, but it is a *contract for services*, as opposed to *a contract of service*. The electrician is an independent contractor, and I am not his employer.

Webster J. in *WHPT Association v. Social Services Secretary* observed that '. . . the difference between a contract of service and one for services must reside, essentially, in the terms of the principal obligation agreed to be undertaken by the employee . . . In a contract of service, it seems to me, the principal obligation undertaken by the employee is to provide himself to serve: whereas in a contract for services the principal obligation is not to provide himself to serve the employer, but his services for the use of the employer'.

- Tests to determine employee status -

Three tests have been formulated by the courts, namely:

1 the control test;
2 the organisation test;
3 the multiple test.

1 Control test

Over a century ago, Bramwell B. stated that 'a servant is a person subject to the command of his master as to the manner in which he shall do his work'.

The essence of the control test is an employer's right to control what an employee does, how he does it, and when and where the work should be done. An employer thus exercises control over the nature of the work, the manner of its performance, and the time and place of accomplishment, i.e. he can exercise much greater control over an employee than he can over an independent contractor.

In *Short v. Henderson*, it was stated that there are four indicia of a contract of service:

(a) the employer's power of selection of his employee;
(b) the payment of wages or other remuneration;
(c) the employer's right to control the method of doing the work;
(d) the employer's right of suspension or dismissal.

The operation of the test can be shown in its application in the following case. In *Midland Sinfonia Concert Society Ltd v. Secretary of State for Social Services*, the Society engaged musicians to play in its orchestra by invitation at irregular intervals. The musicians were paid solely in respect of the occasions when they played, and income tax was not deducted from these payments. It was held that the company's control over the musicians was minimal, in that they assembled as an orchestra to fulfil an engagement and the control exercised by the conductor during the performance of a concert was a fundamental part of orchestral playing. There was no control which could amount to control of the musicians as to the manner in which they carried out their work. They were therefore not employees of the Society.

— 5 —

The control test, although still of importance, has become an unreliable, exclusive test in an ever-changing industrial society. It is unsatisfactory in cases where the traditional test of employer's control cannot be applied: for example, a captain of an aircraft or a hospital doctor.

Other tests have therefore been formulated, as it is now accepted that the degree of control exercised by an employer is no longer the decisive factor in determining the existence of a contract of employment.

2   Organisational or integration test

This test was formulated in response to the limitations of the control test. Lord Denning in his Hamlyn Lectures stated 'I would observe the test of being a servant does not rest nowadays on submission to orders. It depends on whether the person is part and parcel of the organisation.'

In *Cassidy v. Ministry of Health*, a patient sued a hospital for post-operative negligence as a result of which he lost the use of his hand. It was held that the hospital authorities were liable, despite the fact that they were unable to exercise real control over the work performed by those doctors who were employed by them, as the patient had entrusted himself to the care of an organisation.

In *Morren v. Swinton and Pendlebury Borough Council*, a local authority engaged a resident engineer to supervise the construction of a sewage works. He worked under the instructions of a consultant engineer, who was retained by the authority. The local authority paid his salary, national insurance contributions, holiday pay and subsistence allowances. They also reserved the right to dismiss him. It was held that he was an employee as there was a sufficient degree of integration into the organisation, despite the absence of control as to the manner in which he carried out his work.

The organisation test has not received widespread support, partly due to the difficulty in defining 'integration' and 'organisation'. The practice of treating a single test as conclusive has largely been abandoned and has led to the development of the multiple test.

3   Multiple test

This test examines the economic reality and the totality of a relationship before arriving at a conclusion. In *Ready Mixed Concrete (South East) Ltd v. Minister of Pensions and National Insurance*, McKenna J. stated that he considered that a contract of service existed if the following three conditions were fulfilled:

(a)   the servant agrees that in consideration of a wage or other remuneration he will provide his own work and skill in the performance of some service for his master;
(b)   he agrees, expressly or implicitly, that in the performance of that service he will be subject to the other's control in a sufficient degree to make that other master (control includes the power of deciding the thing to be done, the way in which it shall be done, the means to be employed in doing it, the time when, and the place where it shall be done);
(c)   the other provisions of the contract are consistent with it being a contract of service.

The first two conditions listed are self-explanatory. The third allows the courts a degree of latitude to balance each factor and arrive at a conclusion based on all the terms of the contract.

In the *Ready Mixed Concrete* case above, the driver of a ready-mixed concrete lorry bought the lorry on hire purchase by arrangement with the company. He was required to wear the company's livery, obey reasonable orders from the company's servants, maintain the lorry, and use it solely for the company's business. He was paid a mileage rate for work undertaken for the company. He could appoint and pay a substitute driver so that he was not required to drive the lorry in person. The court held that he was not an employee as he operated the vehicle at his own risk, having to meet the expenses and depend upon the mileage rate paid by the company for his livelihood.

The operation of this test can best be illustrated by the following cases. In *Ferguson v. John Dawson Ltd*, a builder's labourer worked on the 'lump' i.e. according to a practice in the building industry where a contractor is paid a lump sum to provide labour to complete a job. Such workers are regarded as self-employed. John Dawson Ltd did not make any deductions from Ferguson's pay in respect of income tax or national insurance contributions, and until Ferguson was injured the parties regarded the plaintiff's status as that of an independent contractor. Ferguson was injured as a result of John Dawson Ltd's failure to provide a guard rail on a flat roof, and was entitled to damages if he could prove that his status was that of an employee. The court held that, despite the label put on the contract by the parties, 'in reality the contract . . . was a contract of service', as John Dawson Ltd's agent was responsible for 'hiring and firing,' moving the workforce from site to site, providing the necessary tools and telling the workmen what particular work they were to do. Ferguson was entitled to damages of £30,000.

In *Massey v. Crown Life Insurance Company*, the plaintiff attempted to claim for unfair dismissal, after electing to become self-employed. Although his duties as a branch manager remained unchanged, he was taxed under Schedule D and paid his own national insurance contributions. It was held that he was self-employed as he had acted on the advice of his accountant and of his own volition. All the indicia were evenly balanced, and as he had elected to become self-employed, he was not entitled to bring a claim for unfair dismissal as he was no longer an employee.

However, in *Davies v. New England College of Arundel*, a professional freelance lecturer was held to be employed under a contract of service, despite the parties' agreement that he should be regarded as self-employed. The reality of the situation was that his employment was clearly under the control of the defendants as his contract was similar to those of the other members of staff who were employed by the defendants. He was therefore entitled to bring a claim for unfair dismissal.

In *Hitchcock v. Post Office*, a sub-postmaster contended that he was a Post Office employee, as the Post Office exercised a degree of control over Post Office business. It was held that, as Hitchcock provided premises and part of the equipment at his own expense and also engaged employees, he was carrying on business on his own account, i.e. he was incurring the chance of profit or loss. Therefore he was held to be self-employed.

However, in *Edwards v. Post Office*, it was held that the sub-postmaster was an employee, for although he owned the premises and some equipment and was able to delegate some of his duties, the Post Office exercised a high degree of control. The sub-post office was not part of a shop; he was paid monthly after the deduction of tax and national insurance and he was responsible for the control of postmen who were post office employees.

Mutuality of obligations between parties is a key fact in determining the status of casual or home workers. If an employer is obliged to provide work and a worker is obliged to take the work offered there is a strong presumption of employee status. In *O'Kelly v. Trusthouse Forte plc*, wine butlers in a large hotel were known as 'regular casuals' and were given preference in work rotas over other casual staff. It was held that they were not employees as they had the right to decide whether to accept the work and the employers were not under a contractual obligation to provide work, although they regularly did so. In *Nethermere (St Neots) Ltd v. Gardiner and Taverna*, trouser machinists who worked from home were held to be employees, as there was a long-standing relationship between the parties that the company should provide and pay for work and the workers should accept and perform the work provided.

The status of company directors has been considered by the courts and tribunals on a number of occasions. A company director who is employed under a contract of employment is entitled to the usual employment rights. If a director does not have an employment contract the presumption is that, as an office holder, the director is not an employee. (The rights and duties of an office holder are defined by the office he holds and exist independently of the person holding the office.) In certain circumstances, a contract of employment is implied despite the lack of a formal employment contract. In *Folami v. Nigerline (UK) Ltd*, the chief accountant of a Nigerian company was appointed managing director of its English subsidiary company. He was paid a salary but was not given a written contract of employment. It was held nevertheless that he was an employee.

Occasionally clarification of the matter is found in the company's articles of association. In *Parsons v. Albert J. Parsons & Sons Ltd*, the sons of the firm's founder were directors of the company. There were no contracts of service, but the articles provided that the directors should be appointed for life. (Such a provision may be subsequently altered unless the appointment was made before July 18 1945.) No formal salaries were paid to the directors and they voted themselves a sum described as 'directors' emoluments' at the end of every year. One of the sons was removed from office and applied to an industrial tribunal claiming that he had been unfairly dismissed. It was held that he was not an employee as he was regarded and remunerated as a director.

In *Eaton v. Robert Eaton Ltd* the EAT set out some of the factors to consider in deciding the status of a director.

(a)　Generally speaking, a director is an office holder and is not in employment.
(b)　The use of a descriptive term, e.g. managing director, technical director, may indicate employee status.

(c)   Drawing a weekly wage or regular or fixed salary as opposed to director's fees may again indicate employee status.

(d)   An agreement to employ a person as managing director minuted at a board meeting or noted by a memorandum in writing is a strong indication of a contract of employment.

(e)   Consideration of the director's functions –was he acting in a directorial capacity or under the control of the board of directors?

The status of priests has also been considered on a number of occasions by the courts. Clergymen are usually classified as office holders and the general rule is that in the absence of a clear indication of a contrary intention in a document, the relationship between a church and a minister is not governed by a contract of employment.

In *Davies v. Presbyterian Church of Wales*, Davies was inducted as pastor of certain churches in South Wales in accordance with the Book of Order and the Rules of the Presbyterian Church. The pastorate was for an indeterminate time and the stipend was to be paid from a Church fund, in accordance with the Rules. He was subsequently dismissed following disciplinary proceedings. It was held that he had not been unfairly dismissed as there was no contract of employment between the minister and the Church. There were no contractual duties imposed upon Davies and his duties were dictated by conscience, not contract. The Church was not contractually bound to pay a stipend as these obligations were found in the Book of Rules. In *Santokh Singh v. Guru Nanak Gurdwara*, a similar conclusion was reached in respect of the status of a Sikh minister of religion. Singh was appointed a priest of a Sikh temple and performed spiritual teaching and ceremonial duties. He did not have a contract of employment. It was held that his spiritual duties outweighed those factors indicating a contract of service, and he was not an employee of the temple.

—————— **The loaned employee** ——————

If an employee is loaned or hired by one employer to another, it may be necessary to determine who is his current employer, to establish who is liable for any torts (civil wrongs) he may commit or who is responsible for his welfare. If a contract exists between the general and special employer, the contract will have to be examined and interpreted to find the answer. If there is no contract, the arrangements and the degree of control which is exercised over the employee will be the decisive factors.

The general rule is that the permanent general employer will be liable for the negligence of any loaned employee. In *Mersey Docks and Harbour Board v. Coggins and Griffith*, a firm of stevedores had hired the use of a crane with its driver from the Board. The Board stipulated in its contract with the stevedores that 'The drivers so provided shall be the servants of the applicants'. As a consequence of the driver's negligence a checker was injured. The court had to determine whether the general employers of the crane driver or the hirer was liable for the driver's negligence. The hirer could instruct the driver where to go and what to carry, but had no authority to give directions as to the manner in which the crane was to be operated. The Board was held responsible for the driver's negligence, as the driver was appointed by them and they alone had the power to dismiss him.

In *Garrard v. Southey and Co.*, an electrician was loaned to the defendant company. His employers, a firm of electrical contractors, continued to pay him and reserved the right to dismiss him. His day-to-day working was, however, supervised by the defendant company's foreman, a skilled electrician. He was injured when he used a ladder at the defendant's factory which proved to be defective. He sued both employers for negligence. It was held that the temporary employers were liable as they owed him a duty of care to ensure his safety at work.

Although control over an employee may pass to his temporary employers, they do not become his employers. They are only responsible to him and for him as if they were his employers. A contract of employment is a personal contract and cannot be assigned without the consent of the parties (*Nokes v. Doncaster Amalgamated Collieries Ltd*).

In *Denham v. Midland Employers Mutual Assurance Ltd*, a company which had engaged a firm of contractors to undertake work on its premises, provided the services of a labourer. The company continued to pay the labourer although he worked under the control of the contractors. He was killed as a result of the negligence of the contractors' employees and his widow brought an action against the contractors. The contractors claimed an indemnity from one of two insurers, namely Midland Employers Mutual Assurance, whose policy dealt with liability for accidental injury to 'any person under a contract of service', or Denham, whose policy covered the death of persons other than 'any person under a contract of service'. It was held that Denham must indemnify, for although control had passed to the contractors, they had not become the labourer's employers.

An employee whose contract of employment is varied to permit him to work for a subsidiary company, nevertheless remains an employee of the parent company for the purposes of the EPCA. In *Cross v. Redpath Dorman Long Ltd*, Cross, who was employed by Redpath Dorman Long Ltd (RDL), was sent to work for British Bridge Builders Ltd (BBB), a company partly owned by RDL. As a construction foreman on the Humber bridge his work was under the control of BBB, and variations were made to his contract to include BBB's terms and conditions. He was made redundant and claimed that he had been unfairly dismissed by BBB or alternatively by RDL. It was held that although BBB had use of Cross's services, and in certain circumstances would have been vicariously liable for his actions, he remained an employee of RDL throughout for the purposes of unfair dismissal.

— Other employment relationships —

There are certain categories of employee that do not fit into the traditional employment pattern. The most important of these are:

1   Crown employees;
2   minors;
3   apprentices.

1   Crown employees

Special provisions apply to Crown employees, for although in practice most civil servants have security of tenure of employment, in theory they may be dismissed at the pleasure of the Crown. Historically the Crown is privileged *vis-à-vis* contract and cannot be sued in its own courts. Although the Crown Proceedings Act 1947 and modern employment statutes have made inroads into this doctrine, the Crown is only bound when this is specifically provided for by an Act of Parliament.

Military personnel may not sue the Crown for breach of contract and may not even claim for arrears of pay. Civil servants hold office at the will of the Crown and may be dismissed with or without notice, at the Crown's pleasure. Theory and practice are often different matters, however, and civil servants are now regarded as having security of employment.

Civil servants are now also granted the majority of the employment rights afforded to other employees. They may sue for unfair dismissal or sex discrimination, and claim equal pay, but they are not entitled to redundancy payments, minimum periods of notice or written statements of the term of their employment.

2 Minors

A minor, i.e. a person under the age of 18, is only bound by certain contracts. These are contracts for necessaries and contracts of a beneficial or educational nature. Contracts of employment or apprenticeship which enable him to earn a living are included in the latter category.

In *Doyle v. White City Stadium*, an infant professional boxer held a licence from the British Boxing Board. He was disqualified for delivering a low punch and forfeited his purse. He sued the promoters on the grounds that his contract was not of a beneficial nature. It was held that a penalty clause of this nature, by which the Board sought to improve standards of safety and fairness in professional boxing, was for his benefit.

In *Clements v. LNWR*, an infant porter claimed that his contract of employment was not of a beneficial character as he had foregone his rights under the Employer's Liability Act 1880 to join the company's insurance scheme. It was held that his claim failed, for although the scale of compensation in the company's scheme was lower, it covered more injuries than the statute.

An onerous term may render a minor's contract void. In *Olsen v. Corry & Gravesend Aviation Ltd*, an infant's deed of apprenticeship contained a clause which relieved his employer from all liability for any injury caused to the infant. Such a clause was not deemed to be beneficial and the infant was not bound by it.

3 Apprentices

A contract of apprenticeship, although a contract of service, is a specialised contract with certain rights and obligations. The essence of the contract is that the master agrees to instruct the apprentice in a trade or calling, and to maintain him. The apprentice agrees to serve the master and learn from him.

The Statute of Artificers 1562 decreed that no person could practice a trade without serving a seven-year term of apprenticeship. This provision was repealed by the Apprentices' Act 1814. Formerly an apprentice was a member of the master's household, but this is rarely found today.

A contract of apprenticeship need not be under seal, i.e. in the form of a deed, but it must be in writing. Although a contract of apprenticeship of a minor is regarded as both necessary and beneficial, it may nevertheless be repudiated by a minor on attaining the age of 18 or within a reasonable time afterwards. It is therefore usual for a parent or guardian to undertake or guarantee that the minor will complete the apprenticeship.

A number of the terms implied in a contract of apprenticeship are vestiges of the past and are now regarded as outmoded. An apprentice has a right to lodging to be provided free when he enters the master's household, and must be provided with medicine and medical attendance should this be necessary. The master has the right to chastise an apprentice moderately, but this is now construed as having the right to exercise stricter control over an apprentice than over other employees.

As an apprentice is contractually bound to serve his term of apprenticeship, he may not give notice to terminate the contract. A master's remedy for breach of this obligation is to sue an adult apprentice for breach of contract, or the guarantor for compensation in the case of a minor. A master may not dismiss an apprentice for ordinary misconduct, but he is entitled to do so in cases of serious misconduct, for example where an apprentice was a thief, where an apprentice refused to learn, or where an apprentice was guilty of habitual loose living.

A contract of apprenticeship requires personal performance by both parties, and the death of either party will terminate the contract. Termination may also occur on the illness of either party, if the illness is of such a nature or duration as to prevent the performance of the contract. The bankruptcy of the master will also terminate the contract, and if a premium has been paid by the apprentice he may request the trustee in bankruptcy to repay as much as is reasonable, or alternatively to transfer the indentures to another master.

An apprenticeship is also terminated by the death or retirement of a partner in a partnership, unless the apprentice is bound personally to one of the surviving partners rather than to the partnership.

An apprentice is entitled, with minor exceptions, to the benefits of employment protection legislation. An apprentice who is dismissed, other than for serious misconduct, may usually recover damages from his employer. The operation of this legislation is illustrated in the following two cases.

In *Paviour and Thomas v. Whittons Transport*, two apprentices were held to be unfairly dismissed when a receiver gave notice to a number of employees. No arrangements had been made with another employer to take over the contracts of apprenticeship.

In *Townrow v. Phillip Davies*, a solicitor's articled clerk was held not to be unfairly dismissed when ill health forced his employer to amalgamate with another firm of solicitors. The other firm were not prepared to allow a transfer of the articles and the master tried in vain to find alternative articles for the clerk. It was held that the master had acted reasonably in the circumstances.

An apprentice may, in these circumstances, bring an action for wrongful dismissal. He may claim in respect of loss of earnings and for loss of future prospects, assuming that he had completed his apprentice-ship (*Dunk v. Waller*).

Elements of contract

A contract of employment is governed by the general rules of contract. It is an agreement between an employer and an employee which will be enforced by the law. The essential elements of contract must be present, namely:

1 agreement, i.e. an offer of employment is made by one party and is accepted by the other;
2 both parties must intend a legally binding relationship to come into existence, with certain obligations imposed on both parties;

3   consideration (usually remuneration for a service) must be present, unless the contract is made under seal, i.e. by deed;
4   both parties must have capacity to contract;
5   the reality of the contract must not be affected by mistake;
6   the contract must not be affected by misrepresentation;
7   the contract must not be illegal.

Certain of these elements merit fuller consideration.

1   *Agreement comprising offer and acceptance*

An offer of employment may be made to one particular individual, to a group of people, or to persons in general. An offer is usually made to a particular individual. It may remain open for a limited time, for example a week or a month, or there may be no time limit stipulated for acceptance. It will remain open until the stipulated time has passed, or a reasonable time has elapsed, or it has been revoked (withdrawn by the person making the offer), or rejected by the other party.

An acceptance must not be qualified (i.e. it must comply with the terms of the offer), and will be effective from the moment of acceptance. In *Taylor v. Furness, Withy & Company Ltd*, a dock worker was allocated by the dock labour board to the defendants. He was given a welcoming letter, an identity card and assigned to work on a ship on his first morning with the defendant company. Later that morning he was informed by the defendant company's manager that he could not be employed as he was not a union member. It was held that he was entitled to be paid his wages from that morning, as a contract of employment was formed when he was handed the letter and the identity card.

2   *Intention to create a legal relationship*

The parties must intend that the agreement and its terms create a legal relationship. This excludes a domestic, social arrangement or 'gentleman's agreement'. This contractual requirement has become increasingly important in determining whether a collective agreement is binding on the parties (see page 24).

3 Consideration

The element of consideration is necessary to distinguish a contract from a promise to perform a gratuitous service. The usual form of consideration in a contract of employment consists of an employer's promise to pay wages in return for an employee's promise to undertake work.

4 Capacity to contract

Most adults are competent to enter into a contract of employment. Certain classes of employees, such as Crown employees, minors and apprentices are subject to special rules (see pages 12–15).

5 Mistake

Only certain categories of mistake affect a contract and render it void. A mistake as to the nature of a document may invalidate a contract, but a mistake as to the contents of a document is inoperative, and the parties will be bound.

6 Misrepresentation

An untrue statement which induces a person to enter into a contract may render a contract voidable at the option of the misled party. An employee is under no obligation to volunteer adverse information, except in certain circumstances (*Sybron Corporation v. Rochem Ltd* – see page 49). In *Fletcher v. Krell*, a governess who described herself as a spinster, although a divorcee, was held not to have misled her employer. She recovered damages for breach of contract when he refused to employ her.

In *Cork v. Kirkby Maclean*, it was held that an employee was not under a duty to disclose to his employer that he was an epileptic.

An employee's dismissal for not disclosing a previous criminal conviction will be unfair if the conviction is 'spent' under the Rehabilitation of Offenders Act 1974. A conviction is 'spent' after varying periods, according to the gravity of the sentence. Certain professions, offices and employments are excluded from the provisions of this Act, e.g. teaching, legal professions, police, medical services, chartered and certified accountant.

The various rehabilitation periods are as follows:

Sentence	Rehabilitation Period
Imprisonment in excess of 30 months	Never spent
Imprisonment of 6–30 months	10 years
Imprisonment of less than 6 months	7 years
Borstal	7 years
Detention centre	3 years
Fine	5 years

7   Illegality

A contract which contravenes the provisions of a statute, or is considered to be contrary to public policy is illegal and will not be enforced. The following are examples of contracts which are *illegal at statute*.

(a)   Section 140 of the EPCA provides that any agreement which seeks to exclude or limit any provision of the EPCA, or which seeks to preclude a person from complaining to an industrial tribunal or bringing proceedings before it, is void (see page 183).

(b)   The preamble to the Sex Discrimination Act 1975 reads: 'An Act to render unlawful certain kinds of sex discrimination and discrimination on the ground of marriage . . .'

(c)   The employment of non-EC nationals in countries without work permits. In *Rastegarnia v. Richmond Design* an Iranian national was granted a work permit on condition that he did not change his job without obtaining permission from the Secretary of State for Employment. He changed employment without permission and was subsequently dismissed. His claim for unfair dismissal was rejected as his employment had become wholly illegal.

(d)   Employment under the Licensing Acts. In *Lay v. Hamilton* a barmaid could not count her period of employment up to her 18th birthday in computing her period of employment. The Licensing Act 1964 did not allow the employment of bar staff under 18. She was unable to bring an action for unfair dismissal as she had insufficient continuous service.

(e) It is unlawful to refuse a person employment or the services of an employment agency on grounds related to union membership:

- because he is, or is not, a trade union member;
- he is unwilling to accept a requirement, i.e. to take steps to become, or cease to be, or to remain, or not to become, a member of a trade union; or to make payments or suffer deductions in the event of his not being a member of a trade union.

A person who is unlawfully refused employment has the right to complain to an industrial tribunal (EA 90 ss1,2).

Various forms of *illegality* may arise *at common law* in relation to contracts of employment. The most important of these – contracts in restraint of trade – are dealt with on page 50. The following cases are examples of illegality at common law.

(a) A contract may contain a servile incident. In *Eastham v. Newcastle United FC*, a footballer sought a declaration that the retain and transfer system used by the Football League was void. Under this system a club was able to place a player on its retained list at the end of his annual contract if he did not agree to the club's new terms. He could only be employed by his club if he accepted those terms and could only be transferred if the fee asked by his club was paid by the other club. The declaration was granted and this led to the abolition of the maximum wage structure, under which professional footballers were paid a pittance for their services.

(b) A contract for sexually immoral purposes is an illegal contract and will not be enforced by the courts. If, however, the immorality occurred in the mode of performing an otherwise lawful contract, an employee will not be debarred from enforcing the terms of the contract. In *Coral Leisure Group v. Barnett*, Barnett was employed as a public relations executive by a casino. In the course of his employment, he alleged that he procured and paid for prostitutes for the use of the casino's customers. He was later dismissed and claimed damages for unfair dismissal. The employers claimed that the dismissal was justified, but questioned Barnett's right to enforce an illegal contract. (The company at no time agreed that Barnett had actually procured on their behalf.) The tribunal held that it had the jurisdiction to hear the case, as, on Barnett's pleadings, the immoral purposes were not part of an otherwise lawful contract.

(c)   A contract of employment involving tax evasion by either the employer or employee is void for illegality in certain cases. The majority of the cases heard by the courts or tribunals under this heading have involved the payment of tax-free sums to individual employees. 'There is nothing necessarily wrong or illegal in agreeing to pay a sum free of income tax to an employee, as long as the employer pays the tax in respect of that payment to the Revenue' (du Parcq LJ in *Miller v. Karlinski*).

If a court or tribunal decides that an employee is aware of the illegal nature of a contract of employment, it will declare the whole of the contract to be invalid. The employee will find that he will not be regarded as an employed person and will be unable to claim the various statutory employment benefits, such as redundancy payments and compensation for unfair dismissal.

In *Corby v. Morrison*, an employee was paid, in addition to her normal wage, an extra £5 a week free of income tax and social security liability. Although the employee did not intend to defraud the Inland Revenue, she knew that she was in receipt of tax-free payments. Mrs Corby was later dismissed and brought an action for unfair dismissal. It was held that the contract was unenforceable and that the tribunal had no jurisdiction to hear the case, as she had knowingly been a party to a deception on the Revenue.

If an employee is unaware of the employer's illegal performance of a contract, the employee can enforce the terms of the contract. This is so, even though the employee ought to have appreciated the position, but did not do so. In *Newland v. Simons and Waller (Hairdressers) Ltd*, a hairdresser was paid her wages out of the shop till every Saturday morning. She never received any pay statement, although she received a form P60 at the end of the financial year. Although she should have realised from the form P60 that proper deductions were not being made from her wages, she did not do so. She was later dismissed. It was held that, as she was unaware of the illegal nature of the contract, she was entitled to bring an action for unfair dismissal.

2

THE SOURCES —— OF A CONTRACT —— OF EMPLOYMENT

Unlike the majority of commercial contracts, few contracts of employment contain all the written details of the terms of a contract. Many of the essential terms of a contract of employment are to be found in works' rules and collective agreements, or are derived from the custom or practice in a particular industry.

Two forms of contracts of employment are required to be in writing, that of a seaman and a contract of apprenticeship (see page 14). The Merchant Shipping Act 1970 requires an agreement for the engagement of a seaman on a ship registered in the United Kingdom to be signed by both parties. The aim and provisions of the 'crew agreement' must be approved by the Department of Trade and Industry.

_____ Written particulars of the _____ contract of employment

An employer is, however, obliged to supply an employee, within thirteen weeks of the commencement of employment, with a written statement of certain terms of a contract of employment (EPCA s1). These are:

1   the names of the parties to the contract;
2   the date of commencement of the employment;
3   whether any employment with a previous employer counts as part of the employee's period of continuous employment, and if so, what period;
4   the scale or rate of remuneration, or the method of calculating remuneration;
5   the intervals at which remuneration is paid, i.e. weekly, monthly, or some other period;
6   any terms and conditions relating to hours of work (including any relating to normal working hours);
7   any terms and conditions relating to:
   (a) entitlement to holidays, including public holidays, and holiday pay (sufficient particulars must be given so as to enable an employee's entitlement to be precisely calculated);
   (b) incapacity for work due to sickness or injury, including any provision for sick pay;
   (c) pensions and pension schemes;
8   the length of notice required on either side to terminate the contract;
9   the title of the job which the employee is employed to do;
10 any disciplinary rules applicable to the employee;
11 the procedure for appeal against any disciplinary action and for seeking redress of any grievance relating to the employment;
12 whether a contracting-out certificate, relating to the state pension scheme, is in force for that employment.

The statement may refer an employee, for all or any of the particulars, to some document which there is reasonable opportunity of reading in the course of employment, or which is made reasonably accessible in some other way.

An employer is only obliged to furnish this statement to employees in full-time employment, i.e. those who normally work more than 16 hours per week. Additionally the obligation to provide details of terms 1–9 applies if these terms exist. If there are no fixed particulars in regard to those items, this fact must be stated. An employer of less than 20 employees is not required to include a note of disciplinary procedures in the written particulars (EA89 s13).

An employee must be informed, within one month, of any changes in the terms of his employment. He must be informed of the nature of the changes either by means of a written statement or by some other means, for example on a notice board, which must be reasonably accessible.

An employee who leaves an employer, but returns to the same employment within six months need not be given these particulars again. However, if any changes have occurred in the terms of the contract, these must be communicated to him.

These written particulars do not constitute a written contract between the parties, but nevertheless provide very strong evidence of the employer's view of the contractual terms. Only if an employer states clearly that the document constitutes the terms of the contract of employment, and the employee signifies his acceptance of the document as a contractual document, will its terms bind on both parties. In *Systems Floors (UK) Ltd v. Daniel* the employer was able to provide oral evidence to prove that an employee's contract of employment commenced at a later date than that shown in the written particulars.

If an employer fails to provide an employee with those particulars, the employee may apply for relief to an industrial tribunal. The tribunal will then ascertain the particulars and state them accordingly.

Works' rules

Many employers lay down works' or company rules. These may form part of an employee's contract of employment, or they may be regarded as instructions to an employee as to how the work should be done. The distinction is important as any variation of the terms of a contract may only be achieved with the agreement of both parties, while an employer may unilaterally vary and amend any instructions to an employee. However, such instructions must be clear, reasonable and unambiguous. The rules may be contained in a rule book given to each employee, a book of rules found in the works' office, or a set of rules pinned to a notice board.

The rules may also be regarded as an indication of company policy on a particular matter. In *Jeffries v. BP Tanker Co. Ltd*, a ship's officer was held to have been fairly dismissed after he had suffered two heart attacks. The company's rules laid down that an employee with a history of cardiac disease should not be employed at sea. The rule was therefore in the nature of company policy.

A failure by an employee to obey new or amended instructions would be regarded as a breach of a duty to obey lawful orders. In *Secretary of State for Employment v. ASLEF*, members of the railway union threatened a 'work to rule' by their literal interpretation of the rule book, which would undoubtedly have disrupted train services. The Court of Appeal held that this would constitute a breach of contract as the employees would be in breach of an implied term in threatening to impede and disrupt their employer's business.

─────── Collective agreements ───────

A majority of the workers in the UK are members of trade unions which have negotiated collective agreements with employers or groups of employers. Collective agreements are regarded as having two main functions:

1 regulating the relationship between the parties, i.e. the trade unions and the employer(s). These are usually procedural agreements which outline the procedure to be taken in the event of disagreement, e.g. defining stages of procedure, setting up machinery for negotiation or conciliation, and so on;
2 regulating the terms and conditions of individual contracts of employment, e.g. pay, hours of work, holidays, overtime.

Collective agreements may also deal with the engagement or non-engagement, termination of employment, or suspension of workers; allocation of work or duties of employment; matters of discipline; membership or non-membership of a trade union; and the right of a trade union to represent workers in these matters (TULRA, s29).

Section 28 of TULRA provides that a collective agreement made before December 1 1971, or after July 31 1974, is conclusively presumed not to have been intended by the parties to be a legally enforceable contract, unless the agreement is in writing and contains a provision that the parties intend it to be legally enforceable. Any collective agreement made between the two previous dates is presumed to be legally enforceable, unless it contains an express exclusion clause stating otherwise. If the collective agreement was not made between the above dates, an employer will be unable to enforce its terms against a trade union and a trade union will be unable to enforce its terms against an employer.

It is generally accepted that in the majority of cases the terms of a collective agreement do not bind an individual employee, who cannot enforce these terms against an employer, and vice versa. Other reasons for this view (apart from the statutory presumption of TULRA s28) are as follows:

1   as the employee was not a party to the agreement, a contract does not exist between him and the employer, i.e. there is no *privity* of contract;
2   the terms of many collective agreements are vague and therefore incapable of being contractual;
3   the courts are reluctant to imply that a trade union is acting as an agent for its members, i.e. bringing its members into a contractual relationship with an employer; and
4   the parties do not intend to be legally bound, i.e. it is regarded as an agreement which is binding in honour only.

In *Ford Motor Co. Ltd v. Amalgamated Union of Engineering and Foundry Workers*, the Ford Company entered into an agreement, by a majority decision, with 19 unions, relating to procedures, conditions and wages. Some of the minority felt aggrieved by the decision and immediately began an unofficial strike. This was contrary to one of the terms of the agreement which provided that certain procedures would be followed before a stoppage of work occurred. The larger unions, who had supported the majority, then decided to make the strike official. Ford then sought an injunction for breach of the agreement. It was held that the agreement was not a contract and was binding in honour only. It could therefore be broken with impunity by either party.

Although the majority of collective agreements do not bind the parties in law, there are nevertheless statutory provisions which seek to encourage and promote collective bargaining. An employer has a general duty to disclose information to an independent trade union for the purposes of collective bargaining. If he fails or refuses to do so, the trade union concerned may complain to the Central Arbitration Committee (CAC), which may make an award relating to the terms and conditions of service which then form part of the employee's contract of employment. This award is binding on the employer.

The Advisory Conciliation and Arbitration Service (ACAS) has produced a Code of Practice which deals with 'the disclosure of information to trade unions for collective bargaining purposes'. The Code gives specific examples of information which could be of relevance in certain bargaining situations. These include pay and benefits, conditions of service, manpower structure, performance and productivity, and the financial structure of the undertaking.

The terms of a collective agreement may however bind the parties if they are incorporated into the contract of employment. Once a term from a collective agreement has become incorporated into an individual's contract it will remain incorporated, even if the collective agreement is later terminated. In *Robertson v. British Gas Corporation* an employee's letter of appointment stated that the provisions of a union agreement applied to an incentive bonus scheme. The employer later gave notice of the termination of the bonus scheme and stopped paying bonuses to Robertson. It was held that he was entitled to the bonuses as the contractual obligation remained and had been expressly incorporated into his contract.

This incorporation may be either express or implied.

Express incorporation

A contract may contain an express provision that it is to be subject to the terms of a collective agreement, i.e. the terms of the collective agreement become incorporated into an individual's employment contract and become legally binding.

In *National Coal Board v. Galley*, a written contract provided that Galley's wages and working conditions should be regulated by such national agreements as might be in force for the time being. A national agreement later signed between Galley's union and the NCB provided that 'deputies should work such days or part days in each week as may reasonably be required.' It was held that Galley's refusal to work a Saturday shift amounted to a breach of contract, as the terms of the agreement were incorporated in his contract of service.

In *Camden Exhibition & Display Ltd v. Lynott*, the written particulars of the contract of employment given to an employee provided that his hours of work were to be in accordance with the terms of the national joint council for the exhibition industry. It was held that these terms had become incorporated in his contract of employment.

Implied incorporation

A term may be incorporated by implication into an individual's employment contract if it is regarded as appropriate. Wages, hours of work and holiday entitlement are appropriate, as they relate solely to the individual. Such matters as machinery for settling disputes are not regarded as appropriate, as they do not relate solely to an individual's contract of employment.

In the last century, agreements between master printers and compositors were regulated by committees of each body. In *Hill v. Levey*, it was held that these agreements had become incorporated into every engagement. In *McLea v. Essex Hire Ltd*, a seaman was bound by the terms of an agreement made by the National Maritime Board, the negotiating body for the industry.

Mention of a collective agreement does not amount to express incorporation of the terms of the agreement into an individual's employment contract. In *Stewart v. Graig Shipping Co. Ltd*, Stewart's letter of appointment specified his pay and stated 'the terms and conditions set out in the National Maritime Board Agreements have been taken into account in the above consolidated figure'. It was held that the terms of the national agreement had not been incorporated into the contract, but merely taken into account in calculating Stewart's pay.

The terms of a collective agreement may be regarded as unsuitable for incorporation in a contract. In *Young v. Canadian Northern Railway*, an agreement between the CNR and a trade union (of which Young was not a member) that, in the event of redundancy, the principle of 'last in first out' should apply, was held not to have been incorporated into Young's contract of employment. His claim for wrongful dismissal, on the basis that the company's redundancy provisions did not accord with the terms of a collective agreement, therefore failed.

Problems are encountered when dealing with the position of non-unionists or individuals who have resigned from a union. In *Singh v. British Steel Corporation*, the plaintiff worked a 15-day shift system over a five-day week. He later resigned from the union. The union later negotiated a new shift system of a 21-day shift over seven weeks. He refused to work the new system and was dismissed. It was held that his dismissal was unfair as he was subject to the terms of the original contract. The new terms had not been incorporated into his contract.

Incorporation by statute

Under the provisions of the EPCA:

1   an application may be made to the Secretary of State for the approval of a dismissals procedure agreement which replaces the right to claim for unfair dismissal (s65); and
2   collective agreements may be made which give the rights to claim:
    (a) redundancy payments (s96);
    (b) guarantee payments (s18);
    under the provisions of the agreement, rather than under the provisions of the EPCA.

Conflicting collective agreements

In cases where there are conflicting collective agreements governing an employee's contract, the law appears uncertain and obscure. In *Loman and Henderson v. Merseyside Transport Services Ltd,* a national agreement provided for a 41-hour week, while the local agreement provided for a 68-hour week. An employee who was made redundant claimed that the computation of the average weekly wage should be based on the local agreement. It was held that the local agreement was a gentleman's agreement, which was not intended to have a contractual effect. In *Clift v. West Riding County Council,* an employee's pay was based on a local agreement, which was not as remunerative as the national agreement. It was held that as the local agreement was later in time, it should prevail.

This principle was not followed in *Gascol Conversions v. Mercer,* where Mercer was employed on a basis of a 54-hour week. A national agreement was concluded in 1971, which provided a 40-hour week with optional overtime. It also provided that a national agreement should take precedence over a local agreement. A local agreement was concluded in 1971, which provided for a 54-hour week. It was held that the terms of the national agreement prevailed.

Many collective agreements now contain provisions as to which agreement should prevail in the case of such conflict.

No strike clause

Any terms of a collective agreement which prohibit or restrict the rights of a worker to engage in a strike or other industrial action, for example a no strike clause, will not be incorporated into a worker's contract of employment unless the following conditions are met.

The collective agreement must be in writing, and must contain a provision which expressly states that those terms shall or may be incorporated into the worker's contract. It must be reasonably accessible to the employee at his place of work and available for consultation during working hours. The trade union which was party to the collective agreement must be an independent union. The worker's contract must expressly or implicitly incorporate these terms into the contract (TULRA s18).

Custom

On occasions, an implied term in an individual contract of employment may be derived from a trade practice or custom in a particular industry or place of employment. Such a custom must be certain, reasonable and notorious, that is, well established.

In *Sagar v. Ridehalgh*, it was held that the practice of deducting sums from a weaver's wages for bad workmanship was an established custom and was a term of each weaver's contract of employment.

In *Bird v. British Celanese* an employee was suspended without pay for two days. It was held that suspension without pay was an established practice of the defendant employer and was an implied term of each employee's contract of employment.

A custom which dates back many centuries is pertinent to the relationship of a domestic servant and an employer. In the absence of other terms, the hiring of a domestic servant may be terminated by a customary month's notice. The close proximity of such a relationship makes it desirable that this type of contract can be terminated without undue delay.

3

EMPLOYER'S DUTIES

The duties owed by an employer to an employee depend on the terms of the contract of employment. In the absence of any specific agreement the following duties are implied:

1 to remunerate the employee;
2 in certain circumstances to provide work for the employee;
3 to indemnify the employee;
4 to treat the employee with respect;
5 to permit time off;
6 to meet safety requirements.

An employer is under no obligation to provide a reference, but should he do so, he owes certain obligations to the employee (see page 36).

An employer also owes a duty (in certain circumstances) to a third party to compensate that person for any damage or injury occasioned by the tortious (wrongful) act of an employee. This is known as the doctrine of *vicarious liability* and is dealt with in the final part of the chapter.

1 To remunerate

An employer must pay the employee the agreed remuneration. If this has not been determined in advance, the employer must pay the employee a reasonable sum. See Chapter 6.

2 To provide work

As a general rule an employer has no obligation to provide work for an employee, as long as he continues to pay the agreed wages. Asquist J.'s statement in *Collier v. Sunday Referee Publishing Co. Ltd* is often quoted as a simple illustration of the rule: 'Provided I pay my cook her wages regularly, she cannot complain if I choose to take any or all of my meals out'.

There are situations where there is an implied duty to provide work as distinct from merely paying wages, as the following examples show.

(a)   Where the work provides the employee with an opportunity to enhance his reputation by publicity, for without the work there can be no enhancement. In *Clayton & Waller Ltd v. Oliver,* an actor was promised a leading role in a West End musical. The offer was subsequently withdrawn, and he was offered a lesser role, but at the previously negotiated salary. He refused and was awarded substantial damages for loss of publicity.

(b)   Where an employee is paid on a piecework or commission basis. In *Turner v. Goldsmith,* a commercial traveller's pay was based on the amount of commission earned. It was held that he must be given a reasonable opportunity to travel and thereby earn his commission.

In *Baumann v. Hulton Press,* a journalist/photographer was paid a retainer of £10 a week and was to be available to undertake commissioned work from the defendants at all reasonable times. It was held that there was an implied term in his contract that the defendants would give him sufficient work to enable him to earn what the parties must have contemplated that he should earn.

In *Devonald v. Rosser,* a piece-worker, given a month's notice by his employers, was entitled to damages when his employers immediately closed down the works where he was employed. It was held that there was an implied term in his contract that his employers would provide him with work during the period of notice.

In *Langston v. Amalgamated Union of Engineering Workers,* an employee was suspended on full pay by his employers in response to a union threat to call a strike if this course of action was not adopted. The employer was held to be in breach of contract as the employee was deprived of the opportunity to earn additional payments for night shift or overtime working.

(c)   Where the employee is a skilled worker, and the provision of work is necessary for the maintenance and development of skills. In *Breach v. Epsylon Industries*, a chief engineer was left with no work after his employers gradually transferred their engineering work overseas. It was held that the failure to provide him with work amounted to a repudiation of the contract.

Where an employer, through no fault of his own, is unable to provide work, he is under no obligation to pay wages. In *Browning v. Crumlin Valley Collieries Ltd*, a mine was closed to enable urgent repairs to be carried out to the mine shafts. It was held that the employees were not entitled to compensation for lost wages during the time of the closure.

3   To indemnify

An employee is entitled to an indemnity if he incurs any expense, loss or liability in carrying out his employer's instructions, if there is an express or implied term to this effect in the contract of employment. The question of indemnity usually arises in situations when an employee is acting, within his authority, as an agent for his employer. In *Re Famatina Development Corporation*, a consulting engineer, in compiling a report for a company, reported matters which were allegedly defamatory of the managing director. He was entitled to an indemnity for the costs incurred in subsequently defending a libel action. As he had been engaged to report fully on the company's activities, his duties were much wider than those of an ordinary consulting engineer.

This right of indemnity extends to the commission of an illegal act, as long as the employee is unaware of its illegal nature. In *Burrows v. Rhodes*, an employee, induced by a fraudulent statement to re-enlist in the armed forces of the British South Africa Company, took part in the ill-fated Jameson raid. As he believed the venture to be legal, he was able to recover damages in respect of the injuries he had received.

A more commonplace situation was encountered in *Gregory v. Ford* when an employee injured a third party by his negligent driving. The employee was not aware that the vehicle was not insured. The third party obtained judgment against both the employer and the employee. As the employee was unaware of the illegal nature of the act, he was entitled to an indemnity in respect of the third party's claim.

An employee who is aware of the illegal character of an act may refuse to carry out such an act, and will not be in breach of a duty to obey his employer. If he is aware of the illegality he is not entitled to an indemnity.

4   To treat with respect

An implied duty of mutual respect exists in every employer/employee relationship. Although this is a vague concept which is often difficult to define, it has nevertheless been re-stated and re-affirmed in recent years. In *Donovan v. Invicta Airways Ltd*, it was stated that each of the parties should treat the other with such a degree of consideration and courtesy as would enable the contract to be fulfilled.

This is clearly shown in the provisions relating to unfair dismissal, and the relevant paragraphs of the Code of Practice dealing with disciplinary practice and procedures in employment. An employer must give adequate training to his employees, keep records and is not entitled (except in the gravest cases) to dismiss his employees without adequate warnings and an opportunity of improvement.

An employer must not behave in an unreasonable manner and thereby damage or destroy the trust and mutual confidence that should exist in the relationship. An employee may treat the contract of employment as repudiated if an employer's conduct is so grossly unreasonable as to be in effect a constructive dismissal (see page 125).

An employer who wishes to rid himself of an employee or alter the terms of the employment, without becoming liable to pay a redundancy payment or compensation for unfair dismissal, cannot do so by making the employee's life so uncomfortable that he either resigns or accepts revised contractual terms. In this situation an employer would be in breach of the duty of mutual respect. In *Woods v. WM Car Services Ltd*, Lord Denning stated: 'Just as a servant must be good and faithful, so an employer must be good and considerate . . . in modern times an employer can be guilty of misconduct justifying the employee in leaving at once without notice'.

5   To permit time off

(a)   For public duties

Employers are required under certain circumstances to permit employees who hold certain public positions to have reasonable time off to perform the duties associated with these positions. These provisions apply to employees who are: justices of the peace; members of a local authority; members of any statutory tribunal; members of a Regional or District Health Authority; members of the managing or governing body of an educational establishment maintained by a local education authority; or members of a water authority.

An employee is entitled to reasonable time off for any duties incurred by membership of any of these bodies. A definition of 'reasonable time off' depends on the circumstances, but the following factors should be taken into consideration:

- how much time off is required in general to perform these duties, and how much time off is required on the particular occasion in question;
- how much time off has already been permitted for this purpose or for trade union duties and/or activities;
- the circumstances of the employer's business and the effect of the employee's absence upon it.

An employer is under no obligation to pay an employee for any time taken off in connection with public duties, unless an agreement to do so has been entered into with the employee or the trade union.

(b)   For trade union duties

An employer must allow an employee, who is an official of an independent trade union recognised by the employer for collective bargaining purposes, reasonable time off with pay during working hours to enable him:

- to carry out those duties which are concerned with negotiations with the employer that are related to matters within the scope of section 29 of TULRA and in relation to which the trade union is recognised;
- to carry out any duties concerned with those matters which the

employer has agreed may be performed, on the employee's behalf, by the trade union.

Matters falling within the scope of section 29 of TULRA include:

(i)   terms and conditions of employment;
(ii)   engagement, non-engagement, termination, and suspension of employment;
(iii) work allocation;
(iv)   disciplinary matters;
(v)   trade union membership or non-membership;
(vi)   machinery for settling disputes (EPCA s27 as amended by EA 1989 s14).

A trade union member is entitled to reasonable time off during working hours, without pay, to take part in the activities of an independent trade union. Industrial action is specifically excluded (EPCA s28).

(c) For industrial relations training

An employee who is a trade union official is entitled to time off, with pay, to undergo training in aspects of industrial relations (EPCA s27).

(d) To look for work or arrange training

An employee who has been continuously employed for more than two years, and who is dismissed by reason of redundancy, is entitled to time off, with pay, during working hours to look for new employment or make arrangements for training for future employment (EPCA s31).

(e) For ante-natal care

A pregnant employee has the right to reasonable time off work, with pay, so that she may keep appointments for receiving ante-natal care (EPCA s31A).

(f) For health and safety representatives

An appointed health and safety representative is entitled to reasonable time off, with pay, for training purposes (Safety Representatives and Safety Committee Regulations 1977).

An aggrieved employee who is not allowed time off under the provisions of the EPCA may, within three months, make a complaint to an industrial tribunal. If the tribunal finds the complaint well founded it may make a declaration to that effect and award compensation.

6   To meet safety requirements

An employer owes a duty at common law and statute to take reasonable care for his employees' safety. This is dealt with in detail in Chapter 5.

—— Provision of a reference ——

An employer is not obliged to provide an employee or former employee with a reference or testimonial, or to answer questions from a third party relating to an employee's character.

A testimonial is usually given to an employee and becomes his personal property, while a reference is usually communicated in confidence to a prospective employer. An employer who provides a reference or testimonial may in certain circumstances incur liability on the document to the employee (or former employee) or to a third party.

An employee may allege that a statement contained in the document was defamatory, i.e. was a false statement which lowered his reputation in the eyes of right-thinking members of society. The employer may plead that the statement was substantially true, but is more likely to rely on the defence of *qualified privilege*. This protects an employer who makes a statement in the performance of a legal or moral duty to a person who has a corresponding interest or duty in receiving it, e.g. a prospective employer. The statement must be made honestly, with a belief in its truth, and must be free from malice.

An employer who recommends an employee to a third party in terms which he knows to be false may incur liability if the third party suffers damage as a result of his recommendation. In *Technovision v. Reed*, the plaintiff hired an accountant, relying on an outstanding reference given by his previous employer, the defendant. The employee stole from Technovision, and it emerged that he had previously stolen from Reed, who admitted that he had put his signature to a blank piece of headed notepaper. Technovision successfully sued Reed for damages.

An employer may also incur liability if a third party suffers financial injury as a result of a statement made carelessly or negligently by him (*Hedley Byrne & Co. Ltd v. Heller & Partners Ltd*).

An employer who is asked for a reference in respect of an employee whose previous conviction is spent, is under an obligation not to refer to any spent conviction or to any circumstances ancillary to it (The Rehabilitation of Offenders Act 1974). It also provides that he shall not incur any liability to a third party for not disclosing a spent conviction.

The Access to Medical Reports Act 1988 gives an employee the right to see, to make written comments upon and correct any errors in a medical report prepared for his employer for the purposes of employment. He has the right to refuse to release the report to his employer. As the Act applies to a report prepared by a medical practitioner who is responsible for the clinical care of the employee, it does not apply to a report or examination made by the company's medical adviser or by a specialist.

Vicarious liability

When an employee injures a third party in a way that gives the third party a legal right to damages, both the employer and the employee are liable to the third party. The employer's liability is known as vicarious liability. It may arise in respect of torts (civil wrongs), e.g. negligence, trespass, as well as for various criminal offences, e.g. assault, theft, fraud. An employer may also be liable for acts of sex or race discrimination committed by an employee unless he takes such steps as are reasonably practical to prevent the employee from committing the act (Race Relations Act; Sex Discrimination Act).

As an employee's wrongful act must arise in the course of his employment, an employer is clearly liable for a tort which he has expressly authorised to be committed. He is also liable for any act or omission which results in the commission of a tort. In *Gregory v. Piper*, an employee who was laying rubble near a neighbour's wall was expressly instructed by his employer not to allow the rubble to come into contact with the wall. Unfortunately the instructions were not carried out and the employer was liable to his neighbour in trespass.

An employer is also liable if an employee 'does fraudulently that which he was authorised to do honestly or if he does mistakenly that which he was authorised to do correctly'. (Salmon on Torts, 18th ed.). The following cases illustrate this principle.

In *Bayley v. Manchester, Sheffield & Lincolnshire Railway*, a railway porter removed a passenger from a train by force, stating 'You are in the wrong train, you must come out'. The Railway Company was held liable for the injury caused to that passenger.

In *Jefferson v. Derbyshire Farmers*, a youth employed by Derbyshire Farmers lit a cigarette when filling a tin with inflammable spirit. The resulting explosion and fire burned down the garage. The employer was held liable for the damage as the youth was acting within the scope of his employment.

An employer will not be liable if the employee's unauthorised act is regarded as an independent act which is not connected with an authorised act. In *GES v. Kingston and St Andrew Corporation*, a fire brigade was operating a go-slow policy in support of a pay claim and deliberately took 17 minutes, instead of three and a half minutes, to reach the scene of a fire. GES's premises were completely destroyed by the fire and they sued the local authority for the fire brigade's actions. It was held that the local authority were not liable, as the employees' unauthorised and unlawful method of performing the act, by going slow and stopping on their way to the fire, could be regarded as an independent act which was not connected with the authorised act.

An employer cannot avoid liability by showing that he had expressly forbidden an employee to use the particular mode of work. In *Limpus v. London General Omnibus Company Ltd*, the company had expressly forbidden its bus drivers 'to race with or obstruct another omnibus, or hinder or annoy the driver or conductor thereof'. A driver nevertheless obstructed one of Limpus' horse-drawn buses and caused damage to the bus and the horses. It was held that the bus company was liable for the acts of its employees.

An employee has implied authority to take reasonable steps to protect the employer's property in an emergency. The employee's actions are often excessive, but in the majority of cases the courts have decided that the employer is liable, for it is his interests that are being protected. In *Poland v. John Parr and Sons*, an employee mistakenly believed that a boy was about to steal a bag of sugar from his employer's wagon. He struck the boy, who fell under the wagon and had his leg amputated as a result of his injuries. It was held that the employer was liable.

In *Dyer v. Munday* the manager of a hire purchase firm went to recover a bed on which instalments were in arrears. He found that the customer had pledged it to his landlady for rent. In the course of a heated argument the landlady was assaulted and the manager was subsequently fined for the assault. It was held that the employer was liable for the manager's criminal offence.

If the act in question is dictated by the personal considerations of the employee, rather than the employer's interests, it may well be outside the scope of the employment. In *Daniels v. Whetstone Entertainments*, a dance-hall bouncer, not content with evicting a reveller from the club, carried on assaulting him outside the club. He subsequently died from those injuries. It was held that the employer was liable for the employee's actions inside the club, but the continuation of the assault outside the club took it outside the scope of the employer's liability.

An employer may be liable if an employee who is authorised to drive a vehicle permits an unauthorised person to drive in his place. This may well constitute a wrongful method of fulfilling an authorised act. In *London County Council v. Cattermoles* a garage worker was instructed to push vehicles about by hand as he had no licence. He moved a van by driving it on to the highway. It was held that he was acting within the scope of his employment as he was carrying out his authorised duty of moving vehicles in an unauthorised manner. In *Ilkiw v. Samuels*, a lorry driver allowed a third party to move a lorry to make room for other lorries, who were waiting to load. The lorry driver, who was at the back of the lorry covering the load, was unaware that the third party was incompetent. The third party crashed the lorry into a conveyor belt and injured the plaintiff. The lorry driver's employers were held liable for the damages resulting from the accident, as the driver was held to be in charge of the vehicle, although he was not at the controls at the time of the accident.

An employer will not generally be liable where, despite orders to the contrary, an employee gives a lift to a third party. In *Twine v. Bean's Express* it was held that the employee's act in giving a lift was outside the scope of his employment. In *Conway v. George Wimpey* it was held that the third party was a trespasser.

Whether an employee is acting in the course of employment when travelling to work depends on whether he is going about his employer's business.

In *Stages v. Darlington Insulation Co. Ltd* the following propositions were laid down:

1 where an employee travels from his home to his regular place of work, even in his employer's transport, he is not acting in the course of employment. If he is obliged, by his contract of employment, to use his employer's transport for the journey, then, in the absence of an express condition to the contrary, he is considered to be acting in the course of his employment;

2 where an employee travels in the employer's time between workplaces, he is considered to be acting in the course of employment;

3 payment of wages, but not travelling allowance, indicates that an employee is travelling in the employer's time, for his benefit and in the course of employment;

4 an employee travelling from his home to a place other than his usual place of work to an emergency is in the course of employment;

5 a deviation, other than a deviation incidental to the journey, takes an employee out of the course of employment;

6 a return journey is to be treated in the same way as the outward journey.

The courts have distinguished between a gratuitous lift, and the situation where an employee, despite orders to the contrary, carries a passenger in furtherance of a purpose which is related to the employer's business. In *Rose v. Plenty*, a milkman used the services of a 13-year-old boy, despite instructions to the contrary. He also paid him a weekly sum for his services. The boy was injured as a result of the employee's negligence. It was held that the employer was liable, as the boy's services were used in furtherance of the employer's business.

An employer will not be liable if the employee's act was outside the scope of the employment, i.e. the employee was engaged on an activity for which he was not employed. In *Beard v. London General Omnibus Company*, a bus conductor, in the driver's absence, drove a bus and injured the plaintiff. The bus company was not liable as the bus conductor's actions were outside the scope of his duties.

In *Keppel Bus Co. v. Sa'ad bin Ahmad* a bus conductor hit a passenger with his ticket punch, causing the loss of an eye. It was held that, although it was part of his job to keep order, there was no evidence of disorder, only of a quarrel with a passenger. The employers were therefore not liable.

For an employer to be liable to a third party, the employee must have been using the employer's property on his employer's business. If an employee injures a third party while using his employer's property in circumstances where there is no connection with the employer's business, the employer bears no liability. In *Rayner v. Mitchell,* a drayman, without permission, took a van out of his employer's stables to deliver a coffin to a relative's house. On the return journey he collected some empty beer barrels and was later involved in an accident. It was held that the employer was not liable as the act of collecting the barrels did not convert an unauthorised journey into an authorised journey.

An employer may not be vicariously liable where an employee deviates from his work or an authorised route to undertake some business of his own. Judges in the last century described an employee's actions in this situation as 'a frolic of his own'. In general, a slight deviation from an authorised route does not detract from the main purpose of the journey which is the delivery of the employer's goods. In these circumstances the employer will be liable for any torts committed in the course of his journey.

In *Hilton v. Thomas Burton Ltd* employees used their employer's van to drive to a café to wait their normal finishing time. On the way back there was an accident due to negligent driving. It was held that, although the employer authorised the use of the van for reasonable purposes, the employees were not engaged in his work at the time of the accident, as they were on 'a frolic of their own'.

In *Heasman v. Clarity Cleaning Co. Ltd* an office cleaner employed by a contract cleaning company made telephone calls while he was working at an office. It was held that the employer was not liable for their employee's dishonesty as the employee's actions constituted 'a frolic of his own'.

An employee's criminal conduct may be regarded as being in the course of his employment if a third party suffers as a result of the employee's criminal act. In *Morris v. C. W. Martin & Sons,* an employee's theft of a mink stole, sent for cleaning to his employers, resulted in his employers being found liable to recompense the plaintiff as the employee had been entrusted with the article in the course of his employment.

An employer who is sued by a third party, following an employee's negligent act, has the right to claim an indemnity from the employee in question, i.e. an employer may recover from the employee the amount paid as damages to the third party (*Lister v. Romford Ice and Cold Storage Co. Ltd* – see page 46).

Where an employer has been negligent and partially contributed to the negligent act, he may not recover the whole amount from the employee, only that proportion that is attributable to the employee's negligence, i.e. a contribution from the employee (*Jones v. Manchester Corporation* – see page 46).

Liability for the torts of an independent contractor

An employer who uses the services of an independent contractor is generally not liable for any torts committed by the independent contractor. In the following circumstances, liability will be imposed:

1   where the employer authorises the commission of a tort, for example instructing the contractor to tip waste on another person's land (the tort of trespass);

2   where the employer instructs an independent contractor to undertake work which is inherently dangerous. In *Honeywill-Stein v. Larkin Brothers Ltd*, an employer was held liable for the contractor's negligence when magnesium flares used for taking indoor photographs set light to theatre curtains and caused substantial damage;

3   where work is being done by the contractor on or in a highway. An employer in these cases usually has a statutory duty to undertake work which would otherwise be classed as a nuisance, but is nevertheless liable for injuries caused by the negligence of an independent contractor. In *Holliday v. National Telephone Company*, a plumber engaged by National Telephone Company negligently used a blowlamp which exploded and injured a passer-by. The company was liable for the contractor's negligence;

4   if a nuisance is created as a result of a contractor's work on the employer's land, the employer will be liable to those parties whose use of their land is affected by the nuisance. Examples of such nuisances are smoke, noise, fumes, dust or vibration;

5   where an absolute duty is imposed by statute on an employer, he cannot evade liability by delegating its performance to a contractor. In *Groves v. Wimbourne*, it was held that a factory owner, under a

duty to fence machinery, was liable for the faulty workmanship of the contractor who had erected the fencing on the employer's behalf.

Where an employer is held liable to a third party for the torts of an independent contractor, he will generally be able to claim an indemnity from the contractor.

4

EMPLOYEE'S DUTIES

The relationship of employer and employee imposes obligations on both parties. Provisions as to remuneration, the hours of work and the main terms of the contract of employment are clearly spelt out in details given to the employee in the Employment Protection (Consolidation) Act. There are, however, certain rights and obligations which are not provided for by statute, but are nevertheless implied in a contract of employment. These are:

1 to render personal service;
2 to render careful service;
3 to obey reasonable orders;
4 to act in good faith;
5 to serve the employer loyally;
6 to share the benefit of an invention;
7 not to disclose confidential information.

1 To render personal service

An employee undertakes to render personal service, i.e. to perform in person the contract of employment. He also warrants that he has the necessary skills to perform the work.

There are certain occupations which demand such a high degree of skill that the slightest departure or deviation from those standards justifies dismissal, e.g. an airline pilot, a driver of an express train, a scientist in charge of a nuclear reactor, a driver of an articulated lorry carrying dangerous chemicals, etc.

In *Taylor v. Alidair Ltd*, an airline pilot was fairly dismissed as the result of an unsatisfactory landing which endangered the lives of his passengers and caused serious damage to the aircraft. The Air Navigation Order provides that 'The operator of an aircraft registered in the UK shall not permit any person to be a member of the crew thereof during any flight . . . unless the operator has satisfied himself that such a person is competent to perform his duties'.

In *Bevan Harris Ltd v. Gair*, a foreman was fairly dismissed after 11 years' service (after four warnings) for failing to carry out his tasks in a satisfactory manner.

A court may not compel an employee to fulfil his or her obligations under (*a*) an order for specific performance (or specific implement) or a contract of employment, or (*b*) an injunction (or interdict) restraining a breach or threatened breach of such a contract.

Although an employer cannot compel an employee to work for him, he can nevertheless prevent that employee from working for a rival company, when the employee has entered into a covenant not to work for another employer in that area of work. In 1936 the actress Bette Davis entered into a contract with Warner Bros for one year, renewable for further yearly periods at the option of Warner Bros. In breach of this agreement she entered into a contract with a rival film company. It was held that Warner Bros were entitled to an injunction to prevent her from working as an actress with a rival company (*Warner Bros v. Nelson*).

An employee cannot compel an employer to continue to employ him. In *Chappel v. The Times Newspapers Ltd*, the National Graphical Association was engaged in a trade dispute with Times Newspapers. Times Newspapers gave notice that, unless the union called off its action, its members would be regarded as having terminated their contracts of employment. The employees sought to prevent the newspaper proprietors from taking such action, but were not entitled to such an order.

2 To render careful service

An employee is under an obligation to render careful service to his employer and must exercise skill and care in the course of his employment. The degree of skill and care will obviously depend upon the nature of the contract and the representations made by the employee, i.e. that he has the degree of skill which he professes to have. In *Lister v. Romford Ice and Cold Storage Company*, a lorry driver, while reversing, injured his 'mate', who subsequently sued the employer for injuries caused by an employee of the firm, i.e. the lorry driver. The driver's 'mate' was in fact the driver's father. He recovered substantial damages for his injuries. The insurance company paid the damages and then sued the driver, in the company's name, to recover the damages paid. It was held that the driver owed the company a duty to perform his work with care and skill and was liable, as he was in breach of this duty.

In practice the employers insure against such contingencies and any damages are paid by insurance companies, who may then seek to recover a contribution from the employee. After Lister's case the employer's liability insurers agreed not to institute claims against employees, unless there was evidence of fraud or collusion.

In *Jupiter General Insurance Co. v. Schroff* the manager of a company's life insurance department negligently recommended granting a life policy knowing that a few days earlier the managing director had refused the insurance. It was held that his misconduct justified summary dismissal.

This principle was re-affirmed in *Janata Bank v. Ahmed*, where the assistant general manager of the bank's London branch was successfully sued for negligence, in that he gave loans to individuals without satisfactory collateral or references. The loans were not repaid and he was held liable in damages.

In *Jones v. Manchester Corporation*, a recently qualified doctor's negligence caused the death of a patient. The hospital was held 80 per cent to blame for the doctor's negligence, but was entitled to recover part of the damages from its employee.

3 To obey reasonable orders

An employee must obey reasonable orders given to him by his employer. What is a reasonable order has on several occasions been discussed by the courts. In the last century a representative of a woollen company was ordered by his employer to card wool. He refused to do so and was dismissed. It was held that he was entitled to refuse to do such a menial task and was awarded damages (*Price v. Mouat*).

In *Pepper v. Webb*, a gardener refused, one Saturday morning, to work beyond his normal hours in order to plant flowers for his employer's wife. As he left he added insult to injury by stating 'I couldn't care less about your bloody greenhouse and your sodding garden'. He was summarily dismissed. As this was not an isolated incident he was held to have been fairly dismissed.

If an order exposes an employee to the dangers of violence or disease he may rightly refuse to obey such an order. In *Ottoman Bank v. Chakarian*, an Armenian employee was sent to its head office at Constantinople. As he had previously been sentenced to death by the Turkish authorities and had escaped, he asked his employers to transfer him to a branch outside Turkey as he feared for his life. His request was refused. He fled from Constantinople and was dismissed without notice. He successfully brought an action for wrongful dismissal.

However, it must be shown that a danger exists for a claim to be successful. In *Walmsley v. Udec Refrigeration*, an employee was dismissed for refusing to work in Wexford, as he considered that area to be a hot-bed of IRA activity. As he could not substantiate his claim his dismissal was upheld by the court.

An employee may well be in breach of contract if he refuses to work overtime in those cases where there is an implied or tacit agreement that overtime will be worked. Colliery deputies had agreed to work 'such days as may reasonably be required by the management'. Six deputies refused to work on Saturday mornings and were each sued for £3.50 by the National Coal Board for loss of production. It was held that the NCB was entitled to recover this sum from each deputy (*NCB v. Galley* (see page 26)).

The Court of Appeal has given guidance as to when it may be regarded as reasonable to refuse to obey a lawful order (*Union of Construction Allied Trades and Technicians v. Brain*). The nature of the order, the circumstances surrounding the giving of that order and the employee's reason for not carrying out the order must all be considered. Brain, the editor of the union's journal, was sued after the publication of a defamatory article relating to an employer in the federation journal. His employers instructed him to settle the libel action but, on the advice of the union's legal officer, he declined to do so. He felt that the undertaking contained in the proposed settlement, that neither he nor the employees or printers should print any further libel relating to the employers' federation, would make him liable for the acts of other parties over whom he had no control. It was held that his subsequent dismissal for refusing to obey a lawful order was unfair, as in the circumstances his refusal was not unreasonable.

The EAT also considered the question of a lawful order in *Davidson v. Maillou Comparisons Ltd.* Employees refused to accept a transfer to different premises when the employers learned that the employees proposed to open a shop in competition a hundred yards from their existing workplace. It was held that they were fairly dismissed as an employer is entitled to take reasonable steps to protect himself against unfair competition.

4   To act in good faith

An employee must show good faith towards his employer. This encompasses a variety of situations. In *Sinclair v. Neighbour*, a manager of a betting shop borrowed £15 from the till to place a bet on horses and deposited an IOU for the money in the till. The following day he retrieved the IOU and repaid the £15. It was held that the employee, though not dishonest, had acted in a manner which was incompatible with his employment as a manager and his summary dismissal was justified.

An employee must not make a secret profit from his employment. The employer will in these circumstances be entitled to recover the value of the secret profit from the employee. In *Boston Deep Sea Fishing Company v. Ansell*, the company's managing director entered into contracts for constructing fishing smacks and was secretly paid a commission on the contract by the shipbuilders. He also owned shares in an ice-making company which paid, in addition to dividends, a bonus to shareholders who were owners of fishing smacks and who purchased ice from the ice company for use in their ships. He was summarily dismissed. These sums were subsequently recovered from Ansell by the plaintiff company.

An employee may not take advantage of his employment to make a profit, which, although not arising in the course of his employment, arises due to his employment. In *Reading v. Attorney General*, Sergeant

Reading, who was stationed in Egypt, made a substantial profit by shepherding convoys of lorries carrying illicit spirit through patrol blocks. This money was confiscated by the military authorities. He later unsuccessfully sued the Crown for its return.

An employee who misuses information received in the course of his employment, or who uses that information for his personal benefit, is liable to account to his employer (or former employer) for any profit made in these circumstances. In *Industrial Development Consultants v. Cooley*, Industrial Development Consultants Ltd provided construction consultancy services for gas boards. Its managing director was an architect named Cooley. The Eastern Gas Board offered tenders for building, and Cooley was informed that it was unlikely that IDC Ltd would be given the contract. He realised that he had an excellent opportunity of obtaining the contract for himself and represented to IDC Ltd that he was ill. IDC released him from his contract and he then obtained the benefit of the contract for himself. IDC successfully sued him for the profit he made on the building contracts.

An employee has a duty to report the misconduct of his fellow employees. In *Sybron Corporation v. Rochem Ltd*, a company recovered a pension payment of £13,208 from a senior executive who had been engaged with his subordinates in a conspiracy to set up in direct competition with the company. As a senior executive, his duty was to report the fraudulent activities of his subordinates.

If an employee accepts a bribe or reward from a third party, there is an irrebuttable presumption that he has been influenced in his dealings by that payment. In *Shipway v. Broadwood*, a sale of horses was conditional on their being passed as sound by a veterinary surgeon. The sale was concluded, but the horses were found to be unsound. As the veterinary surgeon had received a commission from the seller, the sale was put aside. The Court of Appeal ruled that it was immaterial whether the commission had any effect on the judgement of the veterinary surgeon.

An employer may not only rescind the contract but also recover the amount of the bribe from the employee. Additionally the Prevention of Corruption Act 1906 provides that the giving and receiving of bribes is a criminal offence.

5   *To serve the employer loyally*

There is an implied term that an employee shall serve his employer loyally in his business. If an employee harms his employer by any work undertaken in his spare time, there is therefore a breach of this term. In *Hivac v. Park Royal Scientific Investments Company Ltd*, the employees of a firm which manufactured miniature valves worked at weekends and evenings for a competitor, who was also engaged in the manufacture of valves. It was held that an injunction would be granted to prevent this moonlighting.

An employer may insert a clause in a contract of employment which binds the employee's services exclusively to the employer. Such a clause will be upheld if it can be shown to be necessary to protect the employer's legitimate business interests (*Thomas Marshall (Exports) v. Guinle*, see page 117).

This does not prevent an employee from working for a competitor or setting up his own business while in another person's employment. An employee can usefully and profitably employ himself in his free time, in some other capacity, for some other employer. In *Nova Plastics v. Froggatt*, an odd-job man, who worked for a rival company in his spare time, was held to have been unfairly dismissed. Working for a rival employer is not a breach of an implied term of loyal service, unless it can be shown that the employer has suffered harm by the employee's actions.

Restraint of trade

An employer is entitled to incorporate a restraint clause in an employee's contract of service. Such a clause may prevent an employee on leaving his present employment from entering into a similar type of business, either on his own account or with another employer, in a particular area for a certain length of time.

If an employee acts in breach of such a clause his employer may seek an injunction to restrain the former employee from continuing to act in breach. The court has a discretion whether or not to grant relief. In *Provident Financial Group v. Hayward*, Hayward was employed as a financial director. His contract contained a clause stating that he would not work for any other business during its continuance. He tendered his resignation on 1 July 1988 and it was agreed he would be on 'gardening leave' until Dec. 31 1988, i.e. paid in full, provided he did not work for anyone else. He informed his employer in October 1988 of his intention to start work immediately for another employer. The employer was refused an injunction as the court considered that he would not suffer if the injunction was not granted, as the business which the employee wished to work for was unrelated to that of the employer.

As a restraint clause is *prima facie* void, it is for the employer to justify the restraint on the basis that the restrictions placed on the employee are reasonable in terms of the time, the area of the restraint and the interest to be protected.

Generally the interests that can be protected are: trade secrets and other confidential information; and trade connections including business and customer contacts.

Confidential information   An employee may use his own skill and knowledge in competition, but he may not use confidential information which could harm his employer's interests (*Faccenda Chicken Ltd v. Fowler*, see page 55).

In *Forster v. Suggett*, an engineer who worked with a glass manufacturing company and was conversant with secret manufacturing processes, agreed that he would not be engaged in the manufacture of glass products for five years. This covenant was upheld by the courts.

Business and customer connections   An employer is entitled to impose a covenant which protects his business connections and prevents his customers from being enticed away by his former employee. A court will only uphold such a covenant if the former employee had personal contact with the employer's customers. In *Fitch v. Dewes*, a solicitor's clerk agreed that he would not, on leaving his employment, set up in business as a solicitor within seven miles of Tamworth Town Hall. As the clerk had an extensive acquaintance with his employer's clients, this was held to be valid.

In *Office Angels Ltd v. Rainer-Thomas, O'Connor*, a company carried on business as an employment agency, with 34 branches in England, including four within the City of London. One of the defendants worked as a branch manager and the other as a consultant at a City of London branch. They agreed that on leaving their employment they would not, for six months, solicit custom from any customer who had been a client during the time of their employment or engage in or undertake the trade or business of an employment agency within a one-kilometre radius of any branch or branches where they had worked in the previous six months. It was held that both covenants were an unreasonable restriction on competition. The soliciting restriction applied to all the company's clients (6000–7000), while only around 100 were known to the defendants, while the kilometre restriction circle would give the company valuable protection against possible competition.

In *André v. Bashford*, an apprentice hairdresser agreed that she would not set up in competition within three-quarters of a mile of her former employer's place of business, for six months after leaving his employment. This was also upheld by the court. It is interesting to compare these two cases with *Strange Ltd v. Mann*, where the manager of a bookmaker's shop covenanted that on leaving his employment he would not be engaged in a similar business within a 12-mile radius of his present employment. As most of the betting was done over the phone, the defendant had little personal contact with customers. It was held that the covenant was an attempt to stifle competition.

In *Home Counties Dairies Ltd v. Skilton*, a milk roundsman agreed that he would not, within one year after leaving his present employment, sell milk or dairy products to any person who, during the last six months of his employment, had been a customer of the dairy and whom he had served as the dairy's employee. Within days of leaving his employment he started to operate a milk round covering the same area for a competitor. The court granted an injunction to prevent the breach of the restraint. The clause was reasonable and protected a legitimate interest.

In *Spafax Ltd v. Taylor*, a salesman covenanted that he would not, for two years after leaving Spafax's employment, solicit or seek to obtain orders for goods which he dealt with on behalf of Spafax, or any similar goods for anyone to whom he sold goods on Spafax's behalf during the six months prior to his leaving the employment. It was held that the covenant was reasonable.

Area of restraint   Restrictive covenants often contain limitations on the freedom of individuals to compete within a particular area for a certain length of time. In general, the greater the area covered the shorter the permissible time limit and vice versa. (*Fitch v. Dewes*, see page 51.)

A covenant will be invalid if it covers a wider area than is reasonably necessary to protect the employer's interests. In *Marley Tile Co. Ltd v. Johnson*, the defendant agreed that for 12 months after leaving his employment he would not canvass, solicit or deal with Marley's products, or any similar products within any area in which he had been employed during the preceding 12 months. It was held that, although the period of 12 months was reasonable, the restriction as to area (covering practically the whole of Devon and Cornwall) was too wide. The covenant was therefore invalid.

In *Greer v. Sketchley*, a covenant not to engage in any part of the UK in any business similar to that carried on by the employer was held to be unenforceable as the employer's operations were confined to the Midlands and to south-east England.

An employer may be able to enforce a nationwide covenant to protect nationwide business interests.

In *Littlewoods Organisation Ltd v. Harris*, the defendant worked in a senior position for the firm and had access to confidential information as to the organisation and operation of their national mail order business. He covenanted that, on leaving his employment, he would not work for their chief rivals, Great Universal Stores (GUS) for a period of 12 months. He resigned to take up a post with GUS. The restraint was worldwide and covered companies associated with GUS which were not in the mail order business. It was held that the restriction would apply to the mail order business carried on by GUS in the United Kingdom.

Although the courts will not re-write a clause which is an unreasonable restraint of trade to convert it into a reasonable clause, they may on occasion sever an unreasonable clause from the rest of the agreement. This will only be done if the agreement is interpreted as containing separate contractual terms and the unreasonable clause can be severed from the rest of the agreement without altering the nature of the agreement.

In *Putsman v. Taylor*, Taylor was the manager of one of three tailoring establishments owned by his employer in various parts of Birmingham. He agreed that he would not set up in competition within half a mile of any of the three businesses. It was held that the undertaking not to work near his present place of employment was enforceable and could be severed from the other contractual undertakings.

In *Business Seating (Renovations) Ltd v. Broad*, Broad was a sales representative of a company renovating commercial and office furniture. An associated company manufactured and sold office furniture. He agreed that he would not, for one year, canvass customers of the company or the associated company. It was held that the restriction relating to customers of the associated company was void as these were merely potential customers, but the covenant relating to the company's customers was valid. It was therefore possible to sever the covenant.

6   To share the benefit of an invention

The benefit of an invention made by an employee while in his employer's service belongs to his employer if:

(a)   it was made by the employee during his normal duties; or
(b)   it was made outside the course of normal duties, but it was the result of a specific assignment and the circumstances were such that an invention might reasonably be expected to result from those duties; or
(c)   because of the employee's particular responsibilities he has a special obligation to further the interests of the employer's undertaking (Patents Act 1977 s39).

Whether an employee has a special obligation depends on his status. In *Reiss Engineering Co. Ltd v. Harris* a sales manager who sold valves and provided after-sales service invented a new type of valve which eliminated many of the faults found in the valve sold by the company. It was held that the patent belonged to Harris, who had no special obligation to further his employer's interests.

In all other circumstances an employee's invention belongs to him, and any purported agreement to the contrary is invalid. An employee may, if he so wishes, assign or transfer the benefit of a patent to his employer, usually for a cash payment or a percentage of the profits made by marketing the invention.

In certain circumstances an employee may benefit from his invention, even though the patent belongs to his employer. An employee may apply to the court or to the Comptroller General of Patents for compensation, in the following cases:

(a)   if the invention proves to be of outstanding benefit to the employer's business; or
(b)   if the patent had originally been granted to the employee (who had assigned it to the employer), but the benefit derived by the employee from the assignment is inadequate in relation to that derived by the employer.

An employee must receive by way of compensation 'a fair share (having regard to all the circumstances) of the benefit which the employer has derived from the patent . . .' (Patents Act 1977 s40).

7 *Not to disclose confidential information*

An employee is under a duty not to disclose confidential information or material relating to his employer's business or to use such information in an unauthorised manner. In *Thomas Marshall (Exports) Ltd v. Guinle*, it was stated that there are four elements which may assist the court in identifying confidential information or trade secrets which will be protected. These are:

(a) the owner must believe that the release of the information would be injurious to him or advantageous to his rivals;
(b) the owner must believe that the information is confidential or secret;
(c) these beliefs must be reasonable;
(d) the information must be judged in the light of the usage and practices of the particular trade or industry concerned.

An employer may seek an injunction if he considers that the publication of confidential information or material would be harmful to his business.

A former employee is under a duty not to disclose confidential information relating to his previous employment, e.g. trade secrets, secret processes. Not all information acquired by the employee during his employment is confidential. An ex-employee cannot be prevented from using knowledge, know-how and skill which he has acquired in the course of his employment. He may only be restrained by a restrictive covenant in his employment contract.

In *Faccenda Chicken Ltd v. Fowler* the former managing director of a company set up in competition with his former company, using former company employees as his workforce. It was held that he was not in breach of his contract of employment by using information gained in his previous employment, e.g. names and addresses of customers and their requirements; delivery routes; prices charged. The court held that all the circumstances should be considered, in particular:

(a) the nature of the employment;
(b) the nature of the information, which must be such as to require protection;

(c)   whether the employer impressed on the employee the confidential nature of the information;

(d)   the extent to which the information could be isolated from information which the employee is free to use.

An employee is not bound by this duty of confidentiality if he discloses confidential information acquired in his employment which relates to 'misconduct of such a nature that it ought, in the public interest, to be disclosed to others'. The person to whom such information is disclosed must have a proper interest in receiving it. In *Initial Services Ltd v. Putterill*, it was held that a sales manager was entitled to disclose an arrangement by which his former employers maintained prices, which allegedly contravened the Restrictive Trade Practices Act 1956.

5

SAFETY OF EMPLOYEES

An employer is under a duty at common law and under the provisions of the Health and Safety at Work Act 1974 to take reasonable care for the safety of his employees. Section 2(1) of the Health and Safety at Work Act (HSWA) provides that: 'It shall be the duty of every employer to ensure, so far as is reasonably practicable, the health, safety and welfare at work of all his employees'. Section 2(2) states '. . . the matters to which that duty extends include in particular the provision and maintenance of plant and systems of work that are, so far as is reasonably practicable, safe and without risks to health'.

Employer's obligations at common law

In some respects, sections 2(1) and 2(2) of the HSWA restate the general duty which the common law imposes on an employer with regard to the safety of his employees.

An employer does not guarantee that injury will not befall an employee. He merely undertakes that he will take reasonable care, i.e. 'the care which an ordinary prudent employer would take in all the circumstances', and will only be liable if some lack of care on his part fails to prevent an injury to an employee that was reasonably foreseeable. In *Vinney v. Star Paper Mills*, an employee who was instructed to clean a floor on which viscous liquid had been spilt, slipped on the floor while cleaning it. It was held that there was no foreseeable risk in such a straightforward task. Another employer was held not to blame where a worker was injured in the general rush to reach the canteen (*Lazarus v. Firestone Tyre & Rubber Company*).

An employer's duty in respect of his employee's safety was summarised by Swanwick J. in *Stokes v. Guest Keen and Nettlefold Ltd*:

1   an employer must take steps to ensure his employee's safety in the light of knowledge which he has or ought to have;
2   an employer is entitled to follow a recognised practice, unless this is clearly unsound;
3   he must keep reasonably abreast of developing knowledge and not be too slow in applying it;
4   if he has greater than average knowledge of the risk, he must take more than average precautions;
5   he should weigh up the risks in terms of the likelihood of the occurrence of an injury and the potential consequences, and balance that against the effectiveness, expense and inconvenience of the precautions.

This shows that an employer is only liable if he fails to take positive steps to ensure his employee's safety in the light of current recognised practice and knowledge. When there is a developing area of knowledge, he must keep reasonably abreast of it, and must apply it in a reasonably practical manner.

In *Wright v. Dunlop Rubber Co. & ICI*, the employers had, since 1940, used a substance called Nonox S in the manufacture of tyres. The manufacturers, ICI, later discovered that the product carried the risk of cancer and informed Dunlop of the fact, advising them to screen and test all employees who had been exposed to the product. As this was not done for some considerable time, both Dunlop and ICI were liable to the plaintiff.

An employer is entitled to weigh up the risk in terms of the likelihood of injury, and balance that against the effectiveness of the precautions needed to meet the risk, and the economic consequences of taking or not taking the risk. In *Latimer v. AEC*, a company spread sawdust on the factory floor after a storm had flooded the works. The flood had left a film of oil on the floor and some areas were left untreated due to a shortage of sawdust. It was held that it would be unrealistic to close the factory with consequent loss of wages and production until absolutely safe conditions existed. Latimer was therefore unable to claim damages as a result of slipping on the floor, as the company had, in the circumstances, taken reasonable precautions.

The duty is not collective, but is owed to each employee individually. In *Paris v. Stepney Borough Council*, it was held that an employer owes a greater duty of care to an employee suffering from a physical defect than to other employees. The plaintiff, who was blind in one eye, suffered injury to his good eye while working as a fitter, and claimed that he should have been supplied with goggles. It was held that the employer should have taken additional precautions in these circumstances, and the plaintiff was entitled to damages.

An employer's duty is personal and he cannot avoid liability for injury to an employee by delegating his duties, or by obtaining the services of an independent contractor. This is so, even if the employer is compelled by statute, or by lack of the requisite knowledge, to delegate to a subordinate. In *Wilson v. Clyde Coal Co. v. English*, the owner of a mine delegated the task of installing a system of work to an agent. The system proved to be defective and as a result an employee was injured. The owner was held liable, despite the fact that he was bound under the provisions of the Coal Mines Act to delegate this task.

An employer's duty is to provide for the safety of his employee and does not extend to safeguarding the employee's property. A hospital authority was not liable for the loss incurred by a registrar, whose clothing was stolen from a hostel owned by the authority. Neither was a theatre management liable when a Widow Twankey costume was stolen from an actor's dressing room (*Deyong v. Shenburn*).

An employer's duty to provide for his employees' safety may be considered under four headings.

1 The provision of a safe system of work.
2 The provision of safe premises.
3 The provision of safe plant and equipment.
4 The provision of competent fellow employees.

1 Safe system of work

What constitutes a safe system can only be determined in the particular circumstances of the case, and will vary according to the nature of the work involved and the general practice in the particular industry. In many kinds of operations there is no uniformity or regularity in the tasks which are encountered. The actual situation at a given time must then be examined to determine whether a safe system is in operation.

The following factors are relevant in deciding whether a reasonably safe system has been established: the physical layout of the job; the sequence in which the work is to be carried out; the provision of warnings and notices; the issues of special instructions; and general working conditions.

Where a potentially dangerous task is constantly repeated, an employer is under a duty to devise a safe system which will, as far as is reasonably possible, eliminate the danger. If the task is unusual or complicated the employer should organise and supervise the task. In *Rees v. Cambrian Wagon Works Ltd*, a cog wheel weighing 15 cwt, and measuring 125 cm in diameter and 20 cm in width was being removed from a machine, with the aid of a plank and sloping wedge. As the wedge was not wide enough to keep the plank in position, the plank rocked, and the wheel overbalanced and fatally injured an employee. The employer was held liable as he had not devised a safe system of working for that particular task.

An employer must not only devise a safe system of working, but also ensure that the system is enforced. Nevertheless, he is not liable for an injury to an employee if that employee, without the employer's consent or knowledge, departs from the system. In *Woods v. Durable Suites*, the defendant company used synthetic glue in their works with the consequent risk of the employees contracting dermatitis. The employers provided adequate washing facilities and cream, and made widely known to the employees the risk involved if proper precautions were not observed. Unknown to them, an employee had disregarded these precautions and contracted dermatitis. The employer was not liable as 'there is no duty at common law, to stand over workmen of age and experience'. In situations where there is an obvious danger the courts have adopted the attitude that an employee cannot be treated like an 'imbecile child'.

An employee who is indifferent to his own safety and who is subsequently injured may find the courts unsympathetic if his employer has provided equipment which would lessen the danger; for example in *Qualcast v. Haynes,* an employee was injured when molten metal spilt on to his feet from a ladle he was handling. Notices specified that protective boots were available in the stores. As he was not wearing protective boots the employer was held not to be liable.

In *James v. Hepworth and Grandage,* an employee was injured while working in a foundry. The employer displayed notices advising the employees to wear spats. As the employee had not done so, the employer was held not to be liable, despite the fact that the employee could not read. He had seen and understood the use of spats and made a decision not to use them.

In *Smith v. Scott Bowyers Ltd* an employee was injured when he slipped on the greasy factory floor. The employers had supplied their employees with wellington boots which had ridged soles and they were renewed when a request was made by the employee. The employee's wellington boots had worn down. It was held that the employee's failure to renew them was due to his 'own lack of care'. The employer was under no obligation to inspect the condition of the wellington boots.

A similar conclusion was reached in *McWilliams v. Arrol,* when a steel erector, working without a safety belt, was killed when he fell some hundred feet to the ground. The employer was not liable, for although a safety belt was not available on the site, the evidence showed that, had it been available, it would not have been worn by the employee.

If a danger exists which is not obvious to the employees, the employer is under a duty not only to warn of the danger, but also to convince employees of the necessity of taking precautions. In *Crookall v. Vickers Armstrong* a foundry's sandy floor created a risk of silicosis. Although the employers provided exhaust appliances, they did not sufficiently emphasise to the work-force the need to wear masks to overcome the danger of silicosis. The employers were consequently liable for the plaintiff contracting silicosis.

2 Safe premises

An employer must take reasonable care to ensure that the place of work is safe and that steps are taken to minimise any dangers of which he is aware or which are apparent. In *Bath v. BTC*, an employee, working on a narrow ledge on a dry dock, fell and was killed. As the possibility of injury was apparent, the employer was held liable for not providing adequate safety measures such as a safety net.

The employer must also provide safe access to and from the place of work. In *Bryden v. Stewart*, it was held that the owner of a coal mine had not provided a safe access to and from the pit when a stone from the side of the mine shaft fell into an open cage and killed one of the miners.

An employer remains liable for the safety of his employees, even though an employee is working in premises occupied by a third party. However, he cannot be held responsible for the state of premises which are not under his control. In *Cilia v. H. M. James & Sons*, a plumber's mate was electrocuted when installing new plumbing in a building. The employer was not liable as the building was not occupied by him, and he was unaware of the defective electric circuit in the building.

Although the structure of the premises is outside the employer's control, he remains under a duty to exercise reasonable care to safeguard the employee against dangers which he should anticipate and which can be averted. He must provide proper safety equipment and give instructions, if this appears necessary.

In *General Cleaning Contractors Ltd v. Christmas*, a window cleaner, cleaning the outside of the windows of the Caledonian Club, fell when a window sash fell on his hand. Although it was not possible to fit safety belts on the outside of the building, the employer was nevertheless liable as he should have devised a system of work which would have made the work and the premises safe.

3   Safe plant and equipment

An employer is under a duty to provide proper and safe plant and equipment for the work. He must also maintain the equipment in good condition and remedy any known defects. He may incur liability if he fails to provide the appropriate equipment in circumstances where there is an obvious need for such equipment.

In *Lovell v. Blundells & Crompton Co. Ltd*, an employee who was cleaning a ship's boilers needed staging to finish the task. He erected staging with planks he found on the site. The planks were defective and the employee fell and was injured. The employer was held liable as he had failed to provide staging or prescribe a system of working.

An employer will also incur liability if he fails to provide the requisite quantity of equipment required for a particular task. In *Machray v. Stewart & Lloyds Ltd*, only one block and tackle was available on a site when a very large pipe had to be fixed high above ground. An experienced fitter was injured as a result of the pipe swinging out of control, and the employer was held liable for his injuries.

An employer will be in breach of his duty if he provides plant and equipment which he knows, or ought to have known, was defective. In *Bradford v. Robinson Rentals*, an employer who sent an employee in a van with a defective heater on a round trip of 400 miles in severe weather, was liable when the employee contracted frostbite.

This duty is not restricted to the provisions of machinery; for example in *Bowater v. Rowley Regis Corporation*, an employer was liable for injuries sustained by an employee when a horse which was known to be prone to bolting, did in fact bolt. In *Naismith v. London Film Productions Ltd*, sacking draped over a film extra caught fire. The employers were held liable for providing dangerous equipment.

An employer cannot avoid liability by claiming that, although he provided the equipment, the fault is attributable to the third party who supplied him with the equipment.

The Employer's Liability (Defective Equipment) Act 1969 provides that, if an employee suffers a personal injury in the course of his employment as a consequence of a defect in the equipment provided by the employer for the purpose of the employer's business, and the defect is attributable to the fault of the third party, the injury shall be deemed to be attributable to the employer's negligence. The employer may, however, bring proceedings against the third party for an indemnity in respect of the damages which he has had to pay to an employee. Equipment includes any plant and machinery, vehicle, aircraft or clothing.

The provisions of this Act give an employee a right of action when he might not have a right at common law. At common law an employer is not liable for a latent defect in the equipment (i.e. a defect which cannot be discovered and remedied by a reasonable inspection), unless the employee can show that the defect could have been discovered and remedied by proper inspection. Prior to the passing of this Act, an employer had a good defence if he could prove that he had used reasonable care in selecting the tool or machine in question, e.g. he had purchased it from a reputable supplier or manufacturer.

An employer will not necessarily incur liability if he fails to provide the latest and safest equipment available for that particular task. It may well be a factor to be taken into account in determining whether there has been negligence on the part of the employer.

4   Competent fellow employees

An employer is obliged to exercise reasonable care in selecting competent employees. He will be vicariously liable for an injury to an employee caused by the negligence of a fellow employee. An employee who fails to prove negligence may be able to claim damages if he can show that the employer was negligent in selecting those employees, whose actions have caused the injury in question. In *Butler v. Fife Coal Company Ltd*, the widow of a miner killed as a result of a mine explosion was able to prove that the under manager and other responsible mine officials had not evacuated the mine, despite being aware of the presence of gas. The mine owners were therefore liable, as they had failed to appoint and keep in charge persons competent to deal with possible dangers arising at the mine.

The duty extends to the recruitment or the continued employment of individuals who are potentially dangerous, e.g. practical jokers. In *Hudson v. Ridge Manufacturing Co. Ltd*, an employer continued to employ an individual who had been warned on several occasions about indulging in horseplay and skylarking. The employer was held liable for the injuries to an employee caused by the actions of the individual in question.

An employer has a good defence to an action for unfair dismissal if he shows that the reason for the dismissal was the dangerous or potentially dangerous conduct of the employee (see page 132).

An employer may not be liable if an employee acts in a manner which is alien to his known behaviour and character and injures a fellow employee. In *Coddington v. International Harvester of Great Britain Ltd*, an employee kicked a tin of burning thinners towards an employee, who in the agony of the moment kicked the tin away towards Coddington, who was badly burned when he was enveloped by the flames. The employer was not liable as there had been no indication in the first employee's behaviour that he would act in this way, and the act was outside the scope of his employment.

— Employee's action for negligence —

An employee who has been injured at work will only succeed in an action for negligence against his employer if he can prove (*a*) he was owed a duty of care by the employer, and (*b*) there was a breach of that duty which resulted in the injury.

This is often a difficult task. An employee will also be assisted in the action if (*a*) he can show that the employer had acted contrary to the normal practice of the particular trade, and (*b*) he can cite *res ipsa loquitur*. This maxim provides that, if an accident is such that it could not have occurred without there being negligence on the part of the person managing or controlling the operation, he must prove that: (*i*) he had exercised all reasonable care; (*ii*) the accident was due to some specific cause; and (*iii*) he was not negligent.

Sir William Earle CJ in *Scott v. London & St Katherine Docks Co.* stated 'There must be reasonable evidence of negligence, but where the thing is shown to be under the management of the defendant or his servants, and the accident is such as in the ordinary course of things does not happen if those who have the management use proper care, it affords reasonable evidence, in the absence of explanation by the defendant, that the accident arose from want of care'.

In that case, six bags of sugar fell on a customs officer when he was passing the defendant's warehouse. It was held that it was for the defendants to rebut the presumption of negligence on their part.

In *Moore v. Fox & Sons*, an employee was killed as a result of a gas explosion. The gas had accumulated under a de-rusting tank which was heated by a gas burner. It was held that the maxim *res ipsa loquitur* applied, and as the defendants had failed to disprove negligence on their part they were liable for damages.

An employee may also be assisted in an action for negligence by certain provisions of the Health and Safety at Work Act 1974.

(a)   An employee may show that the employer has not complied with the Code of Practice issued under the Health and Safety at Work Act.

(b)   A health and safety inspector may release any information arising out of any accident or occurrence investigated by him, to a potential litigant.

Under the Employers' Liability (Compulsory Insurance) Act 1969, an employer must take out an insurance policy against liability for bodily injury and disease sustained by his employees and arising out of and in the course of their employment. The policy must provide a minimum cover of £2,000,000 for any one occurrence. An employer who is not insured may be fined £500 for each day in default. He must also display a Certificate of Insurance at each place of business.

_____ Employer's defences to an _____
action for negligence

1 Contributory negligence

An employer may allege that, although he was negligent in failing to observe a common law duty, the substantial cause of the accident was the failure of the employee to observe the reasonable degree of care expected in those circumstances. This is known as the doctrine of *contributory negligence.*

If the employer's claim is upheld, the court will estimate the amount that would have been awarded had the employee been blameless, and reduce it 'to such extent as the court thinks just and equitable, having regard to the plaintiff's (employee's) share of the responsibility for the damage' (Law Reform (Contributory Negligence) Act 1945).

The courts must therefore assess: (*a*) the causative potency of the acts of the parties, and (*b*) the degree of blameworthiness to be attached to these acts. The following cases illustrate the working of the rule.

An employer was held liable for not providing a handrail in breach of building regulations. The damages were reduced by 50 per cent as the employee had not disclosed that he was an epileptic and had been advised by his doctor not to work at heights (*Cork v. Kirkby Maclean Ltd*).

An employer did not lock the door to a ventilation shaft and was liable for the injuries sustained by an employee who climbed up the shaft to rescue a bird roosting on machinery. The damages were reduced by 90 per cent because of the employee's gross irresponsibility (*Uddin v. Associated Portland Cement Company*).

2 Volenti non fit injuria

An employer may plead *volenti non fit injuria*, i.e. the employee consented to run the risk of injury. Some occupations are inherently dangerous, e.g. test pilot and deep-sea diver, and an employee engaged in such an occupation, who is aware of the risks involved, may not claim damages from his employer if he suffers injury from his occupation. The pay of such an employee is usually proportional to the risks undertaken and the additional risk payment is generally known as danger money.

However, knowledge of the risks is not synonymous with consent, as an employee is often aware of the risk but does not consent to undertake the risk.

In *Smith v. Baker*, an employee working in a railway cutting was aware that a crane carrying heavy stones often swung its load over his head. No warning was given as to when a load would be swung, and Smith was injured by a stone which fell from the crane. The employer was liable, for, though the employee was aware of the risk, there was no evidence to indicate that he had accepted it.

The defence of *volenti non fit injuria* rarely succeeds in employment cases as an employer is under a duty to provide a reasonably safe system of working. Any change in that system which increases the risk to an employee places a greater burden on the employer to prove the employee's acceptance of that risk.

If a statute imposes a duty on an employee and he disregards that duty, the employer is entitled to invoke the defence of *volenti non fit injuria*. In *ICI Ltd v. Shatwell*, statutory regulations laid down that the testing of detonating wires should only be done from a place of shelter when all the persons in the vicinity had withdrawn from the area. One of a team of three shot firers went to obtain a longer cable, and the other two decided to test the circuit in the open. An explosion occurred and the two were injured. As the employers had also issued instructions in accordance with the statutory regulations, they were able to invoke the defence of *volenti non fit injuria*.

3 Employee's conduct

No liability is incurred by an employer if he can prove that the *employee's conduct* was the sole cause of the accident. In *Horne v. Lec Refrigeration*

Ltd, a tool-setter was killed when working on a press which was insecurely fenced, contrary to the Factories Act 1961. Despite being in breach of the Factories Act, the employers were held not liable as the sole cause of the accident was the employee's failure to observe the safety drill. In *Boyle v. Kodak Ltd*, an employee fell when climbing a ladder to secure the ladder to an oil storage tank he was painting. The ladder was inside the tank, but he could have secured it by climbing a fixed ladder on the outside of the tank. It was held that the employee alone was to blame for the accident.

4   Remoteness of damage

An employer will not be liable for injuries resulting from circumstances which he could not reasonably have foreseen. The courts have applied the rules of *remoteness of damage*, established in the Wagon Mound case, to this situation. In this case the defendant's employees carelessly spilt oil into Sydney Harbour. The oil was carried by wind and tide to the other side of the harbour and spread alongside the plaintiff's wharf. Welding operations were being carried out on the wharf and sparks fell into the water. The oil caught fire and damaged the plaintiff's wharf and ships that were alongside. It was held that a reasonable man could not have foreseen the consequences of the original spillage of oil.

In *Doughty v. Turner*, an asbestos cover fell into a cauldron of molten metal. The resulting explosion, which injured an employee standing nearby, was unexpected and unforeseen. As the explosion and the consequent injuries were not reasonably foreseeable, the employer was not liable.

If it is likely that an injury will result from the employer's negligent act, it is immaterial if the type of accident or injury which does in fact occur is not the one envisaged by the parties, as long as it is reasonably foreseeable that some injury would occur. In *Smith v. Leech Brain*, an employee was burned on the lip by molten metal as a result of the employer's negligence. His lip was in a pre-malignant condition and the employee developed cancer from the burn, from which he died. The employer was nevertheless held liable for this unexpected consequence.

The Health and Safety at Work Act 1974

The various responsibilities and duties of both the employee and the employer are covered by the Health and Safety at Work Act 1974, which is based on the report of the Royal Commission on Safety and Health at Work which was published in 1972. The Royal Commission was set up in 1970 under the chairmanship of Lord Robens to review industrial safety legislation. The report found that, on average, a thousand people were killed at work in Britain every year, and about half a million were injured. Twenty-three million working days were lost annually due to industrial accidents and diseases, and the cost in terms of lost production and diverted resources amounted to nearly one per cent of the gross national product. It concluded that the root cause of ill health and accidents at work was apathy.

The report criticised the existing state of the law. It found that nine separate groups of statutes and some 500 statutory instruments dealt with industrial safety legislation, which was separately administered by five central government departments (Employment, Home Office, Trade and Industry, Environment, and Agriculture) with seven separate inspectorates having responsibility for its enforcement.

The Commission's main proposal was for the enactment of a major statute accompanied by a unified administration with overall responsibility for industrial health and safety legislation. The Report was adopted almost in its entirety and resulted in the Health and Safety at Work Act 1974. Part 1 of the Act deals with health, safety and welfare in connection with work, and with the control of dangerous substances and emissions into the atmosphere. (Only certain aspects of Part 1 are dealt with in the following synopsis.)

The objectives of Part 1 are clearly stated as:

1 securing the health, safety and welfare of persons at work;
2 protecting persons other than those at work against risks to their health and safety arising out of or in connection with work activities;
3 controlling the keeping and use of explosive or highly flammable or otherwise dangerous substances, and generally preventing the unlawful acquisition, possession and use of such substances;

4 controlling the emission into the atmosphere of noxious or offensive substances from those premises prescribed by regulations.

The Act established two new bodies to promote its objectives and to ensure the implementation of its provisions. These are the Health and Safety Commission and the Health and Safety Executive.

The HSWA is superimposed on earlier related legislation, e.g. the Factories Act 1961, the Mines and Quarries Act 1954, and the Offices, Shops and Railway Premises Act 1963, which also deal with the health and safety of employees. The parties concerned must therefore comply with the duties imposed by earlier legislation as well as with those imposed by the HSWA. The majority of the enforcement provisions of the earlier Acts have been replaced by the enforcement procedures of the HSWA, which aims ultimately to replace the earlier regulations by a system of regulations and approved codes of practice operating in combination with the other provisions of the HSWA. The new system aims to maintain or improve the standards of health, safety or welfare established by earlier legislation.

The Health and Safety Commission

The Health and Safety Commission consists of a chairman and from six to nine members appointed by the Secretary of State, including three representing employers and three representing employees. The Secretary of State must consult both employer's and employees' organisations, local authorities and professional organisations on the appointment of members.

The Commission's duty is:

1 to assist and encourage compliance with the Act;
2 to encourage and promote research and training;
3 to establish an information and advisory service;
4 to submit proposals to the Government for regulations under the Act.

The Commission may, with the consent of the Secretary of State, serve a notice on any person requiring him to provide the Commission with information necessary for carrying out its functions; or to supply necessary information to an enforcing authority (i.e. the Health and

Safety Executive or its agencies, the local authority) to enable it to exercise its functions.

The Commission may also initiate an inquiry and investigate any accident, occurrence, situation or other matter which the Commission thinks it necessary or expedient to investigate. (This includes the situation where new regulations might be required.) The Commission may at any time direct the Executive or authorise any other person to investigate and report, or direct any inquiry to be held (with the consent of the Secretary of State). Such an inquiry is usually held in public and the regulations dealing with the conduct of inquiries may include provisions which grant to the person conducting the inquiry a power of entry and inspection of premises, a power to summon witnesses or produce documents, and the power to take evidence on oath and administer oaths, or to require the making of declarations.

The Commission may, after consultation with the Secretary of State, approve and issue codes of practice. It may also approve codes of practice issued by other bodies. Any relevant provision of an approved code of practice is admissible in evidence.

The Health and Safety Executive

The Executive consists of three full-time members who are appointed by the Commission, with the approval of the Secretary of State. The Executive's duty is to exercise on behalf of the Commission any of the Commission's functions which it is asked to carry out, and to make adequate arrangements for the enforcement of legislation.

The Executive's staff includes six Inspectorates (Agriculture, Alkali and Clean Air, Explosives, Factory, Mines and Quarries, and Nuclear Installations), and the Employment Medical Advisory Service.

—— Duties imposed by the HSWA ——

The Act imposes duties connected with health and safety at work on a number of persons. Duties are imposed on employers; manufacturers, designers, importers and suppliers of articles and substances; persons in control of premises; and employees.

Employers

The HSWA imposes the following duties on employers.

1 An employer must provide and maintain plant and systems of work that are, so far as is reasonably practicable, safe and without risks to health.
2 He must make arrangement for ensuring, so far as is reasonably practicable, the safety and absence of risks to health in using, handling, storing and transporting articles and substances.
3 He must provide such information, instruction, training and supervision as is necessary to ensure, so far as is reasonably practicable, the health and safety at work of his employees.
4 He must ensure that, so far as is reasonably practicable, any place of work which is under his control is maintained in a safe condition and does not pose a risk to health. He must also ensure that access to and egress from the work places are safe and without such risks.
5 He must provide and maintain a working environment for his employees that is safe, without risks to health, and adequate as regards facilities and arrangements for their welfare at work, so far as is reasonably practicable.

The Act also requires every employer to prepare a written statement of his general safety policy and to bring it to the attention of his employees. This must set out the employer's aims and objectives for improving health and safety at work, and the organisation and arrangements currently in force for achieving these objectives. Employers with fewer than five employees are exempt from these requirements.

Recognised trade unions are given the right to appoint safety representatives to represent the employees in consultations with the employer in matters of health and safety.

An employer also has a duty to conduct his undertakings in such a way to ensure, so far as is reasonably practicable, that persons who are not in his employment, such as outside contractors and their workers, visitors and members of the public, are not exposed to risks to their health and safety. In general the standard of care required for those persons is similar to the standard required for the health and safety of employees. A similar duty is imposed upon a self-employed person.

Manufacturers, designers, importers and suppliers

The manufacturers, designers, importers and suppliers of articles and substances for use at work must ensure that, so far as is reasonably practicable, any article (by virtue of its design and construction) or substance is safe and is without risk to health and safety when properly used, e.g. fairground equipment.

The article or substance must be tested and examined for the performance of that duty, and adequate information must be available for the use for which an article or substance has been designed or tested. It will not be necessary for a designer, manufacturer, importer or supplier to repeat any tests, examination or research on an article or substance in order to comply with the duties laid down by the Act, if it reasonable to rely on the results of these tests, examinations or research. If an article or substance is known to be inherently dangerous, information should be readily available regarding any safety precautions to be taken for its handling and storage.

It is the duty of designers or manufacturers of an article or substance for use at work to carry out or arrange for the carrying out of any necessary research to identify and, so far as is reasonably practicable, to eliminate or minimise any risks to health or safety caused by the design of the article or substance.

Any person who erects or installs any article for use at work in any premises must ensure, so far as is reasonably practicable, that nothing about its installation makes it unsafe or a health risk.

Persons in control of premises

A person who is in control of premises must use the most practicable means to prevent the emission into the atmosphere from those premises of noxious or offensive substances, and must render harmless and inoffensive such substances as may be emitted. A substance is defined as any natural or artificial substance, in solid, liquid or gaseous form.

A person who is in control of non-domestic premises owes certain duties to persons who are not his employees. He must take measures to ensure, so far as is reasonably practicable, that the premises, and any entry or exit from the premises, and any plant or substance in the premises or provided for use there, is safe and without risk to health.

These duties apply when any person enters such premises by reason of a contract, such as a maintenance engineer. It also applies to premises where machinery or equipment or substances are provided for the use of other persons, such as a launderette or a car wash.

Employees

It is the duty of every employee while at work: (*a*) to take reasonable care for the health and safety of himself, and of other persons who may be affected by his acts or omissions at work; and (*b*) to co-operate with his employer or any other person in any duty or requirement imposed under any of the relevant statutory provisions. The Act also provides that no person shall intentionally or recklessly interfere with or misuse anything provided in the interests of health, safety or welfare.

—— Enforcement of the HSWA ——

Inspectors

Every enforcing authority may appoint suitably qualified persons as inspectors to carry into effect the relevant statutory provisions. Inspectors are given wide powers which include the right:

1   to enter into premises at any reasonable time (or in a situation which he thinks dangerous at any time);
2   to take with him a police officer if he reasonably apprehends any serious obstructions in the execution of this duty;
3   to take with him any other person or any equipment or material on entering premises;
4   to make such examination and investigations as may be necessary;
5   to direct that any premises, which he has power to enter, shall be left undisturbed for the purposes of any examination or investigation;
6   to take such measurements and photographs and make such recordings as he considers necessary;

7　to take samples of any articles or substances or the atmosphere in the premises;

8　to dismantle, or subject to any process or test, any article or substance found on the premises which appears to have caused or to be likely to cause danger to health and safety;

9　to question any person whom he has reasonable cause to believe may be able to give any information relevant to any examination or investigation;

10　to require the production of, inspect, and take a copy of any books or documents required to be kept by a relevant statutory provision or which is necessary to see for the purposes of any examination or investigation;

11　to require any person to afford him such facilities and assistance with respect to any matters or things within that person's control or in relation to that person's responsibilities as are necessary to enable the inspector to exercise the powers granted to him;

12　any other right necessary for carrying out any of the previously listed powers.

An inspector must not disclose information he obtains by virtue of his powers, except in the following circumstances:

(a)　for the purposes of his functions; or

(b)　for the purposes of any legal proceedings or any investigation or inquiry held under the direction of the Health and Safety Commission or Executive, or for the purposes of a report of any such proceedings or inquiry of a special report made by virtue of such a directive;

(c)　with the relevant consent of a person who furnished the information in pursuance of an inspector's examination or investigation, or having responsibilities in relation to the premises where the information was obtained;

(d)　when it is necessary to assist in keeping persons or their representatives, (e.g. safety representatives) employed at any premises adequately informed about matters affecting their health, safety and welfare. He must inform these persons as to any factual information obtained by him relating to these premises and any action which he has taken or proposes to take in connection with these premises. Any information given to employees must also be given to the employer.

Improvement and prohibition notices

If an inspector is of the opinion that a person is contravening health and safety legislation, or has in the past contravened such legislation in circumstances that it is likely that he will do so again, the inspector may serve an *improvement notice* on that person. This requires him to remedy the contravention, or the matters occasioning it, within whatever period may be specified in the notice.

If an inspector is of the opinion that the activities which are being, or about to be, carried on by a person involve, or will involve, a risk of personal injury, he may serve a *prohibition notice* on that person. The notice may be deferred, in which case it will specify the remedial measures to be taken and fix a time after which the work will be prohibited; or it may take immediate effect, in which case the work activity must cease immediately. An inspector will issue an immediate prohibition notice where he is of the opinion that there is an immediate risk of injury.

A person on whom a notice is served may appeal to an industrial tribunal, within 21 days of the issue of the notice. The appeal may challenge the inspector's views regarding the contravention of legislation, the risk of personal injury, the time limit in the notice, or the remedial measures specified in the notice.

Safety representatives

The Act provides for the appointment in prescribed cases of safety representatives who will represent the employees in consultations with the employer. The Safety Representatives and Safety Committees Regulations 1977 became operative on 1 October 1978 and were accompanied by a Code of Practice. The Health and Safety Commission issues guidance notes on the operation of the consultative system.

Only recognised trade unions have the right to appoint safety representatives. The Regulations do not specify the number of representatives that may be appointed, but guidance notes do indicate the criteria to be adopted and suggest that the following factors should be taken into consideration:

1 the total number of employees and their occupations;
2 the size of the work place and the type of work conducted;
3 the shift system and the degree and character of any inherent dangers.

The representatives' functions are set out in the Regulations.

(a)   To investigate potential hazards and dangerous occurrences at the work place and to examine the causes of accidents there.

(b)   To investigate complaints by an employee he represents relating to that employee's health, safety or welfare at work.

(c)   To make representations to the employer on matters of health, safety and welfare.

(d)   To carry out inspections.

(e)   To represent the employees in consultations with the various inspectors and enforcement authorities.

(f)   To receive information from inspectors.

(g)   To attend meetings of safety committees.

An employer should permit a safety representative to take time off with pay during the employee's working hours in order to perform these functions. Safety representatives are entitled to inspect the work place, if they have given the employer written notice of their intention to inspect. Inspection can only be made at three-monthly intervals, unless the employer agrees to more frequent inspections, or there has been a substantial change in conditions of work, or new information on hazards has been published by the Health and Safety Commission. Inspections may also be carried out where there has been a notifiable accident or dangerous occurrence in a work place, or a notifiable disease has been contracted, and the employees' interests are involved. Representatives are also entitled to inspect and take copies of any relevant documents. An employer must establish a safety committee if requested to do so in writing by at least two safety representatives. The committee must be established within three months of the written request.

A breach of the provisions of the HSWA is a criminal offence and upon conviction in summary proceedings in the magistrates court, the maximum fine is £5,000. In cases brought on indictment in the Crown Court the offender is liable to a sentence of up to two years' imprisonment and/or a fine for an unlimited amount. A person who has been convicted of contravening an improvement or prohibition order, or an order of a court is liable to a fine of up to £100 for each day he continues to ignore that order.

The Act provides that there is no right of civil action for an injury which results from a failure to comply with the general duties laid down in Part 1 of the Act. This does not affect any right of action which exists apart from the Act. A breach of any duty imposed by health and safety regulations is actionable unless the regulations state otherwise.

6

—————— WAGES ——————

An employer is under a contractual obligation to pay wages to his employees, whether the contract of employment is in writing or merely a verbal agreement. He is also under an obligation to supply each employee, within 13 weeks of the commencement of employment, with written particulars of the terms of his employment (EPCA, s1). These particulars include:

1 the scale or rate of remuneration or the method of calculating remuneration;
2 the intervals at which remuneration is paid, i.e. whether weekly or monthly or by some other period;
3 any terms and conditions, relating to:
   (a) holiday entitlement, including public holidays, and holiday pay;
   (b) incapacity for work due to sickness or injury including any provision for sick pay;
   (c) pension entitlement.

A statutory statement is not required where a formal contract is in existence which satisfies these provisions. It does not apply to Crown employees and part-time employees.

An employee is also entitled, under section 8 of the EPCA, to an itemised pay statement which contains:

1   the gross amount of the wages or salary;
2   the amount of any variable or fixed deduction made from the gross
    amount and the purpose for which it is made;
3   the net amount of wages or salary payable;
4   the amount and method of each part payment where different parts of
    the net amount are paid in different ways.

In the absence of written particulars, the court will usually imply a term
in an employee's contract of employment that he should be paid a
reasonable sum for his services i.e. on a *quantum meruit* basis (as much
as he had earned). In *Way v. Latilla*, the plaintiff claimed that the
defendant had agreed to pay him a reasonable sum for information and
reports relating to gold mines and concessions in West Africa. It was held
that a contract existed which indicated that the work was not gratuitous.
In view of the defendant's profits of £1,000,000, the plaintiff was held to
be entitled to £5,000 on a *quantum meruit* basis.

In *Powell v. Braun*, an employer offered to pay his secretary a bonus,
based on the net trading profits of the business, in lieu of an increase in
salary. The method of calculating the bonus was never agreed. Nevertheless, it was held that such a bonus was payable on a *quantum meruit*
basis.

In *Fischers Ltd v. Taylor* a Christmas bonus had been paid to all
employees for several years. It was held that the employment contracts
contained an implied term that this bonus would be paid.

However, in *Re Richmond Gate Property Co. Ltd*, it was held that a
managing director was not entitled to payment for the nine months prior
to the company's liquidation. He was to be paid 'such remuneration as the
directors may determine'. As there was a mechanism for determining his
remuneration, he was not entitled to claim on a *quantum meruit* basis.
The directors had not determined the amount of his remuneration, and
consequently he was not entitled to any payment.

An employer may withhold all or part of an employee's pay for taking
part in industrial action, short of a strike, during the course of the
employee's normal duties. In *Miles v. Wakefield Metropolitan District
Council* a superintendent registrar who normally worked a 37-hour
week, refused to work three hours on a Saturday morning, as part of an
industrial action. It was held that his employers were entitled to deduct
$3/37$ of his salary.

In *Sim v. Rotherham Metropolitan Borough Council*, a deduction was made from the salaries of teachers who refused to comply with cover arrangements for absent teachers. It was held that the deduction was lawful.

Wages terms may also be impliedly or expressly incorporated from various documents, e.g. rule books, notices, collective agreements (*National Coal Board v. Galley*, page 26).

Wages and salaries in certain employments may fluctuate according to the number of hours worked and the degree of productivity attained. Certain employees are paid on a piecework basis, or an hourly basis. Other employees are given a bonus or a commission in lieu of, or in addition to, their wages. It is important in the context of modern employment legislation to determine 'a week's pay', and the basis of its calculation, in order to determine the amount of compensation for unfair dismissal, redundancy and guarantee payments.

—— Calculation of a week's pay ——

An employee's entitlement to various payments under employment statutes (e.g. redundancy payments, maternity payments, compensation for unfair dismissal) is based on a formula which includes the amount of a week's pay as one of the main factors. Schedule 14 of the EPCA sets out the method of calculating normal working hours and hence a week's pay. It is sometimes necessary to ascertain an employee's working hours before it is possible to calculate a week's pay. The rules are as follows:

1   if there are normal working hours and the employee's remuneration does not vary with the amount of work done in the period, a week's pay is the amount payable by the employer on the calculation date;
2   if there are normal working hours, but the employee's remuneration varies from the amount of work done, or the hours of work vary from week to week, a week's pay is calculated at the average hourly rate paid over the previous 12-week period, ending on the calculation date;
3   if normal working hours are not worked, a week's pay is the amount of the employee's average weekly remuneration over the previous 12-week period, ending on the calculation date;
4   overtime will only be included as part of an employee's normal

working hours when an employer is under an obligation to provide a fixed period of overtime, and an employee is under an obligation to work this period of overtime, in addition to a fixed number of compulsory working hours;

5   in calculating an employee's remuneration, certain benefits, e.g. travelling allowances and accommodation are disregarded, but bonuses and commissions may be included in the computation, taking $^{12}/_{13}$ of a quarterly bonus or $^{12}/_{52}$ of an annual bonus.

———————— Method of payment ————————

Wages Act 1986

The Wages Act 1986 repealed the Truck Acts and subsequent supplementary legislation, including the Payment of Wages Act 1960.

The Truck Acts from 1831 onwards required manual workers to be paid in current coin of the realm; prohibited the practice of trucking (i.e. the payment of wages in tokens to be exchanged for goods at a local store or one owned by the factory or mine owner); and restricted the payment of fines and deductions from a workman's wages for bad or negligent work. The Payment of Wages Act modified the Truck Acts in that it allowed an employer, at the written request of an employee, to pay wages other than in coin of the realm e.g. cheque, payment into a bank account.

The repeal of these Acts and other Acts covering various industries, e.g. coal mining, tin mining, hosiery manufacture, etc., will encourage the spread of cashless pay, with the payment of wages by credit transfer. The method of payment of wages is now a matter of negotiation between employer and employee.

Section 1 of the Wages Act prohibits an employer from making any deductions from wages and salaries of workers employed by him other than:

1   statutory deductions, i.e. income tax, national insurance contributions;
2   under a relevant provision in the worker's contract, e.g. an occupational pension contribution;

3 a deduction authorised by the contract and agreed to in advance by the worker, e.g. repayment of a loan.

A 'worker' is defined as an employee or apprentice or any self-employed person working under a contract to perform personal services, provided that he is not a professional person or genuinely running his own business.

Certain deductions and payments are permitted by the Wages Act:

1 deductions or payments to reimburse an employer for an over-payment of wages or expenses;

2 deductions or payments resulting from disciplinary proceedings held under a statutory provision, e.g. police and fire service regulations;

3 deductions paid to a local authority under a statutory provision, e.g. payments to the Inland Revenue, DHSS, attachment of earnings order made by a court;

4 payments to a third party agreed to, in writing, in advance by the worker, e.g. check off for trade union dues;

5 deductions in respect of strike or other industrial action;

6 deductions or payments to satisfy a court or tribunal order requiring payment to the employer by the worker (Wages Act s1).

Deductions in retail employment

Special provisions apply to workers in retail employment in respect of cash shortages or stock deficiencies (Wages Act s2).

Retail employment includes:

1 employment involving retail transactions with members of the public, fellow workers, or other individuals in their personal capacities;

2 collecting amounts payable in connection with retail transactions carried out by other persons. The definition covers shop assistants, bus conductors, bus drivers who collect fares, bank cashiers, post office counter clerks, petrol pump attendants, industrial insurance agents, football pools collectors, and so on.

An employer may not deduct from a worker's wages on any pay day, in regard to cash shortages or stock deficiencies, a sum in excess of 10 per cent of the worker's gross wages payable on that pay day. If the deficiency is greater than the sum deducted or demanded an employer may nevertheless deduct or demand the balance on subsequent pay days, provided that the 10-per-cent ceiling is not exceeded on any pay day.

The deduction on demand for payment must be made within 12 months of the date:

(a)   on which the employer became aware of the shortage or deficiency;
(b)   on which the employer ought to have discovered it (if earlier).

The deduction must be authorised by the contract and agreed to, in advance, in writing by the worker.

There is no limit to the amount that an employer can demand or deduct from a retail worker's final instalment of wages, on the ending of the employment, to cover cash shortages or stock deficiencies, as long as he does not infringe the general restrictions on deductions (Wages Act s4). An employer can institute proceedings to recover any balance due if the amount outstanding is greater than the employee's final gross wages, subject to the 12-month limitation period.

This happens in the event of:

(a)   an unauthorised deduction;
(b)   a deduction which a worker has not agreed to in writing;
(c)   a demand for payment not properly notified;
(d)   a retail shortage or deficiency outside the 12-month limit;
(e)   a deduction in excess of 10 per cent in the case of retail shortage or deficiency.

A claim by a worker may only be made to a tribunal, not to the county court. It must be made within three months of the alleged infringement of the Act (Wages Act s5). A tribunal may make a declaration that the complaint is well founded; or order an employer to repay any unauthorised deduction. In retail cases this would mean the repayment of a sum in excess of the 10 per cent deducted lawfully (Wages Act s5).

—— Attachment of earnings ——

An employer may be instructed by a court to make deductions from an employee's wages under the terms of an attachment order. The Attachment of Earnings Act 1971 allows an order to be made in:

1   the High Court, to secure payments under a High Court maintenance order;
2   a County Court, to secure payments under a High Court or County Court maintenance order, under an administration order, or to settle a judgment debt of more than £50;
3   a Magistrates' Court for a Magistrates' Court maintenance order, the payment of a fine, and any legal aid contribution.

The employer must deduct the amounts specified from the employee's earnings and pay these to the specified collecting officer – usually a High Court officer, the County Court Registrar, or a Magistrates' Clerk. He must also inform the appropriate court, within 10 days, if the employee leaves his service. The court must, however, specify a rate of protected earnings. Should an employee's earnings fall below this norm, no deductions can be paid from his wages.

An employer must, on each occasion when a deduction is made, inform the employee in writing of the amount of the deduction, and may charge for administration expenses.

An employer must give particulars of an employee's actual or estimated future earnings when requested to do so by the court. He will be liable to a fine of £100 or 14 days' imprisonment if he fails to comply with the court's request.

Suspension

An employer may suspend an employee without pay if this right is reserved in the contract of employment. Otherwise an employee is entitled to damages for loss of earnings during the period of suspension. In *Hanley v. Pease*, an employee suspended without pay for one day was awarded damages equivalent to a day's pay, as on that particular day he was not given the opportunity to earn a day's pay, and the employer's right to suspend him was not reserved in his contract of employment.

If an employer has reserved the right of suspension in the contract, e.g. in the rule book, there is no breach of contract if an employee is suspended without pay.

Pay during suspension on medical grounds

An employee who is suspended from work by his employer on medical grounds, as a result of certain statutory requirements or the provisions of a code of practice issued under the HSWA 1974, is entitled to a maximum of 26 weeks' pay during his period of suspension. The employee must have been continuously employed for four weeks before the commencement of the suspension.

An employee will be regarded as suspended as long as he continues to be employed by his employer and is not provided with work, or does not perform the work he normally performed before the suspension.

He is not entitled to payment if:

1   he is incapable of work because of disease or physical or mental disablement; or
2   the employer has offered suitable alternative work for that day which the employee has unreasonably refused; or
3   the employee does not comply with reasonable requirements imposed by his employer with a view to ensuring that his services are available.

——— Guarantee payments ———

An employee who is not provided with work by his employer is entitled to guarantee payments in respect of a certain number of 'workless' days. The 'workless' days must be due to a dimunition in the requirements of the employer's business for work of the kind which the employee is employed to do; or to any other occurrence affecting the normal working of the employer's business in relation to work of the kind which the employee is employed to do.

An employee is entitled to guarantee payments for up to five days in any quarter. The maximum entitlement is £13.65 a day, and an employee must be continuously employed for four weeks before the day on which claim is made.

An employee is not entitled to a guarantee payment if:

1 the failure to provide work occurs as a consequence of a trade dispute involving any employee of his employer or an associated employer; or
2 the employer has offered suitable alternative work for that day which the employee has unreasonably refused; or
3 the employee does not comply with reasonable requirements imposed by his employer with a view to ensuring that his services are available.

If an employer refuses to pay part or the whole of a guarantee payment an employee may apply to an industrial tribunal within three months.

———————————— **Sick pay** ————————————

An employee must be given written particulars of any entitlement to wages during sickness. This is one of the items which must be included in the document outlining the terms of his contract.

An individual's contract of employment may contain provisions dealing with an entitlement to sick pay, or reference may be made in the contract to a collective agreement, whose terms will then be incorporated into the individual's contract.

In *Houman & Son v. Blyth*, a term was contained in an employee's contract providing for the payment of sick pay, but no agreed term as to the duration of such pay. It was held that a term should be implied which was reasonable, with regard to normal practice in the industry.

An employer is under no obligation to provide for the payment of sick pay, although most employees are now covered by some form of express contractual sick pay scheme. The only exception is that an employee who has been given notice and 'is incapable of work because of sickness or injury' must be paid by his employer during the period of notice.

If there is no specific provision dealing with sick pay, a term will not necessarily be implied that payment will be made by the employer during a period of sickness. All the facts and circumstances must be considered to establish whether such a term should be implied. Factors to consider are the customs and practice in the industry, and the knowledge and actions of the parties. In *Mears v. Safecar Security Ltd*, an employee was absent from work for a total of seven months out of his 14-month period of employment. There was no reference to sick pay in his written contract, and he did not apply for wages during his periods of absence, having been told by his fellow employees that sick pay was not provided. It was held that in these circumstances there was no entitlement to sick pay from his employer.

—————— Sickness benefit ——————

Under the provisions of the Social Security and Housing Benefits Acts 1982, sickness benefit is payable initially by the employer in the form of statutory sick pay, followed by state sickness benefit for those employees who have paid sufficient national insurance contributions.

Statutory sick pay

An employee is entitled to eight weeks' statutory sick pay from his employer in any tax year. He will not be entitled to claim state sickness benefit until he has exhausted his entitlement to statutory sick pay (SSP).

An employer may recoup 80 per cent of the gross amount of any payment of SSP by withholding the amount from the monthly national insurance contributions sent to the Inland Revenue or from the monthly tax return. Basically, all employees are covered by the scheme if they are absent because of personal sickness for four or more days in a row.

An employee is entitled to SSP if his *day of incapacity* for work forms part of the *period of incapacity* for work; falls within the *period of entitlement*; and counts as a *qualifying day*.

These terms are interpreted as follows:

day of incapacity   a day when he is incapable, because of a specific disease or disablement, of doing work he might reasonably be expected to do;

period of incapacity   a period of four or more consecutive days of sickness;

period of entitlement   this starts with the first day of incapacity and ends when the period of incapacity has ended, or when the contract of employment is terminated, or when entitlement to SSP has been exhausted, or when a woman who is pregnant is disqualified under the terms of the Act;

a qualifying day   usually regarded as a day on which an employee would have been available for work, had he not been sick. An employer and employee should agree on any pattern of qualifying days as long as there is at least one in each week. An employee is not entitled to SSP until he has been off sick for at least three qualifying days (called *waiting days*). Any qualifying day during a four-day spell of sickness can count as a waiting day.

Two or more periods of incapacity for work which are separated by 14 calendar days or less are regarded as linked, and count as one period of incapacity. If an employee has three qualifying days in one period of incapacity and then has a second linked spell, he will be entitled to payment of SSP from the first qualifying day in the second spell.

There are three different rates of SSP. The amount payable depends on the employee's average earnings in the eight weeks before his absence due to sickness.

Rate	*Earnings per week*
£43.50	£52–£184.99
£52.50	£185 or more

Certain employees are excluded from entitlement to SSP: these are listed below.

1   An employee who is incapacitated from work for less than four days.
2   An employee who is over minimum State pension age on the first day of sickness.
3   An employee who is employed under a contract of employment for three months or less.
4   An employee whose average weekly earnings are less than the lower earnings limit for paying national insurance contributions – at present, less than £52 a week.
5   An employee who goes sick within 57 days of a previous claim for one of the following State benefits: sickness benefit, invalidity pension, maternity allowance, or unemployment benefit (in limited circumstances).
6   An employee who goes sick during a stoppage of work at his place of employment due to a trade dispute, unless he can prove that he has not taken part in the trade dispute and has no direct interest in it.

7   A pregnant woman who is off sick in the time starting 11 weeks before her expected week of confinement and ending six weeks after.
8   An employee who has already received eight weeks' SSP from an employer in a current tax year or in one spell of sickness.
9   An employee who is sick while abroad outside the European Community.
10 An employee who is in legal custody.
11 An employee who has not commenced work under a contract of service.

Equal pay

The Equal Pay Act 1970 outlaws discrimination 'as regards terms and conditions of employment, between men and women'. This Act did not come into force until December 1975, so that employers would have sufficient time to comply with its provisions. By this time its provisions had been substantially amended by the Sex Discrimination Act 1975 (the fully amended provisions of the Equal Pay Act are contained in a schedule to the Sex Discrimination Act).

The question of equal pay had been mooted and examined in this country for more than half a century. First examined in 1919, it was reconsidered by a Royal Commission which sat between 1944 and 1946. The British Government was pledged to introduce equal pay legislation, having accepted a Recommendation to Convention 100 of the International Labour Organisation. This provided that each member state should 'promote and . . . ensure the application to all workers of the principle of equal remuneration for men and women to work of equal value.'

The Equal Pay Act provides that, if the terms of a contract under which a woman is employed at an establishment in Great Britain do not include, either directly or by implication, an equality clause, such a clause will be deemed to be included. The provisions of the Act apply equally to men and women. The equality clause operates:

1   where the woman is employed on like work with a man; or
2   where the woman is employed on work rated as equivalent with that of a man in the same employment; or
3   where the woman is employed on work which is, in terms of the

demands made on her, of equal value to that of a man in the same employment (Equal Pay (Amendment) Regulations 1983).

These Regulations implement EC Directive 75/117 on Equal Pay and enable an employee to insist that a job evaluation study be carried out.

Like work

A woman is regarded as employed on *like work* with men if the work is 'the same or of a broadly similar nature, and the differences . . . are not of practical importance in relation to the terms and conditions of employment'.

In *Capper Pass v. Lawton,* the EAT stated that a two-stage enquiry should be adopted to determine whether people were engaged in like work. A tribunal should firstly adopt a broad approach to determine whether the work is similar, without minutely examining the differences between the work. Secondly, if the work is determined broadly similar, a tribunal must then consider whether the differences are of practical importance. In the case in question, a female cook who prepared between 10 and 20 lunches for the firm's directors claimed pay parity with two assistant chefs, who catered for around 350 lunches in the work's canteen. Her work was unsupervised while the assistant chefs worked longer hours under supervision. Despite the minor differences it was held that the work was of a similar nature, involving similar culinary skills and expertise, and therefore she was entitled to equal pay.

In *Eaton v. Nuttall,* and *Capper Pass v. Allan,* it was held that additional responsibilities allocated to male employees amounted to differences which were of practical importance. In the first case, a female dispatcher was not paid the same rates as her male counterpart. She handled a large number of goods of small value, while he dealt with a small number of goods of high value. As an error on his part would have far more serious financial consequences than an error on the part of the female dispatcher, he was entitled to a higher rate of pay.

In the second case, a female canteen employee claimed parity with a male canteen employee, who received an additional shift differential and productivity payment. The additional payments were held to be justified as he was also responsible for stock control and for handling substantial sums of money.

In *Thomas v. NCB*, an action was brought by women canteen assistants at various collieries, comparing their work with that of a male comparator who was a permanent night worker at a colliery at a higher rate of pay. It was held that, as the women worked day shifts and as the man worked permanently alone at night, he was not employed on like work.

The fact that a male employee works different hours to a female employee does not justify a different rate of pay, if the work is similar. An employer may compensate for unsocial hours, night and weekend work by paying special premiums, and as long as he pays the same basic rates to both sexes he does not infringe the provisions of the Act. In *Dugdale v. Kraft Foods*, a female employee was held to be entitled to the same basic rate as her male counterparts, who were obliged to work night shifts, despite the fact that women were debarred from working on night shifts by the provisions of the Factories Act 1961.

When making a comparison, a tribunal must have regard to the frequency or otherwise with which any differences occur in practice, as well as to the nature and extent of these differences. In *Coomes (Holdings) Ltd v. Shields*, a male employee in a betting shop was paid a higher hourly rate than his female counterpart. The employers contended that the extra payment was justified as the man's physical presence was a deterrent to potential troublemakers. It was held that the woman was entitled to equal pay as there was no evidence of past trouble, or that the man was specifically trained to deal with troublemakers. In *Ford v. Weston (Chemists) Ltd*, a female dispensary manager claimed equal pay with a male branch manager, as she occasionally deputised for him in his absence. It was held that as these absences were infrequent she was not entitled to equal pay.

The comparison

Where a woman seeks parity on the grounds of like work or work rated as equivalent, she may specify the person with whom she wishes to compare her work, i.e. the comparator. He must be a real, not a hypothetical, person and the comparison must be realistic, otherwise the employer will be able to rely on a defence of genuine material difference.

Both the applicant and the comparator must either by employed under a contract of service or apprenticeship or a personal contract to execute work or labour. The comparison must be between persons in the *same employment* who need not necessarily be employed in the same establishment. (*Leverton v. Clwyd County Council*, see page 94.)

An applicant may use a former employee as a comparator. (*McCarthy Ltd v. Smith*, see page 99.)

Work rated as equivalent

A woman is to be regarded as employed on work rated as equivalent with that of any man if both jobs have been given an equal value in terms of the demands made upon a worker (under such headings as effort, skill and decision-making) under a job evaluation study conducted within the undertaking, or within a group of undertakings.

When a job evaluation study has been conducted which evaluates a woman's job as equal to a man's, the firm must then modify the terms of the employee's contract to implement the terms of the Equal Pay Act (*O'Brien v. Sim-Chem*). A job evaluation exercise is regarded as conclusive, unless it can be shown that the scheme set 'different values for men and women'.

In *Arnold v. Beecham Group*, the employers had undertaken two job evaluation studies in 1978 and 1980. The employers used the 1980 study to reach agreement on the boundaries of job grades, and the applicant was bracketed with a man as grade 2. There was such an objection to the study amongst the supervisors that the 1980 pay settlement was finally agreed upon on the basis of the 1978 scheme, with certain modifications. It was nevertheless held that, as there had been a complete study, the applicant was entitled to equal pay.

Work of equal value

A woman (or man) may claim equal pay for work of equal value where a job evaluation study has not been carried out or where the provisions of like work do not apply.

In *Bromley v. Quick Ltd*, two female clerical workers brought an equal value complaint comparing their work to that of male managers. Although a job evaluation study had been carried out by the employers it did not satisfy the requirements of the Equal Pay Act as it was not carried out under various headings in relation to demands on the worker, e.g. effort, skill, decision-making. The employer could not rely on the study as it had not been applied individually to the women and their male comparators.

An industrial tribunal has no jurisdiction to hear a case relating to work of equal value unless:

(a)   it is satisfied that there are no reasonable grounds for determining that the work is of equal value – in which case the complaint will be dismissed; or

(b)   it has required a panel of independent experts to prepare a report relating to the question and it has received that report.

The panel of experts is designated by ACAS but must not be officers or members of that body.

When a female employee carries out work of equal value to a male comparator she is entitled to be treated as favourably in respect of individual contractual terms as her male comparator.

In *Hayward v. Cammell Laird Shipbuilders Ltd*, the work of a female cook in a shipyard canteen was held to be of equal value to a painter, a joiner and a thermal engineer. During her period of apprenticeship she was paid the same rates as her male comparators, but thereafter she was paid at a lower rate than the men, but received free canteen lunches and two additional days holiday. It was held that she was entitled to have a term in her contract (i.e. relating to pay) made no less favourable than that of the men, irrespective of whether her contract as a whole provided for her to be treated as favourably as the men.

In *Leverton v. Clwyd County Council*, a nursery nurse brought an equal value claim against Clwyd County Council, using as comparators higher paid male clerical staff who were employed at various establishments on terms derived from the same collective agreement. It was held that Mrs Leverton was in the same employment as the comparators and that common terms and conditions were observed at the different establishments. Nevertheless, the employer was able to justify the difference on the grounds of material factors other than sex, i.e. the differences in working hours and holiday entitlement.

An 'equal value' claim is not barred by the fact that other employees of the opposite sex are employed on similar terms as the claimant. In *Pickstone v. Freemans*, five warehouse operatives claimed that their work was of equal value to male warehouse checkers who were paid £4.27 per week more, even though there was a male warehouse operative who was paid the same wage as the women. It was held, nevertheless, that the claim could be brought.

The results of a job evaluation study may also be challenged. Industrial tribunals may appoint independent experts to assess whether a woman's job is of equal value to that of a man. An employer may, by way of defence, rely on matters that go beyond personal differences between the woman and the man with whom she is compared.

Protected rates of pay

Problems have arisen in deciding whether the payment of an employee at a *protected rate*, i.e. at a higher rate than his fellow employees, is a genuine material difference. This situation may occur when an employee's job is down-graded, but he is offered a lower-grade job at his previous rate as an alternative to redundancy, or when an industrial injury makes it necessary for an employee to do lighter work, but he is paid at his previous higher rates. This is also known as *red circling*, i.e. a red circle around the employee's name on a pay roll signifies that his rate of pay is protected.

An employer seeking to justify a protected payment as a material difference must show that the protected rate is genuine and that 'its origin was not discriminatory'. In *Snoxell v. Vauxhall Motors*, male inspectors were paid at a higher rate than female inspectors, although both groups undertook similar work. The male inspectors were originally part of a male group who received higher wages. As a result of a pay revision, they were re-graded and 'red-circled' until the group was phased out. It was held that the female inspectors were entitled to pay parity.

The payment of a male employee at a higher rate than his female counterpart, for reasons connected with his employment, e.g. market forces, may be justified if the employer is able to show that the pay variation is due to a material fact which is not the result of discrimination.

In *Rainey v. Greater Glasgow Health Board*, the Health Board paid newly recruited prosthetists from the private sector higher salaries than their existing staff who had been recruited directly into the National Health Service some years before. The majority of the existing staff were female, while all the newly recruited staff were male. It was held that the employer's conduct could be justified as the additional staff could only be recruited at their current salaries.

Genuine material differences

An equality clause will not operate in cases where an employer is able to prove that, on the balance of probabilities, the variation in terms and conditions is genuinely due to material differences other than sex. This is so, even if an employee has made out a *prima facie* case for equal pay. The difference must be a factor not previously considered when comparing the work of both sexes.

In *Kerr v. Lister and Co.*, both men and women who worked on the night shift were paid at a higher rate than the women working on the day shift. The difference was therefore a difference between day and night rates, not a difference that was attributable to sex.

However, in *Coyne v. Exports Credits Guarantee Department*, a woman's contract provided that any maternity leave should count against normal sick leave allowance. It was held that the leave provisions were therefore less favourable than those granted to a man in like work, and restricted sickness rights, rather than granting maternity rights. It was therefore not a material difference, but due to the sex of the parties, and the contract had to be modified.

In *Albion Shipping Agency v. Arnold*, a woman took over the running of an office at a substantially lower salary than her male predecessor, who was made redundant following a reduction in the volume of business and profits. It was held that although she was employed on like work, the reduction in the volume of business could amount to a material difference other than that of sex.

Other grounds which have been held to be material differences, and therefore justifying different rates of pay for the same work, include the following:

1   full-time work as opposed to part-time work (*Jenkins v. Kingsgate*);
2   employment in London, as opposed to employment in the provinces (*NAAFI v. Varley*);
3   skill, capacity and experience of male clerks in an insurance firm (*National Vulcan Engineering Insurance Group v. Wade*);
4   the age and ill health of a former engineer who filled a clerical post (*Methven v. Cow Industrial Polymers*);

5 extra responsibility, as a result of greater experience of women communications operators (*Avon and Somerset Police Authority v. Emery*);
6 extra payments to attract skilled staff from the private sector (*Rainey v. Greater Glasgow Health Board*).

Article 119

As a member of the European Community, the United Kingdom is bound by the provisions of the Treaty of Rome. Article 119 is of particular importance in this context as it provides that 'men and women should receive equal pay for equal work'. Pay is defined as 'the ordinary basic or minimum wage or salary and any other consideration, whether in cash or in kind, which the worker receives, either directly or indirectly, in respect of his employment from his employer'.

The European Court of Justice held, in *Defrenne v. Sabena*, that Article 119 is directly applicable in Member States and gives rights to individuals which can be enforced before national courts even where there is no prevailing domestic legislation to deal with the case. These rights may be enforced against Member States and individual employers. In *McCarthy Ltd v. Smith*, see page 99, it was held that the applicant should, under the principle in Article 119, receive equal pay.

In *McKechnie v. UBM Building Supplies*, it was held that a woman who was denied a redundancy payment on the grounds of sex in accordance with United Kingdom law could challenge the discrimination under Article 119. McKechnie was made redundant at 61 at a time when women ceased to be entitled to a redundancy payment at 60. (Since January 1990 both men and women are entitled to redundancy payments to the age of 65.) She complained of discrimination on the grounds of sex as she received a smaller payment on her dismissal than she would have received had she been a man made redundant at 61. (A man was entitled to a redundancy payment up to the age of 65.) Her claim could be enforced by action in an industrial tribunal.

In *Rinner Kuhn v. FWW Spezial-Gebaudereinigung GmbH & Co. KG*, Rinner Kuhn worked up to 10 hours per week and challenged her employer's refusal to make payments to part-time workers who were off work through sickness, i.e. employees who worked 10 hours or less per week or not more than 43 hours per month. German law provided that other employees should be paid sick pay for up to six weeks. The European Court declared that Article 119 prohibits national legislation that enables employers to exclude part-time workers from sick pay entitlement where that legislation affects a much larger number of woman than men, unless a Member State can show that the legislation is based on objectively justified factors which are not related to any sexual discrimination.

The European Court has considered the meaning of 'pay' in a number of cases.

In *Worringham and Humphreys v. Lloyds Bank*, the bank required all its clerical officers to join the company's pension schemes. The women's scheme was non-contributory until the age of 25, while the men's scheme was contributory throughout. The employer paid the men an additional sum to compensate for their contributions. It was held that this additional sum constituted pay within the meaning of Article 119. The female employees were entitled to be paid the same contributions as they would have received had they been male employees employed on like work.

In *Garland v. British Rail Engineering Ltd*, a female employee of British Rail Engineering claimed parity of treatment for retired female employees with retired male employees. Both male and female employees were granted concessionary rail travel for themselves, their spouses and children during their working life. On retirement the concession was withdrawn from the families of former female employees, but was still granted to the families of former male employees. The European Court ruled that travel facilities granted to employees after retirement are 'pay' within the meaning of Article 119.

In *Barber v. Guardian Royal Exchange Assurance*, Barber was a member of a non-contributory pension scheme financed by the employer. The pensionable age was 62 for men and 57 for women, with a proviso that in the event of redundancy a pension would be paid to men who had reached the age of 55 and to women who had reached the age of 50. Barber was made redundant aged 52 and was, therefore, only entitled to a deferred pension at the age of 62. He complained of discrimination in that had he been female he would have been entitled to an immediate pension.

It was held that:

1   a pension paid under a private pension scheme was 'pay' in that it

constituted a consideration paid (indirectly) by the employer and was within the scope of Article 119;

2 benefits paid by an employer in connection with a redundancy are within the scope of Article 119;

3 a scheme which has different age qualifications based on sex is contrary to the principles of equal pay;

4 Article 119 can be relied on before the national courts;

5 the direct effect of Article 119 cannot be relied upon to claim any entitlement to a pension prior to the Court's judgment (17 May 1990) unless legal proceedings have already been instituted.

In *Kowalska v. Freie und Hansestadt Hamburg*, it was held that a collective agreement which restricted severance payments to full-time employees was indirectly discriminatory against women employees, and that severance payments were pay within Article 119. Individuals can therefore rely directly on Article 119 to have the terms of such a collective agreement set aside and are entitled to be awarded benefits proportionate to their hours of work by their national courts.

A woman may compare her work with that of a male employee formerly employed in the same post by the same employer. The principle of equal pay is not confined to situations in which men and women are contemporaneously doing equal work for the same employer. In *McCarthy Ltd v. Smith*, a man was paid £60 a week as a stockroom manager. On his departure, the post was left vacant for four months, when a woman was appointed to the post at a salary of £50 per week. As the duties were similar, it was held that under the principle in Article 119, she should receive equal pay for the same work as her predecessor.

Article 119 defines equal pay in the following terms. 'Equal pay' without discrimination based on sex means (*a*) that pay for the same work at piece rates shall be calculated on the basis of the same unit of measurement, and (*b*) that pay for work at time rates shall be the same for the same job.

Two Directives of the Council of the European Community have extended the 'principle of equal pay' in Article 119 to include 'work to which equal value is attributed' (Directive 75/117) and 'working conditions' (Directive 76/207).

Directive 75/117 also seeks to eliminate all discrimination on the grounds of sex in respect of all aspects and conditions of remuneration. In particular, where a job classification is used for determining pay it must be based on the same criteria for both men and women and drawn up to exclude any discrimination on the grounds of sex.

The European Court in *Jenkins v. Kingsgate Clothing Production Ltd* held that Directive 75/117 is designed to facilitate the practical application of Article 119. In no way does it alter the scope or the content of the Article. The Court decided in that case that Article 119 is directly applicable in Member States where the form of the discrimination is one which may be identified solely with the aid of the criteria of equal work and equal pay referred to by the Article. National or Community measures are not required to define these criteria with greater precision in order for them to apply.

Directive 76/207 seeks the elimination of discrimination in relation to employment, promotion, working conditions and vocational training. The Directive is directly effective against the organs of the Member States and can only be relied on by employees of the state or an emanation of it. (*Foster v. British Gas plc.*)

The Directive can therefore be relied upon against 'a body, whatever its legal form, which has been made responsible pursuant to a measure, adopted by the State, for providing a public service under the control of the State and has for that purpose special powers beyond those which result from the normal rules applicable in relation between individuals'.

Statutory maternity pay

An employee who is absent from work wholly or partly due to pregnancy or confinement will be entitled to statutory maternity pay, as long as certain conditions are fulfilled.

1 She must be an employed earner.
2 She has continued to be employed by her employer until immediately before the beginning of the 14th week before the expected week of confinement.
3 She has (at the beginning of the 14th week) been continuously employed for a period of not less than two years.
4 She informs her employer at least 21 days before her absence begins (or as soon as reasonably practicable) that she will be (or is) absent from work wholly or partly due to pregnancy or confinement.

5 She is employed for a minimum of 16 hours per week. If she has been employed for more than five years, she will be able to claim if she is employed for more than eight hours a week.

6 She must produce a medical certificate stating the expected week of her confinement, if requested to do so by her employer.

Maternity pay is payable for the first six weeks of absence, starting on or falling after the beginning of the 11th week before the expected week of confinement. An employee is entitled to 90 per cent of a week's pay, less the amount of maternity allowance payable, whether or not there is an entitlement to this allowance.

An employee may present a complaint to an industrial tribunal that her employer has failed to pay her the whole or any part of her entitlement to maternity pay. A complaint must be presented before the end of a three-month period, beginning with the last day of the payment period. A tribunal may order the employer to pay the employee the amount of maternity pay which it finds is due to her.

If an employer is insolvent, or refuses to pay the maternity pay due to the employee, she may apply to the Secretary of State who will pay her the due amount. The Secretary of State may then recover from the employer such an amount as he considers reasonable, but this may not exceed the amount which the employer failed to pay. Employers may claim a rebate for the full amount of maternity payments from National Insurance Contributions.

Employer's insolvency

An employer is regarded as insolvent if:

1 he has been adjudged bankrupt;

2 he has entered into a composition or arrangement with his creditors;

3 he has died and his estate is to be administered in accordance with an order under section 421 of the Insolvency Act.

A company is regarded as insolvent on the occurrence of any of the following events:

(a) a winding-up order;

(b) an administration order;

(c) a resolution for voluntary winding up;

(d) the appointment of a receiver or manager;

(e) the approval of a voluntary arrangement;

(f) possession taken by, or on behalf of, the debenture holders.

If an employer is insolvent, an employee's unpaid wages or salary will be treated as a preferential debt, up to a limit of £800, for the four months preceding the insolvency (Companies Act 1985; Insolvency Act 1986). 'Wages' include holiday pay, sick pay, and, by section 122 of the EPCA, any amounts owed by an employer in respect of: a guarantee payment, remuneration during suspension on medical grounds, payment for time off, and remuneration under a protective award. A preferential creditor is given priority over an ordinary creditor.

The EPCA gives an employee additional rights in that he may recover certain amounts owed to him from the National Insurance Fund. These are:

(a) up to eight weeks arrears of pay up to a maximum of £198 per week;

(b) any amount which the employer is liable to pay during the minimum period of notice required by the EPCA;

(c) up to six weeks' holiday pay entitlement for the 12 months preceding insolvency;

(d) any basic award made by an industrial tribunal;

(e) reimbursement of the whole or part of any fee or premium paid by an apprentice or articled clerk.

Pay also includes amounts owed by an employer under the provisions of section 122 of the EPCA. The maximum amount payable in respect of any week is £198.

Payments may also be made out of the National Insurance Fund where an insolvent employer has failed to pay all the contributions to an occupational pension scheme.

If an employer becomes insolvent when he is liable to pay maternity pay or statutory sick pay, liability for payment is transferred to the DHSS, to whom the employee should apply.

An employee may complain to an industrial tribunal if the Secretary of State fails to make a payment, or a payment made by the Secretary is less than the amount which should have been paid. The industrial tribunal may make a declaration that the Secretary of State ought to make a specified payment.

An employee should first claim as a preferential creditor from his employer's assets. If these are insufficient to meet the employee's claim, he should then apply to the National Insurance Fund. If his claim also exhausts these statutory rights, he will rank as an ordinary creditor in respect of any outstanding amounts.

Wages Councils

Wages are determined in certain industries by Wages Councils. Some 26 Wages Councils have been established in industries where employees are without an effective body to undertake negotiations on their behalf, e.g. retailing, and hotel and catering. This is mainly due to weak, ineffective or non-existent trade union representation in that particular industry. The law governing Wages Councils is to be found in the Wages Councils Act 1979 as amended by the Wages Act 1986.

An order establishing a Wages Council may be made by the Secretary of State for Employment in the following circumstances:

1 if he is of the opinion that adequate machinery does not exist for the remuneration of the employees described in the order;
2 if he gives effect to a recommendation of ACAS that a Wages Council should be established, as a result of an application by a Joint Industrial Council or other body representing employers or employees, who habitually take part in wage negotiations.

A Wages Council consists of not more than five individuals, appointed by the Secretary of State as independent persons, and persons representing employers and employees. One of the independent persons will be appointed as Chairman. The Wages Council may make an order dealing with the rates of pay of workers in that particular industry.

A wage order may only set a single minimum hourly rate for all workers and a single minimum hourly overtime rate. It may also set a maximum rate to be deducted from a worker's remuneration or paid by him to his employer to cover the cost of living accommodation provided by the employer. These provisions do not apply to workers under 21.

In setting the minimum rate a Wages Council must consider the effect of that rate on employment levels amongst the workers to whom it applies, especially in the areas where pay rates are generally below the national average.

The basic provisions relating to wage orders apply to time workers. Different rules apply to piece workers, whose pay is calculated by reference to the number of items of work executed by them. Piece rates are set by employers, not Wages Councils, and must be such that ordinary workers would be able to earn, in a given time, not less than the minimum rate for time workers. This must be paid to piece workers even when work is not available as long as they are available for work at the workplace.

A worker to whom a wage order applies, who is paid less than the statutory minimum in any week, is entitled to the difference between what he actually receives and the statutory minimum laid down by the wages order. This additional remuneration is a contractual obligation and the worker may sue the employer in the County Court for recovery of the sum.

7

TERMINATION OF EMPLOYMENT

A contract of employment may be terminated by one of the parties to the contract giving notice to the other. Most employment contracts contain provisions dealing with the length of notice required to be given by either party to bring the contract to an end. In some cases custom or practice in a particular trade or industry may determine the length of the notice required.

A contract may also be terminated by mutual agreement of the parties, with each party releasing the other party from his contractual obligations. Although the majority of employment contracts are terminated by giving the appropriate period of notice, there are certain circumstances in which this does not occur. There are four situations to consider:

1   where the contract is terminated by giving notice;
2   where the contracted is frustrated, i.e. when the original nature of the contract has undergone a fundamental change;
3   the position of partnership and company employees;
4   where an employee claims that the employer is in breach of contract by not giving the required period of notice, i.e. he claims there has been a wrongful dismissal.

1   *Notice*

In the absence of a provision, custom or agreement, either party is entitled to a reasonable period of notice. What is reasonable depends on a variety of factors, e.g. the employee's position, seniority, length of service, rates and frequency of pay (weekly, monthly, quarterly, annually). A chief engineer of a liner and a newspaper editor have been held to be entitled to 12 months' notice, a company director and a manager of estate agencies to three months' notice, a chorus girl to two weeks' notice and a hairdresser's assistant to one week's notice.

These requirements are subject to the minimum periods of entitlement, provided for by the EPCA (see page 121). Any periods of entitlement contained in the contract will be binding on the parties, as long as the terms exceed the statutory minimum. Either party may waive his right to notice, or accept a payment in lieu of notice (EPCA s49). The acceptance of wages in lieu of notice would therefore amount to termination of the contract. It would appear that an employee is under no obligation to accept wages in lieu of notice, and an employee who seeks reinstatement rather than compensation may be advised in the circumstances to refuse the payment.

2   *Frustration*

A contract is frustrated if its performance in its original form becomes impossible, due to a supervening event producing a situation radically different from that envisaged by the parties when they entered into the contract.

The most common events in the present employment field are concerned with the illness and imprisonment of employees. However, these are not the only circumstances in which a contract is frustrated. In *Morgan v. Manser*, a music hall artiste entered into a 10-year agreement to offer his services solely to his manager, in return for an undertaking to secure engagements. Manser served in the armed services during the Second World War and later entered into engagements with other agents. It was held that the period of military service had frustrated the contract.

Illness

The illness or incapacity of an employee may be of such a nature as to lead to the frustration of a contract. In *Condor v. Barron Knights*, a young drummer was unable to fulfil a five-year contract with a pop group and play on seven nights a week. On medical advice he was only allowed to play on four nights a week. As there was no likelihood of his being able to resume normal employment in the near future the contract was held to be frustrated.

If there is no likelihood of the employee returning to work, the court may well decide that it is no longer practical to regard the contract of employment as subsisting. In *Notcutt v. Universal Equipment Co.* an employee with 27 years' service suffered a permanently incapacitating heart attack. He was two years from retirement. It was held that he was not entitled to sick pay during his statutory period of notice. The contract was frustrated as performance of the contract was no longer possible.

If there is a likelihood of the employee recovering and substantially performing his contract it will not be regarded as frustrated. In *Storey v. Fulham Steel Works*, a works manager was engaged on a five-year agreement, with no provision as to notice. After two years' employment he became ill and was absent from time to time. The employer purported to terminate the agreement but was informed by the employee that he had recovered from illness and would shortly be returning to work. It was held that his illness under this agreement was not of such a character as to indicate that he would never be able to perform his contract and that he would have to be reinstated immediately.

The risk of illness of an employee cannot be a ground for frustration of a contract, unless the nature of the employment is such that it would be unsafe for the employee to continue in that employment. In *Converfoam Ltd v. Bell*, a works director who had a heart attack returned to work to be offered an alternative post at a lower salary. He refused and was dismissed. The employers contended that as there was a risk of the employee suffering further heart attacks, the contract was frustrated. It was held that as the employee was fit to resume normal employment, the possibility of an unforeseen risk did not frustrate the contract and he was held to be unfairly dismissed.

Employers have attempted to use the doctrine in situations where an employee has been ill and off work for some time and has not shown any signs of imminent recovery. The EAT, in *Harman v. Flexible Lamps Ltd*, declared that 'in the employment field the concept of discharge by operation of law, that is frustration, is normally only in play where the contract of employment is for a long term which cannot be determined by notice. Where the contract is terminable by notice, there is really no need to consider the question of frustration and if it were the law that an employer was in a position to say "this contract has been frustrated", then that would be a very convenient way in which to avoid the provisions of the Employment Protection (Consolidation) Act'.

An employer who seeks to terminate an employee's contract on the grounds of ill health must therefore be prepared, with few exceptions, to justify the dismissal as reasonable in the circumstances.

The EAT in *Williams v. Watson's Coaches Ltd* set out guidelines for determining whether a contract of employment is discharged by frustration. The test as laid down in *Davis Contractors Ltd v. Fareham UDC* is whether, if the literal words of the contractual promise were to be enforced in the changed circumstances, performance of the contract would involve a fundamental or radical change from the obligations originally undertaken.

The following principles were approved when applying the doctrine of frustration to employment contracts in the event of illness.

(a)   The court must guard against too easy an application of the doctrine, especially in cases of redundancy and where the true situation is a dismissal due to disability.

(b)   Although it is unnecessary to decide that frustration occurred on a particular date, it may help the court if a date is decided upon.

(c)   The party alleging frustration should not be allowed to rely on the frustrating event if that event was caused by that party (*F.C. Sheperd Ltd v. Jerrom*, see page 110).

(d)   There are a number of factors which may be referred to, including:

    (i)   the length of the previous employment;
    (ii)   the expected length of the present employment;
    (iii) the nature of the job;
    (iv)   the nature, length and effect of the illness or disabling event;
    (v)   the need for the work to be done and the need for a replacement;
    (vi)   rights, e.g. redundancy payments, unfair dismissed compensation;
    (vii) whether wages have continued to be paid;

(viii) the employer's acts and statements in relation to the employment;

(ix) whether the employer could have waited any longer;

(x) any contractual terms dealing with sick pay;

(xi) consideration of the prospects for recovery.

These factors (with the exception of the last two) were set out by Phillips J. in *Egg Stores (Stamford Hill) v. Leibovici.*

In *Williams v. Watson's Coaches*, a part-time typist injured her leg at work. She was absent from work for 18 months from June 1986 and submitted a number of medical certificates, the last one dated December 1986. She presented herself for work in January 1988 and was told there was no work for her, as that part of the employer's business where she had worked had been sold as a going concern. The employers claimed that there was no dismissal as her contract of employment had been frustrated by her lengthy absence. It was held that the contract was not frustrated, as the employer was under a duty to make reasonable inquiries in regard to the employee's progress and to consider the employee's position as a consequence of the sale. This had not been done.

A contract may nevertheless be frustrated even though it is of a short duration. Most such cases have involved contracts of theatrical artists. In *Poussard v. Spiers*, an opera singer was taken ill and failed to attend rehearsals or the first four performances of the opera. The replacement singer would only agree to appear if she were offered the complete engagement. It was held that the contract was frustrated. A contract will not be frustrated where the breach consists of a breach of warranty only. In *Bettini v. Gye*, a singer's failure to appear at rehearsals was regarded as a minor breach of the whole contract, i.e. a breach of warranty. The contract was not frustrated, as she was able and willing to appear at the theatre for the opera performances.

Imprisonment

The contract of an employee sentenced to a term of imprisonment may well be terminated by frustration. In *Harrington v. Kent County Council*, the contract of a teacher sentenced to 12 months' imprisonment was held to be terminated by frustration. The employer was entitled to judge the contractual position at the time when the sentence was imposed. It was immaterial that the employer was aware of the employee's appeal against sentence, as the conviction and sentence of imprisonment were events which has frustrated the contract.

In *F. C. Sheperd Co. Ltd v. Jerrom*, it was held that a four-year contract of apprenticeship was frustrated when the apprentice was sentenced to a minimum six-month period of borstal training.

In *Chakki v. United Yeast Co. Ltd*, an employee was sentenced to 11 months' imprisonment at the commencement of his two weeks' annual holiday. His employers immediately arranged a replacement. After spending one night in prison he was released on bail, and on appeal his sentence was varied to a term of probation. It was held that the contract was not frustrated. The EAT stated that the following questions must be considered when deciding whether a contract of employment has been frustrated by a prison sentence.

1 Is it commercially necessary to decide the employee's future and is a replacement necessary?
2 What is the likely length of the employee's absence?
3 If it is necessary to employ a replacement, is it reasonable to employ a permanent replacement rather than a temporary one?

3   Employees of partnerships and companies

Partnerships

Although a partnership is dissolved on the death or retirement of a partner, the death of a partner will not automatically terminate a contract of employment of a partnership employee, unless the contract is dependent on that partner's continued existence. Such a termination amounts to a dismissal for the purposes of redundancy (EPCA s93). However, the retirement of a partner and the subsequent transfer of the business to the remaining partners automatically terminates the contract of a partnership employee, unless there is a stipulation to the contrary in his contract. In these circumstances an employee should mitigate his loss if possible, so that if he is offered employment by the remaining partners on similar terms to his previous employment and refuses, he will only be entitled to nominal damages at common law for breach of contract. This rule must now be viewed in the light of the Transfer of Undertakings (Protection of Employment) Regulations 1981 which provide that, where one person transfers a business in the nature of a commercial venture to another, the transfer shall not operate so as to terminate a contract of employment. An employee of a partnership whose business is taken over by a new partnership would therefore, under these regulations, be unable to claim damages for wrongful dismissal. It would however be regarded as constituting a dismissal for redundancy purposes.

An employee who is offered and who accepts employment in a reconstituted partnership (containing some of the old partners) will preserve his continuity of employment, as will an employee of a business which changes hands. The Transfer of Undertakings (Protection of Employment) Regulations provide that on the transfer of a commercial undertaking, e.g. the sale of a partnership, an employee who was employed by the old employer at the time of the transfer will automatically become an employee of the new employer, as if his contract of employment had originally been made with the new employer.

Companies

The appointment of a receiver by the court automatically terminates the contracts of a company's employees, but in other circumstances such an appointment does not, of itself, constitute a dismissal of the company's employees. A receiver is usually appointed by a creditor, e.g. a bank, when a company defaults on the repayment of interest or principal on a loan secured on the company's undertaking. If the receiver sells the undertaking, or his appointment is inconsistent with the continuance of an employee's contract (e.g. that of the managing director) this will constitute a dismissal.

The compulsory winding-up of a company operates as a notice of dismissal to its employees. The effect of a voluntary winding-up is not so drastic – a company's employees are only dismissed if the company is insolvent and therefore unable to fulfil its obligations under the contract.

4 Wrongful dismissal

Summary dismissal occurs where an employee is dismissed without being given the proper period of notice to which he is entitled under his contract of employment. If there is no justification for the dismissal, or if proper notice is not given, the dismissal is wrongful and he may sue for wrongful dismissal. It is a breach of contract for either party to terminate a contract of employment without giving proper notice. The summary dismissal of an employee may only be justified by showing that the employer had sufficient grounds for taking such action. The numerous examples of such dismissals from the last century and from the early part of this century provide an unreliable guide to present-day tests and changing social conditions.

The breach of a major term of a contract of employment usually provides justification for the dismissal of an employee without notice, e.g. theft from the employer, accepting bribes, incompetence, and immorality. All the circumstances surrounding the dismissal must be examined to determine whether a right of summary dismissal exists. The misconduct of an employee during working hours is far more likely to justify summary dismissal than any misconduct outside working hours.

Examples of summary dismissals which have been held to be justified include:

Pepper v. Webb (see page 47)
Boston Deep Sea Fishing Co. v. Ansell (see page 48)
Jupiter General Insurance Co. v. Schroff (see page 46)
Sinclair v. Neighbour (see page 48)

An employer who is sued for wrongful dismissal may justify the dismissal on grounds which were not known to him at the time of the dismissal but which subsequently come to light. (*Boston Deep Sea Fishing Company v. Ansell*). This is the opposite of the rule developed in unfair dismissal (see page 48).

An employee who is not given the proper period of notice, or whose summary dismissal is not justified, may refuse to accept an employer's repudiation of the contract, as repudiation by one party does not of itself discharge the contract. The contract of employment is only discharged when the repudiation is accepted by the other party. However, the acceptance of new employment and/or claim for damages by an employee implies acceptance of the repudiation.

A fixed-term contract, i.e. a contract made for a specified period of time, will terminate on the expiration of that time. In this situation an employee cannot claim that he has been wrongfully dismissed, but he is entitled to bring an action for unfair dismissal if the contract is not renewed.

A contract of employment will be terminated by the death of either party. There is an obligation to pay any wages which have accrued.

Special provisions are to be found in schedule 12 of the EPCA governing any entitlement to a redundancy payment and compensation for unfair dismissal on the death of either party, after an employee's dismissal.

An employee who is dismissed almost invariably brings an action for unfair dismissal, rather than suing in the courts for wrongful dismissal. An action for unfair dismissal is heard by an industrial tribunal which offers a speedier, cheaper and less formal means of providing redress for a dismissed employee. It also offers alternative remedies to those provided by the courts, i.e. compensation as well as the possibility of reinstatement or re-engagement.

However, there are certain circumstances when a dismissed employee will bring an action for wrongful dismissal.

1 When he is not entitled to bring an action for unfair dismissal as he comes within the excluded categories, or he has less than two years' continuous employment (see page 122).
2 If he is a highly paid employee (e.g. a managing director of a company) who is engaged on a fixed term contract or entitled to a lengthy period of notice, and has been wrongfully and unfairly dismissed. Such an employee would seek damages for wrongful dismissal in preference to a claim for compensation for unfair dismissal, which is subject to statutory limits (see page 148).

__ Remedies following termination __ of the contract

1 *Declaration*   An employee may seek a declaration from the court to determine the rights of the parties in the case.
2 *Damages*   An employee may sue an employer where the employer is in breach of his contractual duties.
3 *Specific performance*   A court order compelling the performance of an act.
4 *Injunction*   An employer may seek an injunction, i.e. an order of the court which forbids the performance of a particular act or course of action.

1 *Declaration*

An employee may seek a declaration as to his legal position, i.e. the court is asked to declare the position in law on a given set of facts. The declaration has coercive effect in that its terms are generally observed by the affected parties. A declaration will not generally be granted to an ordinary employee who is wrongfully dismissed, except in special circumstances.

Employees who enjoy a special statutory status may seek a declaration. In *Vine v. National Dock Labour Board*, a registered dock worker obtained a declaration that his purported dismissal by a disciplinary board was null and void, as his name had not been validly removed from the register. He remained in the employment of the National Dock Harbour Board.

A chief constable was granted a declaration that his dismissal was null and void, and was consequently able to safeguard his pension rights (*Ridge v. Baldwin*).

In *Cresswell v. Board of Inland Revenue*, an employee sought a declaration that the employer was in breach of the employment contract by introducing computer technology and expecting staff to adapt to the new system. The court declared that the nature of the employment had not changed and that employees are obliged to adapt reasonably to new work methods.

The courts will more readily grant a declaration when the facts in issue raise the problem of a right to work rather than the right to remain with a particular employer. In *Nagle v. Fielden*, the Jockey Club refused Mrs Nagle a licence to train racehorses in pursuance of their unwritten policy of not granting a licence to a woman. She obtained a declaration that the practice was contrary to public policy. The parties later reached a settlement and she was granted a trainer's licence.

In *Bonsor v. Musicians Union*, a professional musician was granted a declaration that his expulsion from the Musicians Union was null and void. The branch secretary had removed his name from the register without consulting the branch committee, as was required by the union rules.

2 Damages

An employee who is wrongfully dismissed may sue his employer for damages. The basis of compensation is twofold.

Firstly, the employee should be placed in the same financial position as if the contract had not been broken, i.e. he should be given the wages he would have received had proper notice been given to him on the date of dismissal. An employee on a fixed-term contract will be able to recover as damages the salary or wages payable for the balance of the unexpired term.

Secondly, he should receive such damages as may be reasonably supposed to have been in the contemplation of the parties, at the time of making the contract, as the probable result of the breach (*Clayton v. Oliver*).

An employee will therefore be able to recover the amount of wages that he would have received, but for his wrongful dismissal. He will of course be entitled to any unpaid wages at the date of his dismissal. He will also be entitled to compensation for any loss of fringe benefits, e.g. the use of a car, accrued pension rights.

The purpose of an award of damages is to compensate an employee for any loss sustained as a result of a breach of contract. If an employee obtains other employment before the expiration of the term of the breached contract, earnings from the new employment will be deducted from the damages.

An employee is under a duty to mitigate the loss if possible, by obtaining new or alternative employment. In *Brace v. Calder,* an employee, dismissed on the dissolution of a partnership, refused similar employment offered to him by the new partnership which took over from the 'old' firm. He was awarded nominal damages, as he should have accepted this offer of new employment and minimised his loss.

A court, in assessing damages, may well take into account various benefits paid to the employee, e.g. unemployment benefit, or supplementary benefit. These have been taken into account when assessing damages in personal injury cases. Whether a redundancy payment may be deducted from the assessed damages is questionable and depends on the circumstances surrounding the employee's dismissal.

An employee's liability to taxation must also be taken into account when awarding damages, as the employee's wages would have been subject to income tax if he had continued in that employment (*Beach v. Reed Corrugated Cases Ltd*).

An employee is not entitled to claim damages for the manner of his dismissal, for his injured feelings, or for any loss he may suffer from the fact that the dismissal makes it more difficult to obtain new employment. In *Addis v. Gramaphone Company*, the plaintiff was employed as the manager at its Calcutta office. He was given six months' notice by his employer and was prevented from acting any longer as manager. He was entitled to damages for loss of six months' salary and commission, but there was no entitlement for the way in which the dismissal had been carried out.

However, in *Cox v. Phillips Industries*, it was held that damages may be awarded if the employer's conduct on terminating the contract is such that it causes mental distress to the employee. In this case the plaintiff was relegated to a less responsible position as a result of submitting a letter asking for a review of his salary. Although his salary was un-affected, his new duties were extremely vague, and he became very depressed, anxious and frustrated. Following pressure from the company he was induced to sign a letter of resignation. It was held that the company was in breach of contract by relegating the employee to a less responsible position and by subjecting him to mental distress.

An action for wrongful dismissal must be commenced within a period of six years from the date of the breach of the contract. A claim for £25,000 or less will be heard by a circuit judge in the County Court, unless the case is complex or of particular importance. A claim for £5,000 or less will be tried by a district judge in the County Court. A claim in excess of £50,000 will be tried in the High Court, unless the case is so straightfor-ward as not to merit a trial in the High Court. Cases involving amounts between £25,000 and £50,000 will be allocated between the County Court and the High Court in accordance with the criteria above.

3   Specific performance

A decree of specific performance will not be granted by a court or tribunal to compel an employee to continue to work for a particular employer. Section 16 of TULRA provides that 'no court shall, whether by way of (*a*) an order for specific performance . . . of a contract of employment, or (*b*) an injunction . . . restraining a breach or threatened breach of such a contract, compel an employee to do any work or attend at any place for the doing of any work'.

However, the EPCA provides a remedy, which bears a close resemblance to specific performance. If an industrial tribunal finds that an employee has been unfairly dismissed, it may ask the employee if he wishes the tribunal to make an order for reinstatement or re-engagement. Reinstatement is a restoration of the employee to his former post, while an order for re-engagement requires an employer to find comparable or other suitable work for the employee.

4 Injunction

An injunction (a court order prohibiting the recipient from carrying out an act) is sometimes sought by an employer who seeks to protect certain legitimate business interests. He may allege that an employee is in breach of a restrictive employment covenant or has failed to show good faith towards his employer.

In *Thomas Marshall (Exports) v. Guinle*, a managing director repudiated a 10-year service agreement with the company and resigned after five years and set up his own company and solicited business from the company's customers in breach of his service agreement. The agreement contained clauses against disclosing information relating to the company's affairs, customers or trade secrets during his employment or after it ceased. The company was granted an injunction to enforce the covenant and prevent the defendant from avoiding his obligations under the contract.

As a general rule a court will not grant an injunction where damages provide an adequate remedy, or if it compels the performance of a contract of employment. However, recent decisions have recognised that employees have certain rights which cannot be adequately protected by the award of damages. Where an employee shows that an employer has sufficient trust and confidence in the employee's abilities, an injunction may be granted by the court.

In *Powell v. London Borough of Brent*, a senior benefits officer applied for the post of principal benefits officer. She was informed that she had been selected for the post and a date was agreed for her to start her new post. An unsuccessful candidate complained of the appointment and the Council's appointments sub-committee decided to re-advertise the post.

She was asked to return to her old post. She instituted proceedings to restrain the Council and was granted an interlocutory (temporary) injunction.

In *Hughes v. London Borough of Southwark*, a number of social workers were asked to work in a different area in a newly constituted team, which was not in accordance with their contracts of employment. An interlocutory injunction was granted preventing the Council from varying their contractual duties and retaining the status quo so that the employees could work in accordance with the circumstances existing prior to the dispute.

An injunction may be granted to enforce a negative stipulation in a contract, where damages fail to provide an adequate remedy. In *Lumley v. Wagner*, an opera signer, Joanna Wagner, contracted to sing at Lumley's theatre for a period of three months, and covenanted that she would not sing elsewhere during that time without his written consent. An injunction was granted to restrain her from singing for another party in breach of the agreement, although a decree of specific performance was refused.

The granting of an injunction may have the effect of encouraging an employee to fulfil a contract of employment. In *Warner Bros v. Nelson*, the actress Bette Davis entered into a contract to devote her services exclusively to the film company for a certain length of time. During this time she also entered into a contract with an English film company. The court granted an injunction to Warner Bros, as her contract contained a negative stipulation that she would not work for another person during this time. As the injunction was confined to work on stage and screen she would be able to earn her living in another capacity and would not (in theory) be compelled to work for Warner Bros.

In *Page One Records Ltd v. Britton*, a pop group, 'The Troggs', dispensed with the services of the company, who acted as their manager, in breach of a five-year contract. The company sought an injunction to prevent the group from appointing a manager until an action for breach of contract was heard by the court. This was refused, as it would compel the group to employ the company. The contract was for personal services of a fiduciary nature which could not be continued when one of the parties had lost confidence in the other.

An injunction may be granted to restrain an employer who purports to act in breach of agreed disciplinary procedures. In *Jones v. Lee*, an injunction was granted to prevent managers of a Roman Catholic primary school dismissing the headmaster without affording him the opportunity to be heard and obtaining the consent of the local council. Both these requirements were stipulated in his contract of employment.

8

UNFAIR
DISMISSAL

An action for unfair dismissal will be heard by an industrial tribunal which will enquire into the overall merits of the dismissal. Every dismissal, with or without notice, is presumed to be unfair and it is for the employer to justify the dismissal. At common law an employer may dismiss an employee for any reason as long as he gives the appropriate period of notice, or pays wages or salary in lieu of notice and in these circumstances an employee has no redress whatsoever in the courts.

In order to bring an action for unfair dismissal an employee must have the appropriate period of continuous employment and must not come within the limited categories of employees who are excluded from the unfair dismissal provisions (see page 122).

Continuity of employment

An employee must have been continuously employed for two years before he can bring an action for unfair dismissal.

The minimum periods of notice required to be given by an employer to terminate a contract of employment will vary according to the length of continuous employment of an employee, as follows:

1   one week if employed for more than one month but for less than two years;
2   not less than one week for each year, if employed for two years or more, but less than 12 years (EPCA s49(1)).

An employee must give at least one week's notice if he has been employed for more than one month. Any week in which an employee is employed for 16 hours or more will count as a week in computing a period of employment. If an employee's working week changes from 16 hours or more, to more than eight hours, but less than 16 hours per week, he is entitled to count up to 26 weeks of this reduced working week towards continuity of employment. An employee who has worked for more than eight hours, but less than 16 hours a week, for five years or longer, is deemed to have been continuously employed for the purposes of entitlement to these statutory rights.

Continuity is preserved even when an employee is on strike. The period of time on strike, however, does not count towards the total period of employment. The continuity of an employee who is dismissed during a strike and subsequently re-engaged is preserved, although again the period of time on strike does not count towards the total period of employment.

Continuity is also preserved in the following circumstances, even though there is a temporary break in employment:

(a)   if an employee, whose contract has been terminated because of sickness or injury, is re-engaged under a new contract within 26 weeks of the end of the previous contract;

(b)   if there is a temporary cessation of work of the kind the employee was previously contracted to do. It was held in *Ford v. Warwickshire County Council* that a schoolteacher who had been employed for eight years under a series of contracts commencing each year in September and terminating in July had been continuously employed during that time. The summer holidays were regarded as a temporary cessation of work as the period of absence was short in relation to the length of the actual employment;

(c)   in circumstances in which, by arrangement or custom, the employment is regarded as continuing, e.g. an employee is loaned to another employer;

(d)   where absence is due to pregnancy or confinement, as long as the employee returns to work with the employer or associated employer within 29 weeks of the confinement;

(e)   in the four weeks which are permitted before re-engagement under a different contract of employment.

The periods of employment to be taken into account are those with the present employer. There are, however, certain circumstances where a change of employer does not break an employee's continuity of employment. These include:

(i)   the transfer of a trade or business to another employer;

(ii)   the employees of a deceased employer being offered employment on similar terms by his personal representatives;

(iii)   a change in the partners, trustees or personal representatives who are the employers;

(iv)   employment by an associated company, i.e. a subsidiary or a holding company or a company controlled by the same person;

(v)   a relevant transfer within the meaning of the Transfer of Undertakings (Protection of Employment) Regulations 1981. When a business is sold or disposed of (other than by a share take-over) the employees of the old employer will automatically become employees of the new employer, as if their contracts of employment were originally made with the new employer.

——————— **Excluded categories** ———————

Certain categories of employees are excluded from the unfair dismissal provisions. These are:

1   an employee with less than two years' continuous employment;
2   an employee who, before the effective date of termination of employment, had reached the normal retiring age of his/her employment or, if there is no normal retiring age, had reached 65;
3   an employee who, under his contract of employment, ordinarily works outside Great Britain;
4   a registered dock worker engaged on dock work;
5   the master or crew member of a fishing vessel who is paid solely by a share in the profits or gross earnings of the vessel;

6   a member of the armed forces or the police force;

7   employees covered by a dismissal procedure agreement;

8   a person employed under a fixed-term contract for one year or more who, before the expiry of the contract, has agreed in writing to waive the right of complaint of unfair dismissal on the contract's expiry;

9   a person who did not present a complaint of unfair dismissal within three months of the effective date of termination or within such further time as is considered reasonable;

10 a person who is involved in industrial action at the date of the dismissal.

A claim from a person falling within one of the first three categories will not be excluded if the reason for the dismissal was the employee's membership of a trade union, his trade union activities, or his refusal to join a trade union or to remain a member of a trade union.

——————— Dismissal ———————

An employee is treated as dismissed by his employer if:

1   the employer terminates the contract, with or without notice; or

2   the employee terminates the contract, with or without notice, by reason of the employer's conduct (constructive dismissal); or

3   a fixed-term contract expires and is not renewed.

1 Termination by employer

In the majority of cases, an employee will be given proper notice by his employer in accordance with the terms of the contract. If notice is not given, the intention of the parties must be ascertained. If an employee is told to 'collect your cards' or 'you're fired', the intention is quite clear, but in other cases, words spoken in the heat of the moment may well be viewed in a different light at a later time by the parties.

In *J. J. Stern v. Simpson* an employee claimed that he had been dismissed when Mrs Simpson, who was recuperating from a major illness, rushed into a room following an argument between the employee and her son shouting 'Go! Get out! Get out!' It was held that there was no dismissal as the words were spoken in the heat of the moment.

In *Futty v. D. D. Brekkes Ltd*, a fish filleter in Hull was told by the foreman 'If you don't like the job, fuck off!' He claimed that he had been dismissed. It was held that, in those circumstances, the words were a general exhortation to get on with the job and that Futty had not been dismissed.

If an employee is given a choice of resignation or dismissal, this Hobson's choice will constitute a dismissal. In *Robertson v. Securicor Transport Ltd*, an employee was in breach of a company rule when he signed for a container which he had not received. When this was discovered he was given the option of resigning or being dismissed. Although he resigned, he was nevertheless held to have been dismissed.

However an invitation to resign as an alternative to facing a disciplinary hearing which could result in a dismissal is not in itself a dismissal. In *Salton v. Durham County Council* a social worker terminated his contract by mutual consent when facing a disciplinary hearing where a recommendation for his summary dismissal was to be considered.

It is also important to determine whether there has been a resignation. In *Barclay v. City of Glasgow District Council* a labourer whose general practitioner described as suffering from 'high-grade mental deficiency' shouted at a foreman and said that he wanted his books on the following day, a Friday. His employers treated the demand as a resignation and when he turned up for work on the Monday he was sent home by the foreman. It was held that the employer should have checked that it was a genuine act of resignation and there had been an unfair dismissal.

If an employee who has been given notice by his employer, gives notice to his employer to terminate his employment on an earlier date than that specified in the employer's notice, he will nevertheless be taken as having been dismissed by the employer for the reasons given by the employer.

If an employee gives notice to his employer to terminate the contract of employment and the employer dismisses him, with or without notice, during the period of notice, this will constitute a dismissal rather than a resignation. In *Harris and Russel Ltd v. Slingsby*, an employer ordered off the premises an employee who had given in his notice, when he discovered that the employee intended to work for a rival company. This was held to constitute a dismissal.

2 *Constructive dismissal*

An employee who does not give proper notice to his employer may justify his action on the grounds of 'constructive dismissal', i.e. the employer's conduct was such that he was entitled to terminate the contract without notice. Alternatively an employee may give notice and work the period of notice. In both situations the employer's breach of contract must be fundamental and significant, thereby justifying summary termination by the employee.

In *Western Excavating Ltd v. Sharp*, Lord Denning MR stated: 'If the employer is guilty of conduct which is a significant breach going to the root of the contract of employment, or which shows that the employer no longer intends to be bound by one or more of the essential terms of the contract, then the employee is entitled to treat himself as discharged from any further performance. If he does so, then he terminates the contract by reason of the employer's conduct. He is constructively dismissed. The employee is entitled in those circumstances to leave at the instant without giving any notice at all or, alternatively, he may give notice and say he is leaving at the end of the notice. But the conduct must in either case be sufficiently serious to entitle him to leave at once. Moreover, he must make up his mind soon after the conduct of which he complains; for, if he continues for any length of time without leaving, he will lose his right to treat himself as discharged. He will be regarded as having elected to affirm the contract'.

An employee must also show that the contract had not been terminated by the time the breach occurred, and the breach was the reason for its termination. An employee who continues to work after such a breach may well be regarded as affirming the contract and condoning the breach. If an employee in such a situation clearly objects, the fact that he continues to draw his wages does not necessarily indicate affirmation of the contract and acceptance of the breach.

Examples of constructive dismissals

In *Courtaulds Northern Textiles v. Andrew*, an overseer resigned after 18 years' service, after an argument with an assistant manager when he was told that he could not 'do the bloody job anyway'. It was held that he was entitled to treat the comment as conduct justifying resignation, as it seriously damaged the relationship of confidence and trust between the parties.

In *Post Office v. Roberts*, an employee who had been appraised as capable asked for a transfer to a new area as she was getting married. She was told that there were no suitable vacancies, but later discovered that a senior officer had written a poor assessment of her capabilities containing criticisms of which she had not been informed. She resigned and claimed a constructive dismissal. It was held that the Post Office's conduct was in breach of its implied obligation of mutual trust and confidence, which amounted to a repudiation of the contract.

In *Stokes v. Hampstead Wine Co.*, the employer agreed to pay overtime for Christmas work and an employee worked 88 hours' overtime over the Christmas period. Despite various promises she was not paid for those hours until the following February, when she was paid for 40 hours and was told that this was all she was getting. She informed the employers that she would resign if she did not receive the arrears by the following day. She was not paid, and so she resigned. It was held that this was a constructive dismissal as the employer was in fundamental breach of contract and the employee had acted reasonably.

In *Savoia v. Chiltern Herb Farms*, a company required the employee to change jobs as a result of reorganisation. He was previously supervisor of a packing department and was required to become production foreman. He refused on the ground that he would be exposed to conjunctivitis as a result of heat and smoke, but refused to submit to a medical examination, or provide evidence from his own doctor. It was held that he had been constructively, but fairly, dismissed.

In *McNeill v. Charles Crimin Ltd*, a foreman who was ordered to work under the supervision of an ordinary electrician as a 'temporary' measure was held to be constructively dismissed as his employers were guilty of a major breach of contract.

In *Simmonds v. Dowty Seals Ltd*, a night worker who was threatened with dismissal if he refused to work on day shifts was entitled to claim unfair dismissal as his employers had repudiated his contract by attempting a unilateral change of contract.

In *Wadham Stringer v. Brown*, a company's fleet sales director was constantly moved to cramped offices and provided with fewer and fewer facilities, until he could no longer do his job properly and resigned. It was held that such conduct on the part of the employer amounted to constructive dismissal.

In *Hogg v. Dover College*, a full-time teacher and head of department became ill. After an absence he returned to part-time teaching. The headmaster later wrote to him stating that he could not remain as departmental head because of his health, but he could continue to teach a reduced number of hours at a lower salary. It was held that the headmaster's letter terminated the contract as the changes in the employment terms were so fundamental as to lead to a constructive dismissal.

An employee should not regard a statement by his employer that his employment will cease in the near future, and advising the employee to seek alternative employment, as a constructive dismissal. In *Heseltine Lake v. Dowler*, an employee was told that he no longer had a future with the firm and would be wise to seek other employment or face eventual dismissal. In *International Computers Ltd v. Kennedy*, an employee was informed that the factory where she was employed was to be closed down within the next year and she should seek alternative employment as soon as possible. Both Dowler and Kennedy failed in their respective actions for constructive dismissal, as in neither case was there a dismissal, and there was no evidence that the employers would not have given proper periods of notice.

3   Fixed-term contracts

An employee whose fixed-term contract is not renewed is regarded as having been dismissed. A fixed-term contract which may be terminated before the end of the fixed term, by notice given by either party, is nevertheless regarded for the purposes of the EPCA as a contract for a fixed term. An employee may forgo his right to sue for unfair dismissal if a fixed-term contract is not renewed.

—— Reasons for dismissal ——

If it is established that a dismissal has taken place it must then be determined whether such a dismissal is fair. An employer who seeks to justify a dismissal must show that the reason (or principal reason) for dismissal was one of the following:

1 a reason related to the employee's capability or qualifications for performing the work in question;
2 a reason related to the employee's conduct;
3 that the employee was redundant;
4 that the employee could not continue to be employed in that capacity without contravening a statutory duty or restriction;
5 some other substantial reason which would justify the dismissal of an employee holding the employee's position.

An employer must show that not only did he have a valid reason for the dismissal, but that he acted reasonably in the circumstances (including the size and administrative resources of the undertaking) in dismissing the employee for that particular reason. That question must be determined in accordance with equity and the substantial merits of the case.

The test of reasonableness involves a consideration of the steps leading up to a decision to dismiss the employee, together with a consideration of the way the dismissal was carried out. Previous warnings, hearings and appeals must all be considered to determine the reasonableness of the dismissal. If an employee is dismissed for lack of capability or misconduct, it is necessary to show that he was warned and given the opportunity to improve.

In *Polkey v. Dayton*, it was held that the only test of the fairness of a dismissal is the reasonableness of the employer's decision to dismiss, judged at the time at which the dismissal takes effect. If the decision to dismiss was, in the circumstances, unfair, but the observance of a fair procedure would have made the dismissal fair, the correct approach is a finding of unfair dismissal with a reduction in the amount of the employee's compensation.

An employee who has been continuously employed for two or more years and who is dismissed without notice, or whose fixed-term contract is not renewed, is entitled to receive written reasons for his dismissal, if he so requests. The statement must be provided within 14 days of the request and is admissible in any proceedings.

If the employer unreasonably refuses to provide the statement or provides a statement that is untrue or inadequate, the employee may, within three months, complain to a tribunal. If the tribunal finds the complaint well founded it may make a declaration as to the reasons for the dismissal and make an award of two weeks' pay to the employee (EPCA s53 as amended by EA89 s15).

1 Capability and qualifications

Capability is assessed by reference to skill, aptitude, health or any other physical or mental quality; while qualifications refers to any degree, diploma or other academic, technical or professional qualification relevant to the position which the employee held.

Capability

An employer may dismiss an employee who lacks the capability to perform the contract of employment in a satisfactory manner. Whether a dismissal is fair in these circumstances will depend on a variety of factors, e.g. the position held by the employee, the nature of the incompetence, whether an employee is given the opportunity to improve. The test is whether the employer honestly believes, on reasonable grounds, that the employee is incompetent.

In *Taylor v. Alidair Ltd*, it was held that a landing by an airline pilot was so hazardous and incompetent as to justify instant and fair dismissal. In *Williams v. Mortimer Fashions Ltd*, it was held that an employee, the firm's financial director, was fairly dismissed as he had failed to keep the directors informed as to the company's financial situation, especially as to the extent to which overdue accounts had accumulated.

An employee whose work is criticised should be given an opportunity to improve. In *Tiptools v. Curtis*, an employee with more than 20 years' satisfactory service was held to be unfairly dismissed when dismissed without warning for poor workmanship on an important order. In *Newalls Insulation Co. Ltd v. Blakeman*, an employee was held to be fairly dismissed after being absent on two occasions in a fortnight, following a final written warning for absenteeism.

In the case of a senior employee, one serious case of gross negligence may justify dismissal. In *Comerford v. Swel Foods Ltd*, a factory supervisor was fairly dismissed when he allowed production to continue after realising that a pump was malfunctioning. The output of a whole shift had to be written off.

An employee who is promoted beyond his ability should, if possible, be offered alternative work as an alternative to dismissal. In *Coward v. John Menzies (Holdings) Ltd*, the manager of a branch was considered to be lacking in certain qualities. The employers decided that he needed re-training and proposed that he should be demoted to assistant manager and transferred to a branch 200 miles away, but receive the same salary. Company policy was to re-train employees in this situation, and later re-promote if the re-training was successful. The employee declined the transfer and was dismissed. It was held that the dismissal was fair.

Ill health   A very important aspect of capability is the question of an employee's health. A dismissal of an employee on the grounds of ill health will be judged on the individual's circumstances as well as the nature and size of the organisation.

An employer must make a reasonable effort to establish the true medical position relating to the employee. In *East Lindsay District Council v. Daubney*, an employee who had suffered a stroke was held to be unfairly dismissed as a result of a medical report which merely stated that he should be retired early, but gave no medical details. The report had been obtained without the knowledge or consent of the employee, and there had been no proper investigation of the facts.

An employer acts reasonably if he relies on advice given by his own doctor, even if that advice conflicts with that given by the employee's own doctor. An employer should, if possible, seek alternative work for an employee who has become unfit to follow his present job. In *Carricks (Caterers) v. Nolan*, the dismissal of a maintenance fitter who had been off work with heart trouble was held to be unfair when he refused to work shifts. The employer could easily have re-organised matters to avoid Nolan lifting heavy weights or arranged to offer him a day job.

Although an employer should try to find alternative work for a sick employee, he is not duty-bound to find a new post for him. In *Manweb v. Taylor* an electricity board inspector, who had worked for the board for 38 years, had been absent for 50 weeks out of the last year of employment, due to a heart condition. It was held that, despite his length of service, the employer was not under an obligation to create a special post for him.

Absence from work   The effect of an employee's absence on an employer's business has to be considered on a realistic basis. In *Spencer v. Paragon Wallpapers*, a small firm's only van driver was fairly dismissed for repeated days' absences. If a firm is able to find a temporary replacement it will be difficult for the employer to justify a dismissal.

It was stated in the above case that the factors which should be considered were: 'The nature of the illness; the likely length of the continuing absence, the need of the employers to have done the work which the employee was engaged to do'.

If an employee's absence affects the other employees, e.g. in performance or pay, or his absence is seriously damaging the firm's business, his dismissal may be regarded as fair. In *Tan v. Berry Brothers & Rudd Ltd*, an employee with a record of absenteeism required an operation. His subsequent dismissal was held to be fair as the employers, a small firm, were approaching the Christmas rush, and the continued absence of a single employee was significant in these circumstances.

Although a firm cannot wait indefinitely for the employee's return to work, the likelihood of an employee returning to work in the near future should be taken into account. In *Hawick v. Leeds Area Health Authority* a nurse was absent due to ill health for four months, her period of entitlement to sick pay under the authority's scheme. She indicated that she would be returning to work in eight days' time. Her dismissal by the authority on the termination of the period of entitlement was held to be unfair.

Absenteeism and late arrival at work are forms of misconduct which may, in certain circumstances, justify dismissal. The reason for the absence or lateness and the employee's work and attendance record must be taken into consideration in deciding whether there are grounds for dismissal. This situation usually requires that a warning be given, followed by a reasonable opportunity to improve.

In *London Transport Executive v. Clarke*, an employee was dismissed in 1979 because of his unauthorised absence in Jamaica for a period of seven weeks. He had visited the island in 1977, and the employer had a rule that unpaid leave for overseas visits would only be granted at intervals of three years or longer. This was held to be a fair dismissal, as he had been told that he would be dismissed if he went without permission.

Qualifications

There have been very few cases where the lack of qualifications have been the reason for the dismissal. In *Blackman v. Post Office*, a post and telegraph officer was required to pass an aptitude test within a specified time. He attempted the test on the permitted number of occasions but failed to pass. It was held that his dismissal related to a 'qualification'.

In *Tayside Regional Council v. McIntosh,* a vehicle mechanic who was subsequently disqualified from driving was held to have been fairly dismissed as the nature of the job required a driving licence.

2 Conduct

An employee's misconduct during the performance of the contract of employment may lead to his dismissal if the misconduct is sufficiently grave. Gross misconduct, i.e. a serious breach of contract, justifies instant dismissal while an act of a trivial nature is usually dealt with by a warning. A wide variety of breaches have been dealt with by tribunals, e.g. fighting, swearing, drinking, horseplay, taking drugs, incompetence, wearing unsuitable clothing, betting, clocking-in offences, 'fiddling' expenses, sleeping on duty, theft, etc.

The ACAS Code of Practice gives practical advice to employers on how to deal with disciplinary matters in a fair manner. Although the Code is advisory, a tribunal must consider any provisions of the Code which appear to be relevant in the matter before it. It must also decide to what extent it is necessary and practicable for an employer to follow the provisions of the Code. A tribunal must take into account the size and administrative resources of a business in determining whether an employer acted reasonably.

On joining a firm an employee should be given clear instructions as to the scope of his duties. He should be informed as to what conduct can lead to a dismissal, and in particular those offences which justify summary dismissal for a first offence.

Paragraph 10 of the Code provides that disciplinary procedures should:

(a)   be in writing, specify to whom they apply and provide for matters to be dealt with quickly;

(b)   indicate the disciplinary actions which may be taken and the levels of management which have the authority to take these actions;

(c)   provide for individuals to be informed of the complaints against them and give them an opportunity to state their case before decisions are reached;

(d)   give individuals the right to be accompanied by a trade union representative or by a fellow employee of their choice;

(e)   ensure that, except for gross misconduct, no employees are dismissed for a first breach of discipline;

(f)   ensure that disciplinary action is not taken until the case has been carefully investigated and that an explanation is given for any penalty imposed;

(g)   provide a right of appeal and specify the procedure to be followed.

The Code envisages the following procedures being observed:

(i)   in the case of a minor offence, an individual should receive a formal oral warning. If the issue is more serious, there should be a written   in the case of a minor offence, an individual should receive a formal of further offences. In either case, an individual should be advised that the warning constitutes the first formal stage of disciplinary procedure;

(ii)   further misconduct might warrant a final written warning, which should contain a statement that any recurrence will lead to suspension or dismissal or some other penalty;

(iii)   the final step might be disciplinary transfer or suspension (without pay if provided for in the contract) or dismissal according to the nature of the misconduct. Special consideration should be given before imposing disciplinary suspension without pay and it should not normally be for a prolonged period (paragraph 12 of the Code).

Criminal offences   An employee's dishonesty may justify dismissal. The majority of cases have dealt with theft – from an employer, a fellow employee or a customer. Any of these will usually be regarded as clear grounds for dismissal.

In *Parker v. Dunn Ltd*, an employee admitted to police that he had stolen from his employer. He complained that his subsequent dismissal was unfair as he had not been given the opportunity to state his case to his employers. It was held that his dismissal was fair, as he had not protested his innocence to his employers and had not sought to implement the available grievance procedure.

Theft from a fellow employee is viewed in a similar light. In *Fowler v. Cammell Laird*, an employee stole a car mirror from a fellow employee's car parked in the works car park. His dismissal was held to be fair.

Where there is a suspicion of dishonesty, an employer should carry out an investigation and, where possible, give the employee an opportunity to explain. In *Tesco Group Ltd v. Hill*, an employee was suspended after failing to ring certain items on her till. She was dismissed later the same day after the employer had investigated the matter in her absence. The dismissal was held to be unfair as the employee should have been given the opportunity to offer an explanation.

An employer may dismiss an employee if he genuinely believes, on reasonable grounds, in the employee's guilt. Such a dismissal will be fair even though an employee may later be acquitted of the offence, or the police decline to prosecute.

In *Harris and Shepherd v. Courage Ltd*, two employees were charged with theft from their employer. The employer followed the agreed stages of disciplinary procedure, but the employees did not participate because of the pending trial. The employees were dismissed, but were later acquitted at the Crown Court. Their dismissal was held to be fair, for if an employee chooses not to give an explanation, an employer may consider the evidence and decide whether a dismissal is justified.

In the case of misconduct by a member of a group where an employer is unable to identify the culprit after a thorough investigation, the employer may dismiss all the members of the group.

In *Whitbread plc v. Thomas* an off-licence which was staffed by three part-timers had suffered stock losses over a long period of time. Despite formal warnings and the temporary transfer of all three staff to other shops, the losses continued when they returned to work at the off-licence. The dismissal of all three employees for failure to prevent stock losses was held to be fair.

In such a situation the employer must show:

(a)   the act is such that, if committed by an identified individual, it would justify dismissal;
(b)   the tribunal must be satisfied that the act has been committed by one or more of the group;
(c)   the tribunal must be satisfied that the employer has conducted a proper investigation to identify the person or persons responsible for the act.

The matter was further considered in *Parr v. Whitbread plc* and concerned the theft of £4,600 from an off-licence. The evidence suggested that one out of four employees could have been responsible. The employer, despite investigation, failed to find the person responsible and dismissed all four employees. It was held that the dismissals in these circumstances are justified provided that the employer's beliefs are based on reasonable grounds, that he has sufficiently investigated the matter and that the following criteria are satisfied:

(i)   an act has been committed which, if committed by an individual, would justify dismissal;
(ii)   as a result of an investigation, the employer reasonably believes more than one person could have committed the act;
(iii)   the employer acted reasonably in identifying the group of employees who could have committed the act, and each member of the group was individually capable of doing so, and the employer could not reasonably identify the perpetrator of the act.

Different considerations may apply to an employee who commits a criminal offence outside his employment. The factors to be considered are stated in the ACAS Code of Practice, paragraph 15 (c), which provides that such conduct should not be treated as automatic reasons for dismissal regardless of whether the offence has any relevance to the duties of the individual as an employee. The main considerations should be whether the offence is one that makes the individual unsuitable for his or her type of work or unacceptable to other employees. Employees should not be dismissed solely because a charge against them is pending or because they are absent through having been remanded in custody.

An employee with 20 years' service was apprehended at another store for shoplifting. She signed a form admitting taking the goods without paying. Although she later gave an explanation to her employers which was consistent with her innocence, she was held to have been fairly dismissed (*Moore v. C & A Modes*).

A college lecturer in charge of 16–18 year olds, convicted of gross indecency with another man in a public lavatory, was held to have been fairly dismissed by his employers (*Gardiner v. Newport County Borough Council*).

Disobedience   An employer may dismiss an employee for refusing to obey a reasonable order. What is a reasonable order depends on the type and terms of employment and the employee's position. (*Union of Construction, Allied Trades & Technicians v. Brain* see page 47.)

In *Bloomfield v. Trust Houses Forte Ltd*, an employee called a union meeting at a time when his employer had informed him that it was inconvenient to guests and he would be dismissed if he contravened the order. The dismissal was held to be fair. In another case, a lesbian refused to remove a badge proclaiming 'Lesbians Ignite'. As she was an accounts clerk whose duties involved contact with the public, it was held that her subsequent dismissal was fair (*Boychuk v. Symons Holdings Ltd*).

An employee has a right to object if an order affects or alters terms of employment, the type of work undertaken, his pay, hours of work, or conditions of work. These must be balanced against the employer's needs. In *Johnson v. Nottinghamshire Police Authority*, an employee who refused to change from day working to day, evening and shift working was held to be fairly dismissed (see page 157).

It was stated by Watkins L. J. in *Woods v. W. M. Car Services*, 'Employers must not be put in a position where, through the wrongful refusal of their employees to accept change, they are prevented from introducing improved business methods in furtherance of seeking success for their enterprise'.

An employee who disobeys a disciplinary rule may find that his conduct justifies dismissal. In *Singh v. Lyons Maid Ltd*, an employee, a Sikh, was dismissed for contravening company hygiene rules by wearing a beard. He was engaged in the manufacture of ice-cream, and was told that unless he removed the beard he could not continue as a production worker. He refused to do so on religious grounds. His dismissal was held to be fair.

In *Kingston and Richmond Area Health Authority v. Kaur* a nurse who refused to comply with an order to wear a uniform and persisted in wearing trousers was held to have been fairly dismissed.

However, in *Elliott Brothers v. Colverd*, an employee who was summarily dismissed for clocking in a fellow worker was held to have been unfairly dismissed. The offence had never been specifically defined as one which would result in instant dismissal.

Whether swearing by an employee can justify dismissal depends on the employee's status, the circumstances, the location of the work, and who is in receipt of the employee's invective. An apprentice was dismissed when, on being criticised by the managing director about a job, replied 'you couldn't have done any f....ng better'. It was held that the dismissal was unfair as it was an isolated incident. The employer was also, to some extent, *in loco parentis* to the employee. The apprentice was awarded two years' pay as compensation (*Shortland v. Chantrill*).

In *Rosenthal v. Louis Butler Ltd*, an employee was dismissed for calling the factory manager 'a great fat punk' (his version) or 'a stupid punk' (her version) in the presence of other employees. It was held that her dismissal was unfair. It was 'a small friendly factory in East London where . . . language can be robust at times'. There should have been a warning before dismissal was contemplated.

3 Redundancy

An employee who satisfies certain statutory requirements is entitled, in a redundancy situation, to receive a redundancy payment. This entitlement does not of itself make the dismissal fair, or constitute sufficient grounds for dismissal.

There are certain situations where a selection for redundancy is regarded as unfair (EPCA s59). The dismissal will be held to be unfair if an employee shows that the circumstances constituting the redundancy applied equally to one or more other employees, but they have not been dismissed by the employer, and the reason for selecting the employee was one of the following:

(a)   the employer without special reason disregarded the customary arrangement or agreed procedure relating to the selection of employees for redundancy; or

(b)   the employee was selected for redundancy on account of trade union membership or activities; or

(c)   the employee was selected for redundancy as he did not belong to a trade union.

A comparison must be made with other employees holding similar positions. Tribunals have not relied on titles or gradings, but have looked at the work that is actually done, and its interchangeability with other work in the same undertaking. An undertaking may cover several establishments within a group or a company. In *Oxley v. Tarmac Roadstone Holdings*, two plants situated a quarter of a mile apart had the same works manager. Different hours were worked at the plants, which had different facilities. Nevertheless the plants were not regarded as separate entities.

A customary arrangement is an arrangement which is so well known, clear and certain that it effectively amounts to an implied agreed procedure. It must therefore exist with a degree of notoriety among the work-force. A selection system based on custom and practice in a particular industry may be challenged, and if there is an established procedure it should be followed. An employee cannot merely assert that 'last in, first out' (LIFO) is a general custom which is universally recognised. He must be able to show that this is a customary arrangement which exists in the undertaking in which he is employed.

In the absence of a pre-arranged procedure the general rule is LIFO, with any modifications agreed upon by the unions and management. If a woman who is pregnant or on maternity leave is made redundant because of a fair selection procedure, her subsequent dismissal is fair, as her pregnancy is co-incidental.

An employee who complains that the employer did not follow the agreed procedure must show (*a*) that there was a procedure, (*b*) that he was selected for redundancy in breach of that procedure, and that (*c*) there were no special reasons justifying a departure from that procedure. If there is no agreed procedure an employer may take other factors into consideration, e.g. long service, experience, various skills, hardship caused and so on.

An employer must show that he acted reasonably in the circumstances. In *Williams v. Compair Maxam Ltd*, a union was informed that the company proposed to make 21 employees redundant: by agreement with the union, volunteers were sought, but only seven employees volunteered. The employers then selected the remaining persons to be made redundant, without consulting the union, and dismissed them on the day after the union had been informed of the redundancies, but with no list of names. It was held that the dismissals were unfair. Not only must an employer show that it was reasonable to dismiss an employee, he must also show that it was reasonable to dismiss the employee concerned.

It was stated in *Williams v. Compair Maxam Ltd* that, where employees are represented by an independent union an employer should adopt the following guidelines:

(a) give as much warning as possible of impending redundancies;
(b) consult with the union as to the best means of achieving management's desired result fairly with the minimum hardship to employees;
(c) attempt to agree criteria to be applied in selecting employees for redundancy;
(d) consider together with the union, when a selection has been made, whether the criteria have been applied;
(e) establish criteria (in cases where no criteria have been agreed)

which can be objectively checked against various factors, e.g. attendance record, efficiency, experience or length of service to try to ensure that selection is fair and accords with the criteria and to consider union representations;

(f)   see whether alternative employment can be offered to the employee rather than dismissal.

An employer must therefore show that he acted reasonably in the circumstances. The following have been regarded as unreasonable conduct on the employer's part, rendering a dismissal unfair: unreasonable selection made between comparable employees; failure to adopt a proper procedure of warnings and consultation; and failure to seek alternative employment for an employee before declaring him redundant. An employer also has a duty to consult trade union representatives on impending redundancies.

An employer should consider possible alternatives to redundancy, e.g. the possibility of restricting overtime, recruitment, the redeployment of an employee to another part of the business, or to an associated company, the introduction of short time working and the like.

If the dismissal is found to be unfair, it is possible for an employee to be awarded compensation for unfair dismissal, and a redundancy payment in respect of the same dismissal. The basic award will, however, be adjusted to take account of the redundancy payment.

4   Contravention of statute

An employee may be dismissed if his continued employment contravenes a duty or restriction imposed by the law, e.g. the failure of an employee to obtain a work permit.

In *Appleyard v. Smith (Hull) Ltd*, a mechanic lost his driving licence and he was dismissed. It was held that it was essential for him to test-drive vehicles, and as it was impossible for the firm to employ him in any other capacity until his licence was restored, his dismissal was fair.

In *Gill v. Walls Meat Co. Ltd*, a Sikh employee who dealt with raw meat, grew a beard in accordance with his faith (when he was initially employed he was clean shaven). As it would be an offence under the Food Regulations 1970 to continue to employ him in this capacity, he was offered alternative employment. He refused and his subsequent dismissal was held to be fair.

5   *Some other substantial reason*

If an employer dismisses an employee for some other substantial reason, he must show that the reason warranted dismissal and the dismissal was reasonable in the circumstances.

Section 61 of the EPCA provides for two circumstances which amount to a substantial reason. Both deal with the dismissal of a temporary incumbent, who was engaged to replace a woman who is absent because of pregnancy or confinement, or engaged to replace an employee suspended on medical grounds. In both cases, the incumbent must have been informed in writing of the temporary nature of the employment and that he or she may be dismissed when the absent employee returns to work.

Other cases falling into this general residuary category have dealt with a variety of situations.

In *Priddle v. Dibble*, a farm labourer was dismissed and replaced by the employer's son. The son had farming experience and was competent to do mechanical work on the farm, which the labourer could not do. The employee knew when he was first employed that the son would eventually work on the farm. It was held to be a fair dismissal, as there was insufficient work for both men.

In *Dyer v. Inverclyde Taxis Ltd*, both husband and wife worked for a taxi association – the husband as manager, the wife as secretary/cashier. The husband was made redundant and transferred the two taxis he owned to a rival firm. His wife was dismissed as she had access to confidential information which could be harmful to IT Ltd's business if disclosed to a rival. It was held that the dismissal was fair as she could potentially pass confidential information to her husband.

In *Storey v. Allied Brewery*, a company introduced a rota system of work which included Sunday working. An employee was held to have been fairly dismissed when she refused to work on Sundays, as she wished to attend church. The change in working was necessary in the interests of economy.

An employee was held to be fairly dismissed when he refused to accept a change in pay, as the employer had inadvertently breached government policy in calculating the employee's pay. He refused, even though the amount was a loss of 73p over a period of ten weeks. He left the employment and unsuccessfully complained of constructive dismissal (*Industrial Rubber v. Gillan*).

In *Moreton v. Selby Protective Clothing Co. Ltd,* an employee had a provision in her contract giving her time off for school holidays. She was dismissed when she refused to make alternative arrangements which would allow her to work during those holidays. It was held that the dismissal was fair, as the production difficulties encountered by the firm had priority over domestic arrangements.

Under the Transfer of Undertakings (Protection of Employment) Regulations 1981 the dismissal of an employee before or after a relevant transfer is regarded as unfair if the reason for the dismissal is the transfer or a reason connected with the transfer. An employer may, however, be able to justify a dismissal on the grounds of 'some other substantial reason' if he can show that the dismissal is reasonable and is for economic, technical or organisational reasons which necessitate a change in the work-force.

In *Lister v. Forth Dry Dock and Engineering Co.,* it was held that the transferee (the purchaser) of an undertaking was liable for the unfair dismissal of employees in an undertaking when they were dismissed one hour before the transfer with a view to avoiding the transfer to the transferee of the transferor's rights (seller of business) and liabilities in regard to the employees.

——— Union membership and _____ the closed shop

Union membership

A dismissal by an employer will be regarded as unfair if the reason, or principal reason, was that an employee:

1   was, or proposed to become, a member of an independent trade union;
2   was not a member of any trade union, or of a particular trade union or had refused, or proposed to refuse, to become or to remain a member;
3   had taken part, or proposed to take part, at any appropriate time, in the activities of an independent trade union.

'Appropriate time' in this context is defined as outside working hours, or a time within working hours when, with the employer's consent, or by arrangement, it is permissible to take part in such activities. 'Working hours' means any time when an employee is required to be at work in accordance with his contract of employment.

An employee dismissed for any of these reasons may bring a claim for unfair dismissal, however long his period of service, i.e. it is not necessary to have the normal qualifying period.

Closed shop

A 'union membership agreement,' i.e. a closed shop, is an agreement:

1   made by or on behalf of, or otherwise exists between, one or more employers and employer's associations;
2   relating to employees of an identifiable class;
3   with the effect in practice of requiring all the present employees of the class to which it relates to be or become a member of the union, or one of the unions which is or are parties to the agreement or arrangement, or of another specified independent trade union, whether or not there is a condition to that effect in their contract of employment.

The Employment Act 1988 repealed those provisions of the EPCA which provided that the dismissal of an employee who was not a member of a trade union was fair when there was a valid closed shop agreement (one approved by an overwhelming majority in a ballot) in existence. The new law does not outlaw the closed shop, it merely repeals all those provisions relating to closed shop ballots.

The Employment Act 1990 makes it unlawful to refuse a person employment because he is, or is not, a union member. It is therefore unlawful to refuse a person employment because he is unwilling to accept a requirement to join or leave a union, or to remain in a union, or not to join a union or to make payments or suffer deductions from pay if he fails to join a union.

An employer is free to refuse employment to an applicant because of the applicant's union activities.

The remedy for an applicant who claims to have been unlawfully refused employment is a complaint to an industrial tribunal who will have to establish whether the real reason for the refusal was union membership or union activities, or neither (EA 90 s1).

—— Pressure to dismiss unfairly ——

An employer who is forced to dismiss an employee as a result of the pressure of industrial action (calling, organising or procuring or financing a strike) or the threat of such pressure, may find that such a dismissal amounts to an unfair dismissal. No account must be taken of any pressure when deciding whether the employer had a sufficient reason for the dismissal or had acted reasonably (EPCA s63).

If in proceedings before an industrial tribunal an employer claims that he was induced to dismiss an employee because of the pressure exercised on him by a trade union or other person in calling, organising, procuring or financing a strike, or threatening to do so as the employee was not a member of a trade union or of a particular trade union, he may join that person as a party to the proceedings.

If a tribunal makes an award of compensation, but finds that the employer's claim is well founded, it may make an order requiring that person to pay the employer a contribution in respect of that compensation. The amount of the contribution shall be such as the tribunal considers to be just and equitable in the circumstances, and may constitute a complete indemnity.

———— Industrial action ————

An employee who is dismissed while participating in a strike or other industrial action, or in connection with a lock-out, cannot claim that he was unfairly dismissed if: (*a*) the employer has dismissed all those who took part in the action at the same establishment as the complainant at the date of his dismissal, and (*b*) the employer has not offered re-engagement to any of them within three months of their date of dismissal, without making him a similar offer (EPCA s62).

An employer may therefore dismiss all those employees who are on strike at the date of the dismissal. He is not to be regarded as acting unfairly by not dismissing employees who were on strike, but who had returned to work at the date of the dismissal. An employer may, at any time after three months, re-engage a person dismissed for taking part in a strike. A person who is not offered re-engagement in these circumstances may not claim that he has been unfairly dismissed.

An employer may, however, select for dismissal employees who are participating in unofficial industrial action at the time of dismissal. A strike or other industrial action will be unofficial in relation to an employee unless:

1   he is a member of a union which has authorised or endorsed the action;
2   he is not a union member, but some of those taking part in the industrial action are members of a union by which the action has been authorised or endorsed. A strike or other industrial action is not to be regarded as unofficial if none of the participants are a member of a union.

Authorisation or endorsement is as defined in section 15 of the Employment Act 1982 (page 241) and includes cases of deemed authorisation, e.g. industrial action called by a shop steward or a committee of which a shop steward is a member and is not supported by a ballot. Such action will only become unofficial when repudiated by the union, but only at the end of the next working day after the day on which repudiation takes place.

Whether industrial action was in progress and whether it was official or unofficial is a question of fact to be determined by a tribunal in any contested case. If a tribunal decides that an employee was participating in unofficial industrial action at the time of dismissal they will have no jurisdiction to consider a complaint of unfair dismissal. An applicant may claim a redundancy payment or complain of discrimination if the facts warrant it.

For the purpose of this provision, employees who were trade union members when the action commenced will continue to be treated as union members for the purpose of determining whether the action is unofficial, even if they have since ceased to be union members.

A union will have no immunity in tort in respect of industrial action if the reason, or one of the reasons, for calling the industrial action is the fact or belief that the employer has dismissed one or more employees in circumstances in which they have no right to complain of unfair dismissal, as they were taking part in unofficial industrial action at the time of dismissal. Even if there was a ballot in favour of such action the dispute will not be a lawful dispute in support of employees dismissed while taking part in unofficial industrial action (EPCA s62A).

—— **Pregnancy and confinement** ——

An employee has the right not to be dismissed solely on the grounds that she is pregnant, or for any other reason connected with pregnancy (e.g. a miscarriage, post-natal illness), unless the employer can prove that (*a*) she was incapable of adequately doing her work because of her pregnancy, or (*b*) she could not carry on working without contravening a statutory provision relating to pregnant women. He must also prove that there was no suitable alternative vacancy which she could be offered, or if there was that she had been offered the vacancy, and refused it.

A woman has the right to return to work after her pregnancy or confinement. She can do so at any time before the end of the period of 29 weeks, beginning with the week in which the date of confinement falls. She is entitled to return to her employment on terms and conditions which are no less favourable than those which would have been applicable had she not been absent. She must, however, give appropriate notice and satisfy the conditions for maternity pay listed on page 100.

A woman who is selected for redundancy because she is pregnant is unfairly dismissed. In *Brown v. Stockton-on-Tees Borough Council,* an employee youth training scheme on which an employee was a supervisor was terminated. She was not offered a new post as she would require maternity leave shortly after the date of commencement of the new post and was dismissed for redundancy. She complained that she had been unfairly dismissed. It was held that a need to take maternity leave was a reason connected with pregnancy and her selection for redundancy for that reason amounted to unfair dismissal.

Failure to permit a woman to return to work after her pregnancy or confinement will not be treated as an unfair dismissal in the following circumstances:

1   where, immediately before her absence, the number of employees employed by her employer and any associated employer totalled no more than five, and it was not reasonably practicable to reinstate her in her original job;

2 where it was not reasonably practicable to reinstate her in her
original job (for a reason other than redundancy), and she was offered
alternative employment by her employer or an associated employer,
which she accepted or unreasonably refused.

If there is no vacancy due to a redundancy situation, the employee may
claim a redundancy payment and will be regarded as continuously
employed until the notified date of her return to work. If, however, the
employer can prove that the employee would have been made redundant
on a particular day during her period of absence, her entitlement to a
redundancy payment will be calculated up to that earlier day.

—— Remedies for unfair dismissal ——

The remedies available for unfair dismissal are:

1 reinstatement;
2 re-engagement;
3 an award of compensation.

An employee who complains of unfair dismissal must make an application on form IT1 to an industrial tribunal.

A pertinent question on this form asks 'If the Tribunal decides that you
were unfairly dismissed, please state which of the following you would
prefer: reinstatement, re-engagement or compensation.'

1   Reinstatement

If a tribunal finds the complaint justified it must consider the possibility of
reinstatement. This requires an employer to treat an employee in all
respects as if he had not been dismissed. An employee is therefore
entitled to any arrears of pay and to any benefits which have accrued
during the period of his dismissal, e.g. if other employees on a similar
grading and pay scale receive a pay increase during this time, the order
will provide for the higher rate of pay from the date of its inception. All
rights and privileges, including pension and seniority rights, must also be
restored to the employee.

2 Re-engagement

Having decided that reinstatement is neither possible nor feasible, a tribunal may make an order for re-engagement. This is an order that the complainant be engaged by the employer, or his successor, or an associated employer, in employment which is comparable to his previous employment. Except in cases where an employee has contributed to his dismissal, the terms of the order should be, as far as reasonably practical, as favourable as an order for reinstatement. The order must also stipulate the future employer's identity, the nature of the employment, and the rate of pay.

In exercising its discretion for either of these remedies the tribunal must take into account the complainant's wishes, as an employee may not wish to be reinstated, and may prefer to return to his employment in a different job. If an employee applies for reinstatement or re-engagement, and a tribunal decides against making such an order, it must give reasons for the refusal.

A tribunal must also consider whether reinstatement is a practical proposition for an employer. There may well have been a clash of personality between an employee and his fellow employees, or his supervisor, and this would continue if such an order were made.

A tribunal may not take into account the fact that an employer has engaged a permanent replacement for the dismissed employee, unless:

(a)   the employer can prove that the employee's work could only be done by recruiting a permanent replacement; or

(b)   a replacement was not appointed until a reasonable time had elapsed and the employer had not been informed by the dismissed employee that he wanted to be reinstated or re-engaged.

In calculating the amount of compensation payable for loss of benefits between the termination of the contract and reinstatement or re-engagement, a tribunal must take into account: wages in lieu of notice, *ex gratia* payments, payments from another employer during that period, and unemployment or supplementary benefits.

If a tribunal considers that an employee is partly to blame for his dismissal, it may make an order for reinstatement or re-engagement on less favourable terms, e.g. he should not receive full compensation for the loss of benefits.

The tribunal must also deduct any other benefit received which is relevant in the circumstances. In *Whelan v. Sutcliffe Catering West* the tribunal directed that Whelan be restored to the pension scheme as if he had never left it and that he accordingly refund the lump sum he had received plus pension payments received.

The tribunal's award must be based on what an employee would have earned between dismissal and reinstatement. In *Foot v. Ministry of Defence* the applicant had been unfit for four of the seven months between dismissal and reinstatement. He was therefore awarded three months' full pay, including overtime and four months' half pay.

A tribunal cannot have taken into account any matters of which an employer was unaware at the time of the dismissal, as it has to consider the reason shown by the employer at the time of the dismissal. In *Davis & Sons Ltd v. Atkin*, an employee, the manager of an abattoir, refused to comply with his employers' wish that a considerable proportion of animals should be bought direct from farmers, rather than from dealers. He was dismissed, but was later offered an *ex gratia* severance payment. The employer later withdrew the offer on the grounds that they were treating his dismissal as a summary dismissal, on account of his gross misconduct during his term of employment, and which they were unaware of when he was dismissed. This was held to be an unfair dismissal.

3   Compensation

An award of compensation will be made:

(a)   where an employee indicates that he no longer wishes to return to work for his previous employers; or
(b)   where the tribunal decides that reinstatement or re-engagement is impracticable; or
(c)   where an employer fails to comply with an order for reinstatement or re-engagement.

Most employees who are successful in their claim for unfair dismissal are awarded compensation. The award will usually consist of a basic award.

Basic award

The basic award is calculated on a formula which is based on continuous employment, up to a maximum period of 20 years. An employee is entitled to the following amounts for each completed year of employment: one and a half weeks' pay for each year between the ages of 41 and 64; one week's pay for each year between the ages of 22 and 41; half a week's pay for each year between the ages of 18 and 22.

The maximum amount of weekly pay which can be taken into account is currently £198. The maximum amount which is payable under this provision is therefore $20 \times 1\frac{1}{2} \times £198 = £5,940$.

The basic award may be reduced if the employee:

(a) unreasonably refused an offer of reinstatement;

(b) had received a redundancy payment in respect of the same dismissal;

(c) was within a year of his 65th birthday. The entitlement to the basic award must be reduced by $\frac{1}{12}$ for every complete calendar month after the employee's 64th birthday;

(d) had contributed to or caused the dismissal, or his conduct prior to the dismissal justified the reduction.

Compensatory award

An employee may be awarded compensation for loss suffered as a result of his dismissal. The award is calculated on common law principles.

The various heads of compensation are as follows.

(a) *Loss of earnings*   Loss of net earnings to the date of the hearing. This will include the period of notice if notice was not given. Deductions are not made for any sums earned during the period of notice, or for any supplementary or unemployment benefit received. A deduction will be made for any sickness benefit received, if it is shown that, had the employee remained in employment, this amount would have been deducted from his wages.

(b) *Manner of dismissal*   Although an employee may not claim for any hurt feelings caused by the manner of his dismissal, he may nevertheless claim a sum if the manner of his dismissal could give rise to financial loss at a later date, e.g. by making the employee 'less acceptable to potential employers or exceptionally liable to selection for dismissal' (Sir John Donaldson in *Norton Tool Co. v. Tewson*).

(c) *Estimated future loss of earnings*   There must be evidence of probable future loss before this factor can be taken into consideration. The tribunal will make an assessment of the time it believes an employee is likely to be without employment, and will multiply the number of weeks of estimated unemployment by the employee's net wages. If an employee is likely to obtain employment, but at a lower wage, the tribunal will use the difference in net wages as a basis for its calculation. This is then multiplied by an estimate of the time it will take for the employee to obtain parity with his previous wages.

(d) *Loss of statutory rights*   An award may be made to compensate an employee for the loss of the periods of minimum statutory notice to which he is entitled. If an employee obtains new employment, it will take him two years to obtain protection against unfair dismissal with a new employer. After a period of four weeks' employment, he will be entitled to one week's notice. An employee's entitlement to longer periods of notice is based on his years of continuous employment (see page 120). In *Daley v. Dorsett (Amar Dolls Ltd)*, it was suggested that an employee should receive compensation of half a week's net wages for the loss of every week of statutory notice. In this case the complainant, having worked for eight years, received an additional four weeks' pay under this heading.

(e) *Loss of pension rights*   Any employee unfairly dismissed from pensionable employment may claim under this heading. The burden of proving the loss and its extent lies on the dismissed employee. There are two distinct types of loss. Firstly, the loss of the pension position which has already been earned. Secondly, the loss of future pension opportunity, i.e. the opportunity of improving this position until the time at which the pension becomes payable.

Two different methods of calculation are used:

(i)   the employee and the employer's contributions to the date of dismissal are initially calculated. Compound interest from the date of payment is then assessed on these contributions. The grand total will then constitute the basis of the award;

(ii) a calculation of the capital sum required to purchase an annuity which is equal to the pension which he would ultimately receive.

The second calculation basis is appropriate for an employee who is close to retirement age.

Deductions

A tribunal must deduct a sum for an employee's contributory fault, for any redundancy payment received by the employee and for any failure of an employee to mitigate his loss. Sir John Donaldson, in *Bracey Ltd v. Iles*, stated: 'It may not be reasonable to take the first job that comes along. It may be much more reasonable, in the interests of the employee and the employer who has to pay compensation, that he should wait a little time. He must, of course, use the time well and seek a better paid job which will reduce his overall loss and the amount of compensation which the previous employer ultimately has to pay . . .'

In *Field v. Leslie & Goodwin Ltd*, an applicant, a placing broker, failed to register with agencies who might have been able to find him similar employment and also neglected to take up a good reference which had been promised. A tribunal assessed compensation on the basis that he would not have been out of work for more than four months if he had taken steps to mitigate his loss.

In *McGoldrick v. Robinson*, an employee was held to have failed to mitigate his loss when he refused the offer of his old job back, one week after being unfairly dismissed.

Failure to comply with an order

A tribunal cannot compel an employer to comply with a reinstatement or a re-engagement order.

(a)   If an order is made for reinstatement or re-engagement and the terms of the order are not fully complied with, a tribunal must make an award of compensation, having regard to the loss sustained, up to a maximum of £10,000, unless the employer can satisfy the tribunal that it is not practicable to comply with the order.

(b)   If an employer fails completely to comply with a tribunal order for reinstatement or re-engagement, the tribunal *must* make an additional award. The amount will depend on the reason for the original dismissal.

   (i)   The award will be for a minimum of 13 weeks' pay, but no more than 26 weeks' pay.

   (ii)   If the order for reinstatement or re-engagement relates to a dismissal which is in breach of the Race Relations Act or Sex

Discrimination Act, the tribunal's award will be for a minimum of 26 weeks' pay, but not more than 52 weeks' pay.

(c)   There are special compensation rules where an employee is dismissed for trade union membership or non-union membership. There are four possible situations:

(i)   *reinstatement or re-engagement order made and complied with.* The employee will be fully compensated for all losses incurred between dismissal and re-employment. There is no maximum.

(ii)   *Reinstatement or re-engagement order is not sought.* Compensation will consist of a basic award calculated in the normal way, subject to a minimum award of £2,650, *and* a compensatory award based on actual financial loss, up to a maximum of £10,000.

(iii)   *Reinstatement or re-engagement order sought, but no order made by a tribunal.* Compensation will consist of a basic award (as above), *and* a compensatory award (as above), *and* a special award of 104 weeks' pay, subject to a minimum award of £13,180 and a maximum award of £26,290.

(iv)   *Reinstatement or re-engagement order made, but not complied with.* Unless the employer can satisfy the tribunal that it was not practicable to comply, compensation will consist of a basic award (as above), *and* a compensatory award (as above), *and* a special award of 156 weeks pay, subject to a minimum award of £19,735. There is no maximum.

(If an employer satisfies the tribunal that reinstatement or re-engagement is not possible the special award will be calculated as in (iii) above.)

9

—— REDUNDANCY ——

The redundancy provisions of the EPCA provide for the payment of a lump sum to an employee who is dismissed due to redundancy, or who is laid off or kept on short time for a substantial period. The Act recognises the fact that an employee has an 'accrued right in his job' and provides a redundant employee with monetary compensation for its loss.

Redundancy provisions apply (with certain exceptions) to employees under 65 who have been employed, after the age of 18, under a contract of employment, for at least two years. Certain workers are not included within the scope of the redundancy provisions, as they are not employees, or are covered by other arrangements, or their terms and conditions of employment are such that the application of the provisions would be inappropriate. These include:

1 share fishermen;
2 apprentices whose service ends at the end of the apprenticeship contract;
3 the majority of merchant seamen;
4 Crown servants;
5 employees who normally work outside Great Britain, unless recalled before the termination of the contract;
6 domestic servants working in private households, who are closely related to their employers;

7   persons employed on fixed-term contracts for two years or more who agree in writing, before the expiry of the contract, to waive their entitlement to redundancy payments;

8   persons covered by approved redundancy agreements, i.e. approved by the Secretary of State.

——— Dismissal for redundancy ———

An employee is treated as having been dismissed by his employer if:

(a)   the contract of employment is terminated by the employer, with or without notice;

(b)   the employee is employed under a fixed-term contract which has expired without being renewed;

(c)   the employee terminates the contract, with or without notice, in circumstances such that he is entitled to terminate it without notice by reason of the employer's conduct (EPCA s83).

There is also deemed to be a dismissal on the dissolution of a partnership, the death of an employer, or the winding-up of a company (EPCA s93).

When an employee claims, in proceedings before an industrial tribunal, an entitlement to redundancy compensation, it is presumed that his dismissal is for redundancy. This presumption may be rebutted by evidence given by the employer showing that the dismissal was for a reason other than redundancy.

A dismissal is due to redundancy if it is attributable wholly or mainly to the following facts:

1   the employer has ceased, or intends to cease, to carry on the business for the purposes for which the employee was employed by him;

2   the employer has ceased, or intends to cease, to carry on the business in the place where the employee was so employed;

3   the requirements of that business for employees to carry out work of a particular kind, or for employees to carry out work of a particular kind in the place where they were employed has ceased, or diminished, or is expected to cease or diminish (EPCA s81).

1 The cessation of a business

The interpretation of this provision has caused relatively few problems, as the majority of dismissals under this provision are self-evident. It has been held that even a temporary cessation of business may amount to a redundancy situation. In *Gemmell v. Darngival Brickworks Ltd*, the applicant was held to be entitled to a redundancy payment when he was dismissed from the brickworks, which closed down temporarily for 13 weeks for repairs to be made to machinery.

2 Change in the location of a business

An employee will not be justified in refusing to move to another location if his contract, or a collective agreement, or custom permits such a move. The majority of contracts of employment do not contain such provisions, and each case must be judged according to its merits. In *O'Brien v. Associated Fire Alarms*, the employee was an electrician employed to supply, install and maintain fire and burglar alarms in the Cheshire and Liverpool area. He was based at Liverpool and worked within a commutable distance from the city. The company proposed that he and fellow employees should work in Barrow-in-Furness, some 120 miles away. He refused and was dismissed. It was held that there was nothing in his contract to imply a term of mobility of that nature, and he was entitled to a redundancy payment.

A different conclusion was reached in *Stevenson v. Teesside Bridge & Engineering Ltd* where a steel erector, who had worked at various times in different parts of the country, refused to work away from his home. It was held that his refusal was not justified, and that his subsequent dismissal was fair.

The removal of a business to a nearby location does not usually have the effect of constituting dismissal. A company which closed one of its restaurants in London offered its waitresses similar employment at another of its restaurants nearby. They refused, and it was held that their dismissal was fair (*Margiotta v. Mount Charlotte Investments Ltd*). Similarly in *Stevens v. Stitcher and Sons Ltd*, an employee who refused to transfer to a shop 400 yards down the road was not entitled to a redundancy payment. However, in *Buck v. Edward Everard*, a Bristol printing company moved its premises to a suburb some seven miles away. It was held that Buck's refusal to move was justified, as mobility was not a factor which was normally encountered in the printing industry. He had been employed by the firm for 25 years, and such a move would mean a revision of working hours and the provision of travelling allowances.

3   Surplus labour

A dismissal is due to redundancy if a decline in the volume of trade or work means that an employer requires fewer employees for the existing work, or there is less work for the existing employees; or if the introduction of new business methods or new technology means that fewer employees are required to achieve the same output.

In *Dixon v. Everden*, an employee was informed on her return from holiday that, as the business had operated smoothly with reduced staff, her services were no longer required. It was held that her dismissal was due to redundancy.

In *European Chefs v. Currell*, a pastry cook specialising in making éclairs and meringues was dismissed when his employers decided to discontinue the manufacture of these products and concentrate on the manufacture of continental pastries. He was entitled to a redundancy payment, as the manufacture of these products involved different skills, and his employers' requirements for work of a particular kind had ceased.

In *Yusuf v. Aberplace*, a decline in demand led an employer to reduce the working week from 60 hours to 40 hours, reduce pay, introduce seven-day working and abolish weekend overtime payments. An employee who refused to accept these new terms was not entitled to a redundancy payment as the need for the same number of employees remained the same, although the volume of work was reduced.

In *Haden Ltd v. Cowan*, a divisional contracts surveyor was dismissed by his firm owing to changed economic circumstances. His contract required him to undertake 'any and all duties which reasonably fall within the scope of his capabilities'. It was held that this clause only required him to perform those duties within the scope of his capabilities as a divisional contracts surveyor. As the post had ceased or diminished there was a redundancy situation.

In *Vaux Breweries v. Ward*, a brewery changed the character of a public house and introduced a discotheque and games room in order to attract a younger clientele. They dismissed a middle-aged barmaid with 18 years' service as they wanted a young blonde 'bunny-girl' type barmaid as part of the new image. The barmaid was not entitled to a redundancy payment as the nature of the work remained the same.

If, however, an employee is replaced by an independent contractor, the presumption is that the requirements of the business for employees of a particular kind have ceased. In *Bromby & Hoare Ltd v. Evans*, two employees were dismissed by their employer and replaced by self-employed contractors. It was held that they were entitled to a redundancy payment as the employees had not been replaced by other employees and there was therefore a decline in the amount of work available for employees.

If an employer seeks to abolish night work in order to concentrate on daytime production, an employee who works night shifts is entitled to a redundancy payment if he refuses the offer of daytime employment. The requirements of the employer for work of a particular kind, i.e. night work, have ceased (*Morrison and Poole v. Ceramic Engineering Ltd*).

An undertaking will often re-organise its working hours in order to achieve maximum efficiency. An employee who does not agree to a variation of his working hours in these circumstances may not be entitled to a redundancy payment. If the exercise is merely a means of discarding surplus labour, there is then an entitlement to a redundancy payment.

In *Johnson v. Nottinghamshire Police Authority*, two clerks were employed to work five days a week from 9.30 am to 5.30 pm. The police authority, seeking to achieve greater efficiency, proposed to introduce six-day working, divided into two shifts of 8 am to 3 pm, and 1 pm to 8 pm. Both clerks refused to change over to the new system of working and were dismissed. Their dismissal was not due to redundancy as the work remained the same and it was 'the same job done to a different schedule'.

If in the course of a re-organisation an employee is dismissed, the presumption is that the dismissal is not due to redundancy. In *Lesney Products Ltd v. Nolan*, night work at a factory was stopped after a fall in sales. The previous day and evening shift on which overtime was worked was split into two day shifts, on which the equivalent work was done. Employees were offered work on the new day shifts. Those who refused were dismissed and were not entitled to a redundancy payment. The re-organisation of shifts with the loss of overtime did not create a redundancy situation as the employer's requirements remained the same.

If a work-force is expanded to meet a scale of production which never materialises as the employer has been over-optimistic in his forecast, this is not a cessation or diminution of work as the work never materialised initially. An employee dismissed in these circumstances is not entitled to redundancy payment (*O'Hare & Rutherford v. Rotaprint Ltd*).

If an employee becomes surplus to requirements in one section of the business and is moved to another section, and in doing so displaces a second employee, that employee will be dismissed for redundancy (*Eliot Turbomachinery v. Bates*).

A distinction must be drawn between redundancy and the needs of employees to adapt themselves to new methods and techniques. If an employee fails to adapt, his subsequent dismissal will not be due to redundancy. In *Hindle v. Percival Boats*, the company, who were boat builders, changed from the use of wood to fibreglass in the manufacture of boats. Hindle, a skilled craftsman, was dismissed as 'he was too good and too slow', and therefore unable to adapt to a new technology because of the decline in the use of wood. It was held that the dismissal was not due to redundancy. Similarly in *North Riding Garages v. Butterwick*, a workshop manager failed to adapt to new working methods when new employers took over the business. As there was no change in the nature of the work his subsequent dismissal was not due to redundancy.

Offer of further or alternative employment

An employee will not be entitled to a redundancy payment if he unreasonably refuses an offer by his employer and either: (*a*) the provisions of the renewed contract, or of the new contract as to the capacity and place in which he would be employed, and as to the other terms and conditions of employment would not differ from the corresponding provisions of the previous contract; or (*b*) the terms and conditions differ, but the offer constitutes an offer of suitable employment.

An employee has been held to have had reasonable grounds for refusing an offer of re-engagement when he sold his house (after being given notice), in anticipation of moving to another area.

The alternative employment offered must be suitable. Factors to be considered are the differences as to capacity, terms and conditions of employment, the place of work when compared with the employee's previous employment.

In *Taylor v. Kent CC*, a headmaster was made redundant and was offered a post as a supply teacher. Although there was no reduction in salary, it was held that his refusal was justified in that the consequent loss of status and authority made the offer unsuitable.

In *Ramage v. Harper McKay*, a salesman was offered alternative employment as a warehouse/relief representative. It was held to be unsuitable as it involved not only loss of status, but also loss of bonuses, trade contacts and the use of a car.

In *Standard Telephone Cables v. Yates*, a card wirer for 10 years was made redundant and was offered alternative employment as an assembly operator with an associated company taking over the works. It was held to be unsuitable as the work offered was less skilled than her previous work.

In *Bowman v. NCB*, a colliery worker was offered a post which involved a 20 per cent loss in wages, downgrading and a possibility that the work might not last longer than three years. It was held to be unsuitable.

If the new employment is at a greater distance than the old from an employee's home, it does not of itself make the new employment unsuitable. Factors which must be considered as a consequence of the additional travelling involved are the employee's health, age, domestic circumstances, possible marital problems and the time and cost involved in travelling. If the change involves an employee having to move house, this might well indicate that the offer is unsuitable.

Employment with an associated employer

If a redundant employee is offered employment with an associated employer then in general the two employers are regarded as the same, and continuity of employment is preserved. If an employee refuses the offer he must, in order to qualify for a redundancy payment, show that the offer was unsuitable. Section 153 of the EPCA provides that 'any two employers are to be treated as associated, if one is a company of which the other (directly or indirectly) has control, or if both are companies of which a third person (directly or indirectly) has control'.

The various area boards of the nationalised industries are not regarded as associated employers, within the meaning given to the phrase by the Act. In *Southern Electricity Board v. Collins*, an employee transferred from the Southern Electricity Board to the Central Electricity Generating Board for six and a half months in 1965. He returned to the SEB until he was made redundant in 1968. It was held that although he had been employed by the SEB since 1951, he was only entitled to three years' redundancy payment as his transfer to the CEGB broke the continuity of employment.

Change of ownership of a business

Section 94 of the EPCA and the Transfer of Undertakings (Protection of Employment) Regulations 1981 apply when there is a transfer of a business to a new employer.

If there is a change in the ownership of the business, an offer by the new employer to engage the employee on the terms of the old contract or re-engage him under a new contract will be regarded as an offer of renewal. An employee cannot claim a redundancy payment in these circumstances, unless he can show reasonable grounds for refusing the offer (EPCA s94).

Where there has been a change of ownership of part of a business, the correct test for redundancy purposes is to determine whether there is a transfer of a going concern, i.e. does it remain the same business in different hands. If there has been a transfer of physical assets, the new owner may use these assets in whatever business he chooses. In *Melon v. Hector Powe Ltd*, the appellants manufactured men's suits. They sold their factory in Scotland to another company which agreed to take over the business and retain most of the employees. It was held that as the purchasing company operated a different business, there was a transfer of certain assets, and the employees were entitled to redundancy payments.

Where a new owner purchases premises and carries on a completely different type of business, or purchases the physical assets of a business, there is no continuity of employment, and employees may claim redundancy payments.

In these circumstances, an employee remaining at work, who does not claim a redundancy payment from his former employer, can subsequently only claim a redundancy payment for the time spent with the new employer. In *Woodhouse v. Peter Brotherhood,* a company manufacturing diesel engines sold its factory premises to another company. Some plant and machinery were sold, as the purchasing company manufactured other types of machinery. Employees of the old company who accepted employment with the new company were eventually made redundant by the new company. They were not entitled to count the years spent with the old company in computing their entitlement to a redundancy payment, as there was only a transfer of the physical assets. They would have been eligible for a redundancy payment from their old employers had they applied for payment at the time of the transfer of the assets.

In *Crompton v. Truly Fair Ltd,* a company manufacturing children's clothes sold its premises, plant and machinery to another company, and its employees were offered employment in a different capacity, manufacturing men's trousers by the new company. As only the physical assets had been transferred, not the business itself, the employees of the old company were entitled to a redundancy payment from the old company, even though they were re-engaged by the new company.

The Transfer of Undertakings (Protection of Employment) Regulations 1981 applies to the transfer of a trade or business. The Regulations do not apply to the sale or transfer of shares, but to the take-over of a business as a going concern.

The Regulations provide that, on such a transfer, an employee's contract of employment with the transferor (seller of the business) is not terminated, but is treated as if made between the employee and the transferee (the buyer of the business). Continuity of employment is therefore preserved.

All the transferor's rights, powers, duties and liabilities are transferred, so that an employee may seek redress from the transferee in respect of any breach of contract which occurred prior to the transfer. An employee must, however, have been in the transferor's employment immediately before the transfer. If an employee is dismissed before the transfer, liability for any redundancy payment will fall on the transferor; if after the transfer, the transferee will be liable.

An employee who is dismissed before or after the transfer may claim for unfair dismissal if the transfer or reason connected with the transfer is the reason, or main reason, for the dismissal (*Lister v. Forth Dry Dock and Engineering Co.,* see page 141).

An employer may seek to justify such dismissals on economic, technical or organisational grounds which entail a change in the work-force.

Such dismissals would therefore be for 'some other substantial reason' (see page 140). In these circumstances an employee would be able to claim a redundancy payment.

Trial period

An employee whose contract is renewed on the basis of new terms and conditions is entitled to a trial period of four weeks (or such longer period as may be agreed by the parties for the purpose of re-training the employee), to decide whether the employment is suitable.

The new agreement must be made in writing, before the employee starts work under the renewed or new contract. It must specify the date of the end of the trial period and the terms and conditions of employment which will apply after the end of that period.

During this period both parties are free to terminate the new contract or give notice of termination. In either case the employee will be treated as having been dismissed at the termination of the original contract. However, if the employee, either before or during the trial period, unreasonably terminates the contract, he will not be entitled to a redundancy payment. The burden of proof is on the employer to prove that the employee's conduct was unreasonable in refusing the offer of re-engagement.

An employee is entitled, in certain circumstances, to a common law trial period, which has the effect of prolonging the total trial period to which he or she is entitled.

This applies to an employee who is constructively dismissed and who is offered new terms by an employer. The employee is entitled to a reasonable period within which to decide whether or not to accept these terms. If he decides not to accept the new contract, he may resign within a reasonable time and claim constructive dismissal. If he accepts the new terms, the statutory trial period will then commence from the time of the acceptance.

In *Air Canada v. Lee*, a switchboard operator agreed to move to her employers' new premises on a trial basis. There was no mobility term in her contract and she gave notice after two months at the new premises. It was held that she had been made redundant, as she had by consent merely postponed the decision as to whether to treat the contract as repudiated. In this case the statutory trial period had never commenced.

Her original contract only terminated when she decided 'before the expiry of the reasonable period of the common law and trial period' that 'she did not wish to continue to be employed'.

In *Turvey v. C. W. Cheney & Sons Ltd*, a polisher was offered work in a different department. The company had no power to insist on the change and indicated that he would take the new work on trial. He decided after more than four weeks that the job was not suitable. It was held that he had been dismissed for redundancy, as he had never in law accepted the new contract, and he had left before the expiry of the reasonable common law trial period.

Dismissal during period of notice

An employee who is dismissed for conduct which justifies summary dismissal (e.g. theft) is not entitled to a redundancy payment. An employee who has been given notice because of redundancy, and who is dismissed for misconduct during that period of notice, does not automatically lose his entitlement to a redundancy payment. He may appeal to a tribunal, which has the discretion to award him the full payment, or part of the payment, or no payment as it thinks fit. In *Jarmain v. Pollard*, an employee aged 53 stole scrap from his employers during his period of notice of redundancy and was subsequently convicted of theft. As he had worked for the company for seven years, he was awarded half the redundancy payment he would otherwise have received.

An employee who takes part in a strike during his period of notice, and is dismissed for so doing, is entitled to the payment which would have been due on the expiry of the notice (EPCA s92). The employer may request that the employee returns to work after the strike, and remains at work after the date of the expiration of the notice for the number of days which were lost due to the strike. If the employee refuses to do so, and the employer withholds the redundancy payment, the employee may appeal to a tribunal. If the tribunal decides that the employee had reasonable grounds for not complying with the employer's request, it may award the full payment, or part of it, according to the circumstances.

An employee who is on strike and is made redundant is not entitled to a redundancy payment. Section 82 of the EPCA provides that, if an employer terminates the contract of employment by reason of the employee's conduct, in circumstances where he is entitled to do so, the employee is not entitled to a redundancy payment.

Departure before notice expires

An employee, given notice terminating his employment, may wish to leave before the notice expires. He may give the employer notice in writing to terminate the contract of employment. If the employer does not object to the employee's premature departure, the employee's entitlement to a redundancy payment is unaffected. If the employer objects, he may serve a written notice on the employee, stating his objection, and requesting the employee to withdraw the notice. The notice must also state that, unless the employee does so, the employer will contest any liability to pay him a redundancy payment. If an employee leaves after such a notice has been served on him, and the employer withholds a redundancy payment, the employee may appeal to a tribunal. The tribunal must examine the case on its merits in order to consider the employee's reason for leaving and the employer's reasons for wanting the employee to stay. It may award the employee the full payment he would have received if notice had been worked, or part of the payment, or no payment.

An employee who leaves his employment without being dismissed, on being told of the possibility of a redundancy situation arising in the future, will forfeit his right to a redundancy payment. In *Morton Sundour Fabrics v. Shaw*, a foreman was warned of impending redundancies. He left the firm to take other employment. It was held that as he had not been dismissed, he had not been made redundant. In *Scott v. Coalite Fuels and Chemicals*, Scott was given notice of redundancy to take effect three months later. Before the end of the three-month period, he accepted voluntary early retirement as an alternative to redundancy and received a lump sum and a reduced pension. It was held that Scott had not been dismissed as he had elected to retire early.

Lay-off and short-time working

An employer may lay off his employees or put them on short time working if there is insufficient work available for his labour force, e.g. a recession or shortage of business. A lay-off occurs where an employee is not entitled to remuneration as the employer does not provide work for him. Short-time working occurs when less than half a week's pay is earned, due to shortage of work.

A lay-off or short-time working may constitute grounds for constructive dismissal unless an employer has reserved the right to do so in the contract of employment. In *Jewell v. Neptune Concrete Ltd*, a labourer who had worked for a company for four years was given his cards by the company, but was told that he was merely laid off. He found other employment, but the first company informed him one month later that his employment was to be resumed. It was held that there had been a dismissal.

An employee, whose employer has retained a contractual right to lay off or put his employees on short time, is nevertheless entitled, in certain circumstances, to a redundancy payment. He may claim if he has been laid off or put on short time for more than four consecutive weeks, or for at least six weeks in any period of 13 weeks. The employee must give written notice to the employer, no later than four weeks after the lay-off or short time has finished, stating that he intends to claim a redundancy payment (EPCA s88).

The employer may agree to the claim, or he may consider that there are reasonable prospects of resuming normal working for at least 13 weeks, and serve a counter notice to this effect on the employee. If the claim or counter claim is not withdrawn, a tribunal will have to decide whether there were such prospects. An employee is entitled to a redundancy payment if the counter notice is withdrawn by the employer, or the 13 weeks' employment fails to materialise.

—— Calculation of redundancy pay ——

The amount of compensation paid to a redundant employee is calculated on a formula which is based on the employee's age, the amount of his weekly earnings and the length of continuous employment. A similar formula is used to calculate the basic award in a compensation order for unfair dismissal (see page 148).

An employee is entitled to the following amounts for each completed year of employment: one and a half week's pay for each year between the ages of 41 and 64; one week's pay for each year between the ages of 22 and 41; half a week's pay for each year between the ages of 18 and 22. Not more than 20 years' service may be taken into account and earnings of more than £198 a week are disregarded in a calculation. The maximum possible payment is therefore $20 \times 1\frac{1}{2} \times £198 = £5,940$.

An employee's entitlement is reduced if the redundancy occurs after the employee's 64th birthday. The amount is reduced by $\frac{1}{12}$ for each month employed after the age of 64.

The employee's entitlement is computed by reference to a week's pay (see page 81). Most employees have normal working hours and these can be easily ascertained from the written particulars of their terms of employment, together with any relevant working agreement entered into with their employers.

To qualify for a redundancy payment, an employee must have the appropriate period of continuous employment (see page 120). Absences due to pregnancy, sickness, holidays, lay-offs or short time do not affect continuity as the contract of employment remains in being. Continuity is also maintained in the week(s) when an employee is on strike, or locked out, or on service with the armed forces or employed abroad.

Consultation and the protective award

An employer is required to consult with the appropriate trade union if he proposes to make any of his employees redundant. Notification of his proposals will enable the trade union to examine his plans to see if there is any way of reducing the numbers involved, or mitigating the effects of the redundancies. Consultation is required even where the employees have volunteered for redundancy.

Section 100 of the EPA sets out minimum periods of consultation, which vary from 30 days for between 10 and 99 dismissals, to 90 days for dismissals of 100 or more employees. The employer must notify the union in writing of the reason for the proposals, the number and descriptions of employees involved, the method of selection, the proposed method of carrying out the redundancies and the dates of dismissal.

If an employer fails, without good reason, to give notice or consult with the appropriate trade union, it may, within three months, request an industrial tribunal to make a protective award. A protective award requires an employer to pay those employees covered by the award their normal week's pay for a specified period, i.e. the protected period. This period varies from 28 days to 90 days depending on the numbers involved, and will apply to employees whom the employer plans to dismiss, or has already dismissed for redundancy.

An employer who proposes to make redundant more than 100 employees at one establishment within 90 days, or more than 10 employees within 30 days must notify the Secretary of State of his proposals within 90 days, or 30 days respectively. He must also notify the representatives of any trade unions whose members are affected. If he fails to give notice he may be prosecuted in the magistrate's court and is liable to a fine on conviction.

10

DISCRIMINATION IN EMPLOYMENT

Discrimination on the grounds of sex or race

The Sex Discrimination Act 1975 'renders unlawful certain kinds of sex discrimination and discrimination on the grounds of marriage', and establishes a Commission whose function is to work towards the elimination of such discrimination, and to promote 'equality of opportunity between men and women generally'. Although the Act is drafted in terms of unlawful discrimination against women, it is also unlawful to discriminate against men on similar grounds, or against a married person of either sex, solely on the grounds of that person's marital status. The Act has been amended by the Sex Discrimination Act 1986 to comply with Community Law and the rulings of the European Court.

The Race Relations Act 1976 is modelled on the Sex Discrimination Act, and makes provision with respect to discrimination on racial grounds, and relations between people of different racial groups. Discrimination may take three forms: direct discrimination, indirect discrimination, or victimisation.

Direct discrimination

A person discriminates against another if, on the grounds of sex or marital status or race, he treats that person less favourably than he treats or would treat other persons.

In *James v. Eastleigh Borough Council*, a 61-year-old pensioner was charged for admission to the local swimming pool. As his 61-year-old wife was of state pensionable age, she was admitted free. It was held that, as the state pensionable age was directly discriminatory, any differential treatment based on it was also discriminatory. If he would have received the same treatment as his wife, but for the fact that he was a man, he had suffered less favourable treatment on the grounds of sex.

In *Skyrail Oceanic Ltd v. Coleman*, the appellant was dismissed by her employers on the day after her marriage to a man who worked in a rival agency. Both employers agreed that there was a risk of disclosure of confidential information, and as the husband was the breadwinner, the wife was dismissed. It was held that the dismissal of a woman based on the assumption that men are most likely to be the main supporters of the family amounts to sex discrimination.

An intention to discriminate must be shown, for if there is some other genuine reason for treating a woman less favourably, this is not discrimination on the grounds of her sex.

Discrimination cannot be justified on the grounds of convenience. In *Hurley v. Mustoe*, a married woman with four young children was refused employment as a waitress. The employer's policy was not to employ persons who had young children, as he had found them unreliable in the past. There was no evidence to suggest that the employer would refuse to employ men with small children, and the employer's policy was therefore held to be discriminatory. Browne-Wilkinson J. stated: 'Even if . . . one concedes that some women with small children are less reliable than those without, it does not follow that it is necessary in order to achieve reliability to exclude all women with children'.

In *Horsey v. Dyfed County Council*, a local authority refused secondment to a trainee social worker to attend a course in the London area. Her husband was employed in the London area and the authority was afraid that she would not return to her employment at the end of the course. It was held that the authority had committed an act of discrimination as it had made a general assumption about a married woman's behaviour, which could not be lawfully made.

Evidence of direct discrimination is rarely available, and a tribunal is entitled to draw an inference of discrimination from indirect evidence.

In *Owen and Briggs v. James*, a coloured girl answered an advertisement for a typist with a firm of solicitors, but did not obtain the post. Later she saw a differently worded advertisement and returned, not realising it was for the same post. She was told not to come back. The employer made a comment about employing coloured girls (which was possibly racist) to the successful applicant. It was held that the solicitors were in breach of the Race Relations Act.

In *Zarczynska v. Levy*, it was held that a white barmaid who was dismissed for refusing an order by her employer to apply a ban on coloured customers, could claim that she had been treated less favourably on racial grounds even though she had not been discriminated against on the grounds of her race.

In *Noone v. N.W. Thames Regional Health Authority*, Dr Noone, a Sri Lankan, was not appointed to a post as a consultant microbiologist despite the fact that her qualifications, experience and publications appeared to be better than the successful candidate. It was held that the reason for this was discrimination on the grounds of race.

Indirect discrimination

This occurs when a requirement or condition is applied to a person of one sex, or to single persons, or to persons of other racial groups:

1 which is such that the proportion of the complainant's sex or racial group or married persons is considerably smaller than the proportion of persons of the other sex, or of another racial group or single persons, who can comply with it; and
2 which cannot be shown to be justifiable irrespective of the sex, race or marital status of the person to whom it applied; and
3 which is to that person's detriment because he or she cannot comply with it.

There is little authority on what constitutes a requirement or condition. In *Clarke v. Eley (IMI) Kynoch Ltd*, it was held that an agreed redundancy procedure which provided for the dismissal of part-time employees before full-time employees amounted to a requirement or condition. This was discriminatory, as the majority of part-time employees were women and a large proportion would be unable to comply with the requirement or condition to work full-time in order to avoid redundancy. The EAT nevertheless stated that the standard of 'last in, first out' should be regarded as justifiable, even though its effect is indirectly discriminatory.

In *Steel v. Union of Post Office Workers*, it was conceded that the allocation of postal work by seniority amounted to a 'requirement or condition' (see page 172). In *Price v. Civil Service Commission*, it was alleged that an imposition of an age limit of 28 for a Civil Service post was discriminatory. The applicant was 35, and claimed that women tended to return to work after bearing and rearing children. The words 'can comply with' meant practically possible, not theoretically possible. The case was remitted to an industrial tribunal to determine on statistical evidence whether the proportion of women who could comply was considerably smaller than the proportion of men who could comply, and it was held that the age limit was discriminatory.

In *Hussein v. Saints Complete House Furnishers*, an employer stipulated that he would not interview job applicants who lived in the Liverpool City Centre area, as experience had shown that they attracted their unemployed friends, who stood in front of the shop. He was held to have discriminated indirectly against black and coloured applicants, as 50 per cent of the population of the City Centre area was black or coloured, while outside the area the percentage was two per cent.

In *Perera v. Civil Service Commission*, it was held that placing an upper age limit of 32 on trainees for certain Civil Service posts was potentially discriminatory. It was more difficult for coloured immigrants to apply, as a large proportion of those immigrants are adult.

An employer who seeks to justify such discrimination must satisfy the burden of proof, i.e. that on the balance of probabilities such discrimination is not merely convenient, but necessary.

'Justifiable', when referring to the requirement, means 'reasonably necessary' or 'right and proper in the circumstances', i.e., although a requirement or condition may have a discriminatory effect, it was implemented for reasons that were not connected with sex or race and it was necessary for business or organisational needs. In *Ojutiku v. Manpower Services Commission*, it was held that the Commission's refusal to sponsor for training persons who lacked managerial experience was justified by the subsequent inability of those persons to find jobs, even when trained. The discrimination was therefore justifiable, despite its indirect discriminatory effect on coloured people.

No award of damages will be made against an employer who fails to prove that a discriminatory practice was justifiable, if he can show that the requirement or condition was not applied with the intention of treating the complainant less favourably.

In *Kingston and Richmond Area Health Authority v. Kaur*, it was held that it was justifiable for a health authority to require its nurses to wear a uniform 'without alteration'. A Sikh trainee nurse who wished to wear trousers under her uniform had therefore not been discriminated against.

In *Panesar v. Nestlé Company*, it was held that a rule that no beards were allowed in the chocolate-making part of the factory was reasonable and that, although the rule was apparently discriminatory as the applicant was a Sikh, it was nevertheless justifiable.

Although the provisions of the Acts are not retrospective, they will nevertheless apply to acts of a continuing discriminatory nature. In *Steel v. Union of Post Office Workers*, the Post Office awarded postal routes according to seniority, which was judged according to the length of an employee's permanent status. Women had only been able to attain permanent status since 1975. A route was given to a man whose permanent status was longer, but whose total length of service was shorter than that of the complainant. It was conceded that the ruling amounted to 'a requirement or condition', and was discriminatory.

'Detriment' is defined by its ordinary literal meaning of being placed at a disadvantage. In *Schmidt v. Austicks Bookshops*, a company laid down a rule that female employees were not allowed to wear trousers and must wear overalls. A female employee persisted in wearing trousers and was dismissed. She complained that the overall restriction was an unlawful detriment, and that both restrictions were less favourable treatment. It was held that the restriction was not serious enough to be a detriment, and as male employees were not allowed to wear T-shirts, there was no less favourable treatment of female employees.

It is a detriment to the complainant if he or she is unable to comply with the requirement or condition. It is not detrimental if they do not wish to comply.

In *Turner v. Labour Party and Labour Party Superannuation Society*, a divorcee was required to join an occupational pension scheme which provided for pension entitlements for dependants (including a surviving spouse) on her death. She contended that, as she was unlikely to marry, these provisions were detrimental and the scheme discriminatory. It was held that, although she may not wish to marry, it could not be said that she was unable to marry. She was able to comply with the requirement, which could not be said to be to her detriment.

In *B.L. Cars v. Brown*, several black employees complained of racial discrimination, as the employers had issued an instruction to the security men at the gates to check the identity of every black employee trying to enter the premises. This followed the arrest of a black employee who had been charged with theft. It was held that the black employees had been unlawfully discriminated against, in that they had been subjected to a detriment.

An employer cannot buy a right to discriminate by paying extra to employees who are the subject of discrimination. In *Ministry of Defence v. Jeremiah*, both male and female examiners were employed at a government ordnance factory. Overtime was voluntary, but any men working overtime had to make colour bursting shells and were paid an extra 4p an hour. This was very dirty work which women were not required to do. It was held that the practice discriminated against the male employees.

The European Court has, in two recent decisions, held that a woman who suffers a detriment on account of her pregnancy is subjected to direct discrimination on the grounds of sex. There does not have to be a male comparator and, as pregnancy is unique to one sex, any decisions that are based on pregnancy are therefore decisions that are based on sex.

In *Dekker v. Slichting Vormingscent voor Jong Volwassenen (VJV-Centrum) Plus (1991)*, an applicant for a job as a training instructor was refused employment, despite the recommendation of the selection committee, as she was three months pregnant. Although she would have been entitled to maternity leave and pay, it was conceded that VJV's insurers could refuse reimbursement of wages where a foreseeable absence occurred within six months. Nevertheless it was held that direct discrimination occurs when the main reason for an employment decision applies exclusively to one sex. As the refusal of employment was connected with the sex of the applicant it was discriminatory.

In *Handels-Og Kontorfunktionaerernes Forbund i Danmark v. Dansk Arbejdsgiverrforening*, a part-time cashier and saleswoman became pregnant and, due to complications, was absent from work for most of her pregnancy. After the birth she had 24 weeks' statutory maternity leave and for the next six months was able to work without problems. In the following year she was absent for 100 days due to ill health and was dismissed. The Court stated that a dismissal for reasons of pregnancy or for absence during maternity leave was sexually discriminatory. Where a woman was ill after that time it was not necessary to distinguish it from any other illness having its origin in pregnancy or confinement, and if she was dismissed in circumstances where a man would also have been dismissed, there was no sex discrimination.

Victimisation

It is unlawful to treat a person less favourably than another because that person has brought proceedings, or given evidence, or information, or alleged a contravention of the Sex Discrimination Act, Equal Pay Act or Race Relations Act; or if it is known that a person intends to do any of these things, or it is suspected that he or she has done, or intends to do any of them. There is no protection if the allegation was false and was not made in good faith.

_____ Discrimination before and _____ during employment

Discrimination before employment

Discrimination *before employment* may occur in any of the following ways:

1   in the arrangements made for the purpose of selecting employees and making offers of employment; or
2   in the terms on which employment is offered; or
3   by refusing or deliberately omitting to offer employment because of a person's sex or race.

It is unlawful for an applicant to be asked questions which might not be asked of a person of the opposite sex, e.g. to ask a married, or even unmarried, woman if she has plans to start a family.

It is discriminatory if an applicant responds to an advertisement only to be told it is 'man's work' (or woman's work). In *Batisha v. Say and Longleat Enterprises*, a woman applied for the post of cave guide. She was informed that only men would be appointed, but she could attend for the interview if she so wished. The posts had already been filled by local male applicants before she was interviewed. It was held that there had been discrimination, as the posts could have been held by women.

If a woman is not considered for a vacant post because of her sex and the post is not filled, there is nevertheless discrimination (*Roadbury v. Lothian Regional Council*).

In *Grieg v. Community Industry*, two women were employed as a decorating team. When one woman did not turn up for work, the employer refused to allow the other woman to do the work, as there had been problems in the past when there was only one woman in a team. It was held that the employer's motive was irrelevant, as his action was discriminatory.

An employer retains the right to appoint whomsoever he wishes to fill a vacant post. The fact that the appointee is not as well qualified as another applicant is not in itself evidence of discrimination. An employer may therefore use any criteria he so wishes in an appointment, as long as there is no evidence of discrimination on the grounds of sex or race.

Discrimination during employment

Discrimination occurs *during employment* if an employer discriminates, on the grounds of sex or race, against an employee:

1   in affording access to opportunities for promotion, transfer or training or any other benefits, facilities or services or by refusing or deliberately omitting to afford access to them; or
2   in dismissing or subjecting the employee to any other detriment.

It was held in *Steel v. Union of Post Office Workers* that the Post Office had contravened this provision by refusing to recognise an employee's total length of service as a criterion for promotion and thereby discriminating against women.

In *McGregor Wallcoverings v. Turton*, the employer's redundancy scheme provided higher rates of pay for employees over the age of 60. This was held to be discriminatory, as women employees had to retire at 60, and were therefore unable to qualify for the higher rates of payment.

In *Barclays Bank v. Kapur*, employees of Asian origin were initially employed by the bank in Africa. In 1970 they were offered posts in the United Kingdom on condition that their employment in Africa would not count towards the bank's pension scheme, although the previous service of European employees was counted for pension purposes. It was held that the lack of pension rights equivalent to their European colleagues amounted to discrimination and a detriment.

———— Lawful discrimination ————

Discrimination is permitted under certain circumstances, under the provisions of the Sex Discrimination Act and the Race Relations Act.

1 Discrimination on the grounds of sex

This is permitted in the following circumstances:

(a)   provisions relating to death or retirement (SDA s6);

(b)   where a charitable instrument confers benefit on one sex;

(c)   training for members of one sex by a training body where it appears that, at any time within the 12 months immediately preceding the start of training, there were no persons of that sex holding that post or the numbers were comparatively small (SDA s48);

(d)   where the sex of the person is a genuine occupational qualification for the job (SDA s7). This applies in the following circumstances:

(i)   where the essential nature of the job calls for a man or woman for reasons of physiology, and for reasons of authenticity in dramatic performance or other entertainments;

(ii)   when there is a need to preserve decency or privacy, e.g. taking inside leg measurements in a gent's outfitting department;

(iii)   when the employee is required to live in because of the nature or location of the establishment, and there are no separate sleeping or sanitary facilities;

(iv)   employment in a hospital, prison or other establishment;

(v)   employment as a welfare or education counsellor;

(vi)   when there are traditional restrictions on the employment of women;

(vii)   in employment likely to be performed outside the United Kingdom, in a country whose laws or customs preclude a woman from performing those duties;

(viii)   when the job is one of two to be held by a married couple;

(e) when differentiating between male and female police constables with regard to the requirements for height, uniform, equipment, pensions and the special treatment offered to women in pregnancy and childbirth;

(f) provisions relating to the height of prison officers;

(g) employment as a minister of religion.

In *Timex Corporation v. Hodgson*, an employer selected two male supervisors for redundancy, contrary to company policy of 'last in, first out'. A woman supervisor was retained, as she could deal with women's personal problems in addition to her ordinary job. It was held that the employer was not liable, for although there had been discrimination, the sex of the employee was a genuine occupational qualification, as in (d) above.

The SDA provides that nothing in the Act 'shall render unlawful any act done by a person if it was necessary for him to do it in order to comply with a requirement' of earlier legislation, or to safeguard national security. In *Page v. Freight Hire (Tank Haulage) Ltd*, a 23-year-old woman was employed as an HGV driver. Her employers refused to allow her to drive loads of a chemical (DMF) which the manufacturers warned was potentially dangerous to women of child-bearing age. It was held that discrimination was lawful, to comply with the Health and Safety at Work Act 1974.

In *Hugh-Jones v. St John's College, Cambridge*, a woman was barred by college statutes from being appointed a research fellow. As the college statutes had been enacted before 1975, the discrimination was not unlawful.

2 Discrimination on the grounds of race

This is permitted in the following circumstances:

(a) when providing persons of a particular racial group with access to:
(i) facilities or services to meet their special needs in regard to their education, training or welfare or any ancillary benefits; or
(ii) facilities and training or encouraging them to take advantage of those opportunities, where, during the preceding 12 months, there were no persons of that race doing that work or their numbers were comparatively small.

(b)   when providing persons not ordinarily resident in Great Britain with access to facilities for education or training or ancillary benefits;

(c)   where being a member of 'a particular racial group is a genuine occupational qualification for the job'. This applies in the following cases:

(i)   participation in a dramatic performance or other entertainment where authenticity is required;

(ii)   employment as an artist's or photographic model where authenticity is required;

(iii)   employment in a place where food or drink is provided and consumed, and a person of that racial group is required for authenticity, e.g. a Chinese restaurant;

(iv)   provisions of personal welfare services which can be most effectively provided by a person of that racial group.

In *Lambeth London Borough v. Commission for Racial Equality*, the council advertised two posts with its Housing Benefit department. As more than 50 per cent of its tenants were Afro-Caribbean or Asian, the council advertised the posts as restricted to applicants of these racial groups. It was held that, as the posts were managerial and administrative and did not therefore involve personal (i.e. direct) contact with the tenants, membership of a particular racial group was not a genuine occupational qualification.

There is also a provision in the RRA that nothing in the Act will render unlawful any act done by a person if it was necessary to comply with earlier legislation or to safeguard national security.

The Commission for Racial Equality's Code of Practice came into operation on April 1 1984. The Code gives practical guidance on the provisions of the Race Relations Act, and how to prevent racial discrimination and achieve equality of opportunity.

Advertisements

It is unlawful to publish an advertisement indicating an intention to discriminate. The use of a job description with a sexual or racial connotation, e.g. waiter, salesgirl, postman, stewardess, will be taken as an indication of such an intention, unless the advertisement contains an indication to the contrary.

In *Equal Opportunities Commission v. Robertson,* Robertson placed an advertisement for "a good bloke" (or blokess to satisfy fool legislators)'. It was held that the advertisement might reasonably be understood to indicate that the post was not open to women and therefore contravened the Sex Discrimination Act.

The publisher of an advertisement which proves to be discriminatory will not be liable to any penalty if he can prove that he relied on a statement that the advertisement was not unlawful and that it was reasonable for him to do so.

It is also unlawful for a person who has authority over another to instruct that person to commit a discriminatory act, or for a person to induce, or attempt to induce a person to commit a discriminatory act. It was held in *Commission for Racial Equality v. Imperial Society of Teachers of Dancing* that a request from the Society to the careers section of Camden School for Girls not to send anyone coloured as a prospective employee was not an attempt to induce and did not therefore contravene the RRA in that respect.

—— Discrimination by other bodies ——

Discrimination against contract workers is also unlawful. (A contract worker is an individual who is not employed by the principal, but by another person, who supplies under a contract made with the principal.) The Acts also prevent discrimination by: a partnership of six or more partners; trade unions, employees and workers' organisations; professional and trade associations; qualifying bodies for various trade and professions; vocational training bodies; employment agencies; Manpower Services Commission, and other allied agencies.

—— Enforcement of legislation ——

Anti-discrimination legislation may be enforced in two ways.

1 By an individual bringing proceedings before an industrial tribunal.
2 By the Equal Opportunities Commission (EOC) or the Commission for Racial Equality (CRE).

1   *Proceedings before a tribunal*

An individual must present his complaint within three months of the discriminatory act taking place. An application out of time may be considered if it is just and equitable to do so.

Although the burden of proof rests on the complainant, he is nevertheless given help to obtain information by submitting questions to the respondent on a prescribed form. The respondent is not obliged to reply, but if he fails to do so, or his replies are evasive and equivocal, the tribunal is entitled to infer that he committed an unlawful act.

The EOC and CRE may, at their discretion, give assistance to an individual who is an actual or prospective complainant, if they consider that the case raises a question of principle, or is complex, or it is unreasonable to expect the applicant to deal with the case unaided. The assistance may take the form of advice, procuring or attempting to procure a settlement of the dispute, arranging for legal advice, assistance or legal representation.

A conciliation officer may intervene if requested to do so by both the parties, or if he considers that there is a reasonable prospect of achieving a voluntary settlement of the complaint.

A tribunal may make any of the following orders which it considers just and equitable:

(a)   an order declaring the right of the parties in relation to the act to which the complaint relates;

(b)   an award of compensation, subject to a maximum of £10,000;

(c)   a recommendation that the respondent takes, within a specified period, practical action to obviate or reduce the adverse effect on the complainant of any act of discrimination to which the complaint relates.

A declaration states that there has been discrimination and that the complainant's rights have been violated. It may be combined with an order for compensation or a recommendation or both.

A tribunal may award compensation where it considers that making an award is just and equitable. The maximum award may not exceed £10,000 and where an employee claims an additional award for an employer's failure to comply with the tribunal's recommendation, the total award must not exceed the maximum figure. The amount of damages must be assessed by a tribunal in the same manner as a court of law. Damages will be awarded under two headings.

- *Special damages* Those losses which are easily identified and quantified, e.g. lost wages, financial benefits, etc.
- *General damages* Those intangible losses which must be assessed by a tribunal, e.g. injury to feelings, loss of career opportunities, loss of future earnings, etc.

A tribunal may only make a declaration and/or recommendation if an employer is able to satisfy the tribunal that, in the case of indirect discrimination, he applied a requirement or condition without intending to discriminate. An award of compensation may not be given, even if the complainant shows that he or she has suffered direct financial loss.

If, without reasonable justification, a respondent fails to comply with a recommendation, a tribunal may increase an order for compensation (up to the maximum amount) where an award of compensation has been made or, if no order was made, make such an order.

A person who is dismissed, and who alleges that the dismissal is discriminatory, is more likely to succeed in an action for unfair dismissal. The burden of proof in a case of unfair dismissal rests on the employer and an industrial tribunal may make an order for reinstatement or reengagement, or may grant compensation if the case is proven (see page 146). A claimant in a discrimination action may be granted damages which may include compensation for injury to feelings. Although a claimant may bring a complaint under both headings, he or she cannot be awarded double compensation.

2 Proceedings by the appropriate Commission

Each Commission consists of a chairman and up to 14 members, who are appointed by the Secretary of State on a full-time or part-time basis. The duties of the Commissions are:

(a) to work towards the elimination of discrimination;
(b) to promote equality of opportunity between men and women and between persons of different racial groups;
(c) to review the workings of the Acts, and, if necessary, to draw up and submit proposals for amendment.

The main functions of each Commission are:

(i)   to conduct formal investigations, either on its own initiative or at the request of the Secretary of State. Any person may be required to give information, provide relevant documents and attend the hearing. The Commission may make recommendations in the light of those investigations. A Commission may recommend changes in policy or procedure, or a change in the law;

(ii)   where an investigation discloses an unlawful practice, a Commission may serve on the party concerned a non-discrimination notice requiring him to cease the practice or otherwise comply with the law. There is a right of appeal within six weeks to an industrial tribunal;

(iii)   if, within five years of the service of a discrimination notice or a (iii) Commission that, unless restrained, the respondent is likely to act unlawfully again, it may apply to a County Court for an injunction;

(iv)   to institute proceedings in respect of discriminatory advertisements, instructions to discriminate or pressure to discriminate;

(v)   to give assistance to individual complainants to prepare their cases;

(vi)   to undertake or assist research and any educational activities;

(vii)   to submit an annual report on its activities.

11

INDUSTRIAL —— TRIBUNAL —— PROCEDURE

An individual who seeks to enforce a statutory right, or obtain a remedy for breach of that right, may apply for relief to an industrial tribunal. The complaint must be presented within the time specified by the appropriate statute, although an industrial tribunal has a general discretion to hear a complaint presented out of time if it considers that it was not reasonably practicable to present it earlier.

The majority of claims must be presented within three months of the date when the act or omission occurred. There are exceptions to this rule in that:

1   a claim for redundancy must be brought within six months of the dismissal;
2   a claim for interim relief for dismissal on the grounds of membership or non-membership of a trade union must be brought within seven days of the termination of employment.

The majority of industrial disputes are settled informally by the parties to the dispute without recourse to any outside agency. One party may agree to accept a sum of money in full and final settlement of any claim arising from the dispute. Most companies have procedures for dealing with discipline, works practices and redundancies. The EPCA encourages the provision of voluntary procedural agreements in respect of guarantee payments (s18), unfair dismissal (s65), and redundancy (s96).

The ACAS Code of Practice on Disciplinary Practice and Procedures in Employment and its advisory handbook on Discipline at Work give practical guidance for promoting good industrial relations.

Jurisdiction

Industrial tribunals have jurisdiction in a wide range of matters including:

1 Industrial Training Act 1964: s12 imposition of industrial training levy;

2 Docks and Harbour Act 1966: s51 definition of dock worker;

3 Equal Pay Act 1970: s2 breach of equality clause in employment contract;

4 Health and Safety at Work Act 1974: s24 appeals against improvement and prohibition notices;

5 Sex Discrimination Act 1975: s63 complaints of discrimination on grounds of sex or marital status; s68 appeals against non-discriminatory notices; s72 applications by the Equal Opportunities Commission relating to discriminatory advertisements;

6 Race Relations Act 1976: s54 complaints of discrimination on racial grounds; s68 appeals against non-discriminatory notices; s72 applications by the Commission for Racial Equality relating to discriminatory advertisements;

7 Employment Protection Act 1975: s101 complaint by a trade union on failure of employer to consult on redundancies; s103 application for protective award;

8 Employment Protection (Consolidation) Act 1978: s11 failure to give written particulars of terms of employment (s1), changes in terms of employment (s4), or give itemised pay statement (s8); s17 failure to pay guarantee payment; s22 failure to pay medical suspension payment; s24 taking action (short of dismissal) on grounds of trade union membership or non-membership; ss27, 29, 31, 31A time off work for trade union activities, public duties, looking for work or making arrangements for retraining, antenatal care; s53 failure to give written reasons for dismissal; s67 complaints of unfair dismissal; s77 interim relief pending determination of complaint of

unfair dismissal; s91 entitlement to redundancy payments and the amounts of those payments; s122 rights on employer's insolvency; s130 jurisdiction of referees under certain statutory provisions;

9   Employment Act 1980: s2 secret ballot on employer's premises; s4 unreasonable exclusion or expulsion from trade union;

10   Wages Act 1986: s5 unauthorised deductions or payments, deduction of amount in excess of the 10-per-cent limit permitted for retail shortages or deficiency; s11 wage deduction not notified on itemised pay statement;

11   Employment Act 1988: s3 right not to be unjustifiably disciplined;

12   Employment Act 1990: ss1, 2 refusal of employment or refusal of service of employment agency on grounds related to trade union membership;

13   Safety Representatives and Safety Committee Regulations 1977: time off work for safety representatives;

14   Transfer of Undertakings (Protection of Employment) Regulations 1981: failure to inform or consult with trade unions; failure to pay compensation.

Administration

Separate Central Offices of Industrial Tribunals have been established in London, Glasgow and Belfast for England and Wales, Scotland and Northern Ireland respectively, dealing with the appointment of personnel and the processing of applications. The principal administrative officer for each Central Office is known as the secretary of tribunals.

Regional Offices have been established at 16 centres throughout England and Wales. Each has an assistant secretary who deals with the administration of applications, after their initial registration at the Central Office. Industrial tribunals sit at numerous centres within each region; an average of 60 tribunals sit in England and Wales on each working day.

Composition

Each tribunal consists of a chairman (a barrister or solicitor of at least seven years' standing) and two lay members, one of whom is usually a nominee of an employer's organisation and the other a trade union nominee. It is desirable for a tribunal hearing a sex discrimination case to have both male and female membership and for a tribunal hearing a race discrimination case to have a member with experience of race relations, but this is not a legal requirement.

A tribunal may proceed with a claim in the absence of one of the lay members, if the parties to the action consent. In *Yardley Plastics v. Heathcote*, one party did not attend the tribunal hearing and submitted written representations. The tribunal heard the case with only the chairman and one lay member present. It was held that, as the consent of both parties to a reduced tribunal membership had not been obtained, the hearing was invalid.

The chairman and the lay members have equal voice in the decision reached by the tribunal. A clerk is also attached to each tribunal, who advises and assists the parties and the tribunal, before and during the hearing.

Procedure

The procedure is governed by the Industrial Tribunals (Rules of Procedure) Regulations 1985.

Proceedings are commenced by the applicant submitting an originating application form IT 1 to the Central Office of Industrial Tribunals, in writing, to the secretary of tribunals. This sets out the applicant's name and address, the respondent's name and address and the grounds on which relief is sought. It is unnecessary to state what relief is sought, as this allows the tribunal discretion as to what relief (if any) to grant the applicant. This form and the accompanying booklet is obtainable from a number of sources, including job centres.

The secretary of tribunals enters details of the application in the register and sends a copy of the application to the respondent, together with details of how the respondent may enter an appearance and contest the applicant's claim. If the respondent intends to enter an appearance, he must inform the secretary within 14 days of receiving his copy of the originating application of his intention to do so and on what grounds he intends to resist the claim. A copy of this must be sent to the applicant. Documents of a confidential nature may be examined by the chairman of the industrial tribunal to ensure that discovery is essential for the proper conduct of the case.

Either party (or the tribunal) may require further particulars of any ground relied on together with any relevant facts, and may require the attendance of any person (including a party to the proceedings) as a witness. Discovery of documents may be granted and an order may be made for the production of any relevant documents.

A tribunal may sometimes hold a preliminary hearing where it appears that it does not have the power to consider the complaint or where there is a dispute between the parties about this. If the tribunal concludes that it does have the power it will arrange a further hearing to consider the merits of the complaint.

Each party must be given at least 14 days' notice of the hearing, which takes place in public, unless the tribunal considers that a private hearing is appropriate in the circumstances.

A private hearing is only considered appropriate in cases where disclosure would involve matters of national security; contravene any enactment; expose a confidential relationship; or cause substantial injury to an undertaking other than in respect of collective bargaining.

The tribunal may conduct a hearing in such a manner as it considers most appropriate to the just handling of the proceedings, and to the clarification of the issues before it. A tribunal's proceedings are fairly informal and flexible. As a general rule the burden of proof is on the applicant, who should therefore give evidence first to support his allegations, e.g. of sex discrimination, racial discrimination, that an employee was not dismissed, etc. In cases of unfair dismissal where an employer does not contest the fact that a dismissal has taken place, he will be required to give evidence first and must establish the reason(s) for the dismissal, that it was a statutory reason and that he acted reasonably in the circumstances. It is not bound by the strict legal rules relating to the admissability of evidence.

At the hearing, a party and any person entitled to appear may appear in person and has the right to be represented by counsel, or by a solicitor, or by a trade union or employers' association representative, or by any other person whom he desires to represent him. A party to the proceedings may give evidence, question witnesses and address the tribunal. A witness may be required to give evidence on oath or affirmation.

In *Aberdeen Steak Houses Group v. Ibrahim*, the EAT summarised the established guidelines relating to the presentation of evidence at tribunal hearings.

1   The party concerned, not the tribunal, decides the order in which that party calls his/her witnesses.
2   It is the duty of the parties to ensure that all the relevant evidence is presented to the tribunal and not for the tribunal to ensure that this is done.
3   A tribunal should not allow a party to be taken by surprise by an allegation of dishonesty, made at the last minute, but should adjourn and give directions.
4   Where a party specifically states that he will not be calling evidence, he will normally be bound by his evidence.
5   A tribunal cannot refuse to admit evidence which is admissible and probative of one or more issues.
6   The party opening the case should call all his relevant evidence and should then close his/her case.

If a party fails to appear, or is not represented at the hearing, the tribunal may, if that party is an applicant, dismiss or dispose of the application in the absence of that party or may adjourn the hearing to a later date.

The tribunal's decision is recorded in a document, which is then sent to the secretary of tribunals. He enters the decision in the Register and sends a copy of the entry to each party. In many cases a tribunal gives its decision, and the reasons for arriving at that decision, at the end of the hearing. If it is not possible to give a decision immediately, the tribunal will reserve its decision, and the parties will be notified at a later date of the decision and the reason behind it.

Written reasons for a tribunal's decision may be given in either full or summary form, but in the majority of cases summary written reasons will be sent to the parties. Full written reasons will be given in the following cases:

(a)   complaints of dismissal, action short of dismissal, selection for redundancy on the grounds of trade union membership, or activities or non-membership of a trade union;

(b)   applications for interim relief in respect of dismissal on the grounds of trade union membership or activities or non-membership of a trade union;

(c)   complaints of expulsion or unreasonable exclusion from a trade union in a closed shop;

(d)   complaints of racial discrimination;

(e)   complaints of sex discrimination;

(f)   claims of equal pay;

(g)   in other cases, where a party requests full written reasons, the request may be made orally at the hearing or in writing within 22 days of sending summary written reasons.

A tribunal may, in limited circumstances, review its decision. It may do so if:

(a)   the decision was wrongly made as a result of an error on the part of the tribunal staff;

(b)   a party did not receive notice of the proceedings leading to the decision;

(c)   the decision was made in the absence of a party or a person entitled to be heard;

(d)   new evidence has become available since the conclusion of the hearing, provided that its existence could not have been reasonably known of or foreseen;

(e)   the interests of justice require such a review.

—— Pre-hearing assessment ——

A tribunal may, on the application of either party (or of its own accord), convene a pre-hearing assessment. If at this stage it considers that the originating application is unlikely to succeed, or that a particular contention made by one of the parties is without merit, it may advise the party concerned that to proceed with the application or to reassert the contention would lead to an order for costs.

As it is an informal hearing, only the party whose case appears to have no reasonable chance of success need attend. The other party may attend if he or she wishes. No evidence from the parties or from witnesses will be taken, but either party may address the tribunal.

A tribunal has no power to decide or to dismiss a case at a pre-hearing assessment; nor can it order a party to withdraw an application. It can advise a party that it considers a case to be without merit and that to persist with the case will probably lead to liability for the other party's costs if the case is subsequently unsuccessful. This does not prevent the warned party from continuing to a full hearing and does not mean that costs will automatically be granted against that party at that hearing – that is a matter for the tribunal at that hearing to decide.

Section 20 of the Employment Act 1989 empowers the Secretary of State for Employment to replace the present system of pre-hearing assessment with a pre-hearing review. This will enable the tribunal chairman sitting alone, or the full tribunal, to conduct a pre-hearing review of a case, in advance of the full tribunal hearing. If it is considered that a case has no reasonable prospect of success or that the pursuit of it is frivolous, vexatious or otherwise unreasonable, either party may be ordered to pay a deposit of up to £150 as a condition of proceeding with or defending the case. The deposit will be returned, unless the case goes to a full hearing and the party who has been ordered to put down the deposit loses and has a costs order made against him or her. In that case the deposit will be paid to the other party in part-settlement of the costs.

Award of costs

An award will not normally be made in respect of any costs or expenses incurred by either party, but if the tribunal considers that a party has acted frivolously, vexatiously or unreasonably in bringing or conducting proceedings, then it may make an award of costs. An award of costs may follow a warning given at a pre-hearing assessment. It may make an order for that party to pay the whole or part of the other party's costs, or it may order that party to pay to the Secretary of the State part or the whole of any sum paid as allowances to the other party. It may also award costs where a hearing has been postponed or adjourned on the application of one of the parties.

The following cases illustrate the power of a tribunal to make an award of costs.

In *Banai v. N.E. Thames Health Authority,* a claim was brought for race and sex discrimination. Banai was warned at an interlocutory hearing that his allegations of racial discrimination were unfounded. He raised irrelevant points in cross examination and put the other party to considerable expense in preparing parts of a case which he abandoned in his final speech. He was ordered to pay £7,000 costs.

In *Keskar v. Governors of All Saints Church of England School,* it was held that, although a teacher had a sincere belief in the case of racial discrimination brought against the Governors, he was motivated by spite as the Governors had not appointed him headmaster and had endorsed disciplinary action against him. The Governors' costs were £5,000 and the tribunal ordered him to pay £4,000 costs.

Conciliation

The secretary of the tribunal must, in all cases where an enactment provides for conciliation, inform the parties that the services of a conciliation officer are available to them. A copy of a complaint presented to an industrial tribunal must also be sent to the conciliation officer.

A conciliation officer may offer his services to a party to a dispute before a complaint is lodged. As his aim is to promote a settlement, he may, where appropriate, encourage the parties to use any other procedures which are available for the settlement of grievances, but the parties are under no obligation to co-operate or communicate with him.

Conciliation officers are given specific functions when a complaint of unfair dismissal is presented to an industrial tribunal. A copy of the complaint is sent to a conciliation officer, who must endeavour to promote a settlement without recourse to an industrial tribunal, if requested to do so by either party, or if he considers that he has a reasonable prospect of success. If the employee is no longer employed by the employer, the conciliation officer must seek to promote the employee's reinstatement or re-engagement on terms which appear to the conciliation officer to be equitable. Where the employee does not wish to be reinstated or re-engaged, or where those remedies are not practical, and both parties wish him to act, the conciliation officer may seek to promote agreement as to the amount of compensation to be paid by the employer.

Although section 140 of the EPCA states that any provision in an agreement is void if it precludes any person from presenting a complaint to, or bringing any proceedings under the Act, a settlement reached under the auspices of the conciliation officer is binding on the parties. It may be enforced in the same way as an award made by a tribunal and will bar an employee from presenting an unfair dismissal complaint to a tribunal.

In 1989, 31,913 applications were registered:

- 34 per cent proceeded to a tribunal hearing;
- 32 per cent were settled with the involvement of ACAS;
- 34 per cent were withdrawn;
- 57 per cent of the applications involved unfair dismissal claims;
- 15 per cent dealt with claims under the Wages Act;
- 42 per cent of the cases heard resulted in a favourable decision for the applicant.

The median compensation awarded for unfair dismissal was £1,786. five hundred and forty five pre-hearing assessments were ordered by tribunals. Costs were awarded in 185 cases.

– Employment Appeal Tribunal (EAT) –

The Employment Appeal Tribunal was established under the Employment Act 1975, is regulated by section 135 of the EPCA, and is a superior court of record. It consists of High Court Judges and lay members who are required to have special knowledge or experience of industrial relations, either as employer's or employee's representatives. One of the judges is nominated as the president of the appeal tribunal.

The tribunal may sit at any time and in any place in Great Britain, either as a single tribunal or in two or more divisions concurrently. When sitting as a single tribunal, it consists of a judge and either two or four appointed members, equally representative of employers and employees.

Jurisdiction

It considers appeals on questions of law from the findings of industrial tribunals under the Equal Pay Act 1970, the Sex Discrimination Act 1975, the Employment Protection Act 1975, the Race Relations Act 1976, the Employment Protection (Consolidation) Act 1978 and the Employment Act 1980.

An appeal may be made on one of the following grounds:

1 the tribunal misdirected itself in law, or misunderstood or misapplied the law;
2 the tribunal's findings are in conflict with the evidence;
3 the decision was such that no reasonable tribunal could have reached it.

An appeal can also be based on a question of fact or law from a decision of a tribunal relating to unreasonable exclusion or expulsion from a trade union.

The EAT also hears appeals, on questions of law, from the decisions of the certification officer in respect of objections by trade union members to contributing to the union's political funds; the application of trade union funds for political purposes; the provision of ballots to approve union rules; complaints in respect of resolutions passed in cases involving the amalgamation of trade unions or transfer of engagements from one trade union to another.

An appeal also lies to the EAT from a certification officer's ruling that a trade union is not independent, and his refusal to enter a trade union or an employer's association in the lists of trade unions and employer's associations. An appeal on those grounds may be made on questions of fact or law.

It has original jurisdiction to determine applications for compensation in cases dealing with: unreasonable exclusion or expulsion from a trade union (EA 80 s5); and the right not to be unjustifiably disciplined (EA 88 s5).

Procedure

The appeal must be lodged within 42 days of the date on which the decision or order appealed against was sent to the appellant. The appellant must submit a notice of appeal, a copy of the industrial tribunal's decision and the full written reasons for the decision. The EAT has a discretion to authorise an appeal, without the submission of the full reasons if it considers that it would lead to the 'more expeditious or economic disposal of any proceedings or would otherwise be desirable in the interests of justice'. If it appears to the registrar of the EAT that the grounds of appeal are not within the EAT's jurisdiction, he must notify the appellant of this fact, and no further action may be taken on the appeal. The appellant may in these circumstances serve a fresh notice of appeal within 28 days of the registrar's notification, or before the expiration of the 42 days. He may also express his dissatisfaction, in writing, with the registrar's decision and the registrar must then place the papers before a judge or the president for his direction.

On receiving notice of appeal, the registrar seals the notice with the EAT's seal. He then serves a sealed copy on the appellant and the respondent, and the secretary of industrial tribunals in the case of an appeal from an industrial tribunal. A notice is served on the certification officer in a case involving an appeal from any of his decisions.

If the respondent wishes to contest the appeal, or cross-appeal, he may do so by delivering his answer, or his cross-appeal, in writing, to the EAT. The appellant may, in reply to a cross-appeal, set out the grounds on which he replies. The registrar will provide copies of the answers and replies to a cross-appeal to the other parties.

If the respondent does not wish to contest an appeal, the parties may deliver to the EAT an agreed draft of an order allowing the appeal. The tribunal may, if it approves, make an order allowing the appeal on the agreed terms.

The registrar informs the parties of the arrangements for the hearing. Provision is made for holding a meeting for directions, prior to the hearing, if it appears that this would facilitate the future conduct of the proceedings.

If, at any stage of the proceedings, it appears to the appeal tribunal that there is a reasonable prospect of an agreement being reached between the parties, it may take such steps as it thinks fit to enable the parties to avail themselves of any opportunities for conciliation.

The hearings are in public, but the EAT may sit in private, in similar circumstances to those in which an industrial tribunal may conduct its proceedings in private (see page 187). It may order the attendance of witnesses and compel the production of documents. Costs may be awarded in any proceedings if it appears that the proceedings were unnecessary, improper, vexatious, or there has been unreasonable delay or other unreasonable conduct in bringing or conducting the proceedings.

In *Ballantine-Dykes v. Bedales School*, the EAT were of the opinion that the appellant had acted unreasonably in bringing an appeal, as the tribunal's findings could not be overturned and there was no prospect of success. He had also issued a number of superfluous letters and writs. He was ordered to pay £1,000 costs.

The EAT may, either of its own accord or on the application of a party, review any order made by it. It may, after review, revoke or vary that order on the grounds that:

1   the order was wrongly made as the result of an error on the part of the tribunal or its staff; or
2   a party did not receive a proper notice of the proceedings leading to the order; or
3   the interests of justice require such review.

A clerical mistake in any order, due to an accidental slip or omission, may at any time be corrected by, or on the authority of, a judge or member.

A further appeal, on a question of law from a decision of the EAT, lies to the Court of Appeal and to the House of Lords.

The Courts

Although the majority of actions are dealt with by industrial tribunals, certain matters are dealt with by the civil courts. These include:

1   actions for wrongful dismissal (see page 111);
2   actions for damages following injury at work (see page 65);
3   actions for breach of contracts (see page 50), including an action for a breach of a covenant in restraint of trade.

Any court or tribunal can refer a case to the European Court of Justice for a ruling where there is perceived to be a conflict between Community Law and the law of the United Kingdom. In the recent case of *Barber v. Guardian Royal Exchange Assurance* (see page 98), the European Court was asked by the Court of Appeal to give a ruling in a case involving occupational pension schemes.

12

THE SETTLEMENT
—— OF INDUSTRIAL ——
DISPUTES

While the courts and industrial tribunals enforce individual rights and duties, other bodies engage in settling disputes at collective level between employers and trade unions as well as assisting in the settlement of individual disputes between employers and employees.

—— Advisory, Conciliation and —— Arbitration Service (ACAS)

ACAS was established in 1974, and is charged with the general duty of promoting the improvement of industrial relations. In particular, it is intended to encourage the extension of collective bargaining, and the development and reform of collective bargaining machinery.

Composition

Its work is directed by a council, which consists of a full-time chairman and nine other members. Three of the members represent employers' organisations, three are representatives of workers' organisations, and the remainder are independent members. All appointments are made by the Secretary of State, who may appoint a further two members, and up to three full-time or part-time deputy chairmen. The appointments will be for an initial term of five years, and may be renewed for a further term.

The council may, with the approval of the Secretary of State, appoint a secretary and such other officers and servants as may be necessary for its work. It may maintain such offices in those major centres of employment in Great Britain as it thinks fit for the purpose of discharging its functions. Although its functions are performed on behalf of the Crown, it is not subject to directions of any kind from any minister of the Crown as to the manner in which it exercises any of its functions. These functions are: collective conciliation, arbitration, mediation, advice, individual conciliation, and inquiry.

Collective conciliation

ACAS may offer its assistance to the parties when a trade dispute exists, or is apprehended, in order to bring about a settlement. This may be at the request of the employer and/or the trade union concerned, or the approach may be made on the initiative of ACAS.

The essential characteristic of conciliation is its voluntary nature. As the settlement of dispute is a matter for the parties themselves to resolve, the involvement of ACAS is only requested when the parties have exhausted their own procedures for the settlement of disputes without resolving the dispute, or when the parties agree that overriding considerations require the services of a conciliator. All agreements subsequently reached in conciliation are the responsibility of the parties in dispute.

During 1990 ACAS received 1,260 requests for collective conciliation: 50 per cent related to pay and terms and conditions of employment; 14 per cent related to recognition; 13 per cent related to dismissal and discipline.

Arbitration

Three conditions must be fulfilled before ACAS may refer a dispute to arbitration. The consent of each of the parties must be obtained; the agreed procedures for settling disputes must have been used and have failed to produce a settlement; and the likelihood of an agreement being reached by conciliation must have been considered and rejected.

There are three modes of arbitration, namely the use of a single arbitrator, the appointment of a special board of arbitration and reference to the Central Arbitration Committee.

A single arbitrator is appointed by ACAS from a panel of experienced arbitrators. This method is speedy and confidential and is especially suitable for the settlement of local disputes.

Boards of arbitration are usually set up for the larger or more significant disputes. The board consists of an independent chairman, appointed by ACAS, and an equal number of members, representing employer and trade union interests in the dispute. The parties to the dispute are asked to agree that, if the members of the board fail to reach unanimous agreement on their award, the chairman will have the full powers of an umpire to decide the matter. Both a single arbitrator and a board may call upon the services of assessors to provide professional or expert knowledge where technical or complex matters are in issue. Assessors take no part in the award-making process.

Central Arbitration Committee; ACAS may refer a dispute to the Central Arbitration Committee (CAC) at the request of the parties to the dispute. The CAC is a permanent arbitration tribunal and consists of a chairman and members representative of employees' and employers' interests. The chairman has the powers of an umpire where the Committee fails to reach a unanimous decision.

Mediation

Mediation is another method of helping to resolve disputes. It is mid-way between conciliation and arbitration, in that the mediator commences by way of conciliation, but nevertheless formulates proposals or recommendations, which the parties may accept, or use as a basis for negotiations which will lead to a settlement.

As the parties are not bound to accept the mediator's proposals or recommendations, it is an acceptable format where the parties are unwilling to commit themselves to arbitration and a binding award. A single mediator or a board of mediation may be appointed, and all such appointments are from outside ACAS.

Advice

ACAS also provides free advice to employers, employers' associations, employees and trade unions on various aspects of industrial relations and employment policies. It offers a wide range of services including advisory visits to firms, conducting diagnostic and other surveys, instituting projects, organising seminars and conferences, and setting up working parties to examine deep-seated industrial relations problems.

Individual conciliation

ACAS conciliation officers are under a statutory obligation to endeavour to settle complaints made by individuals alleging infringement of certain employment rights. A copy of a complaint presented to an industrial tribunal must also be sent to a conciliation officer, who must seek to resolve the complaint without recourse to a tribunal hearing. ACAS received 52,071 cases for individual conciliation in 1990; 56 per cent reached a conciliated settlement; 21 per cent proceeded to a tribunal hearing; 23 per cent were withdrawn.

Inquiry

ACAS may inquire into any question relating to industrial relations generally, or in a particular industry, undertaking or part of an undertaking. The results of the inquiry may be published, if considered desirable, after sending a draft of the findings to the parties and taking account of their views.

Codes of practice

ACAS may issue Codes of Practice containing practical guidance for employers and trade unions, with the object of promoting the improvement of industrial relations. Every code must be published initially in a draft form, and any representations as to its content must be considered before its eventual publication. It must also be approved by both Houses of Parliament.

Three Codes of Practice have been issued dealing with: disciplinary practice and procedures in employment, disclosure of information to trade unions for the purposes of collective bargaining, and time off for trade union duties and activities.

Central Arbitration Committee (CAC)

The Committee is a permanent, independent arbitration body maintained at the Crown's expense, but not subject to any directions from any minister of the Crown as to the way in which it exercises any of its functions.

Composition

It consists of a chairman, a deputy chairman and two panels consisting of members with experience as employers' or employees' representatives. Each member has experience of industrial relations and arbitration and is appointed for an initial term of five years.

Cases are usually heard by a committee of three, consisting of a chairman and two members, drawn from each panel. The Committee may, however, sit in two or more divisions with such membership as the chairman directs, and may be advised by assessors.

Jurisdiction

The Committee fulfils a traditional role as an arbitration body, with its origins in the Industrial Court, set up in 1919. It may arbitrate in any matter relating to a trade dispute, if one party so requests and the other party (or parties) agree. The dispute must have been initially referred to ACAS, who must have concluded that conciliation or the existing dispute procedures could not produce a satisfactory agreement.

The Committee may arbitrate, at the request of one party, when an independent recognised trade union may present a complaint that an employer has failed to disclose certain information necessary for collective bargaining. If the Committee finds the complaint justified, it makes a declaration as to what information is to be disclosed. If the employer refuses to comply, a claim may then be made to the Committee for improved terms and conditions for those employees.

The Committee may also amend any collective agreement, employee pay structure or wage regulation order which contains a provision applying to men or women only. In such a case, reference may be made to the Committee by any party to a collective agreement, by the employer concerned in the pay structure, or in all cases by the Secretary of State.

Procedure

The Committee is not bound by precedent, but nevertheless seeks to achieve consistency in its decisions. The parties are invited to submit and exchange evidence before the hearing. The procedure at the hearing seeks to avoid the formality of a court of law, by amplification of the written evidence, by explanation, question and discussion, rather than by examination and cross-examination of witnesses. A hearing may be adjourned if it appears that the parties may be able to reach an agreement on their own, or with the aid of conciliation, and they are prepared to try to do so. Costs are not awarded.

Although the parties usually agree on the terms of reference and undertake to honour any award made, an award does not bind the parties in law.

The Committee does not usually inform the parties at the hearing of its decision. They are notified in writing of the decision in a report which also contains an indication of the considerations which have led to the decision. The report may also contain advice or comments which may be of assistance to the parties.

Voluntary arbitration cases are held in private and the awards will not be published, unless the parties so wish.

13

TRADE UNIONS

Definition

A trade union is defined in section 28 of TULRA as an organisation (whether permanent or temporary) which either:

1 consists wholly or mainly of workers of one or more descriptions, and whose principal purposes include the regulation of relations between workers and employers' associations; or

2 consists wholly or mainly of:
(a) employers or individual proprietors whose principal purposes include the regulation of relations between employers and workers or trade unions;
(b) constituent or affiliated organisations with those purposes or representatives of such constituent or affiliated organisations whose principal purposes include the regulation of relations between employers and workers or between its constituent or affiliated organisations.

An employer's association is defined in similar terms in TULRA s28(2).

Status

Section 2 of TULRA defines the status of a trade union in the following terms:

(a)   it is capable of making contracts;

(b)   all trade union property must be vested in trustees in trust for the union;

(c)   it is capable of suing and being sued in its own name;

(d)   criminal proceedings may be brought against it in its own name;

(e)   any judgment, order or award made in proceedings against a trade union is enforceable against its trust property.

It further states that a trade union shall not be a body corporate, i.e. formed as a company. An exception is granted in the case of those organisations who were on the register created by the Industrial Relations Act 1971, i.e. professional organisations engaged in collective bargaining on their members' behalf, whose status was derived from their charter of incorporation or from their incorporation under the Companies Acts. Other than these, any purported registration by a trade union as a company, industrial society or provident society is void.

As a trade union does not have a legal personality it may not sue for libel, in respect of its reputation, as it does not have the legal personality which could be protected under the Defamation Act (*EEPTU v. Times Newspapers*).

A rule or purpose of a trade union is not unlawful or unenforceable by reason only that such a rule or purpose is in restraint of trade.

Although the characteristics of an employers' association are similar to (a)–(e) above, it differs from a trade union in that it may be incorporated under the Companies Act, i.e. a company, or it may be an unincorporated association (TULRA s3).

Classification

1   Listed trade union

An organisation of workers which satisfies the statutory definition of a trade union has the legal status of a trade union. It is therefore entitled to have its name entered on the list of trade unions. The list is kept by the certification officer, an official whose functions were previously carried out by the chief registrar of friendly societies, and is available for public inspection, free of charge, at all reasonable hours. It also includes the names of organisations registered as trade unions under earlier legislation, organisations affiliated to the TUC, and organisations formed by amalgamations of organisations previously registered as trade unions. The fact that an organisation is included in this list is evidence that it is a trade union and that it is entitled to a certificate stating that it is listed.

One advantage of obtaining this certificate is that the trade union is entitled to certain tax exemptions on its provident fund income. The issue of a certificate is the first step in obtaining a certificate of independence.

The certification officer may remove a trade union from the list if requested to do so by the organisation. He may also remove an organisation from the list if it appears to him that it is not a trade union, or if he is satisfied that the organisation has ceased to exist. There is a right of appeal to the Employment Appeal Tribunal against a decision of the certification officer.

2 Independent trade union

A listed trade union may apply to the certification officer for a certificate that it is independent. It must show (*a*) that it is not under the domination or control of an employer or a group of employers or of one or more employers' associations, and (*b*) that it is not liable to interference by an employer or any such group or association (arising out of the provision of financial or material support or by any other means whatsoever) tending towards such control.

The larger unions have little difficulty in satisfying these criteria. The smaller unions, especially staff associations, must be looked at very closely to see whether that degree of independence exists.

The decision as to whether a trade union is independent is taken by the certification officer after consultation with other interested parties, e.g. other trade unions. The decision is subject to a right of appeal, on a question of law or fact, to the Employment Appeal Tribunal.

Factors to be taken into consideration by the certification officer in deciding whether a union is independent include:

(a)   the degree of participation (if any) of the company's senior management in the union's affairs, and the restrictions (if any) placed on that participation;

(b)   the financial independence of the union, i.e. its non-dependence on the employer;

(c)   the facilities provided by the employer, and the effect on the union of a withdrawal of those facilities;

(d)   its record of collective bargaining with the employer and its status in disputes procedures;

(e)   its membership base, e.g. a union composed entirely of employees of a single company is more likely to be influenced or dominated by that employer.

An independent trade union has certain advantages.

(a)   Its representatives are entitled to receive information for bargaining purposes and to be informed and consulted in cases of redundancy and under the Transfer of Undertakings (Protection of Employment) Regulations 1981.

(b)   Employees who are members of independent trade unions are entitled to time off for trade union activites. Employees who are officials of such unions are entitled to time off work (with pay) in order to undertake industrial relations training.

(c)   Employees have a right to join an independent trade union and take part in its activities. A union member who claims that he was dismissed for trade union membership may apply for interim relief.

(d)   It may obtain payments from the certification officer in order to hold secret ballots. It may also use an employer's premises to hold a ballot.

(e)   It may appoint safety representatives from among the employees.

(f)   It is entitled to be consulted about contracting out of occupational pension schemes.

3   Recognised trade union

An independent trade union must be recognised by the employer for the purposes of collective bargaining in order to enjoy certain rights conferred by statute. A recognised trade union is entitled to: receive bargaining information; be consulted on impending redundancies; appoint safety representatives; and be notified and consulted with regard to company pension schemes. Its members are also entitled to time off work for union duties and activities.

4   *Special register bodies*

These are organisations whose names were entered on the special register maintained under the Industrial Relations Act 1971. They consist of companies registered under the Companies Act 1948 or incorporated by charter or letters patent, e.g. British Medical Association, Royal College of Nursing.

Although these organisations are principally concerned with the maintenance and advancement of professional standards and training, they nevertheless take an active interest in the regulation of industrial relations.

The main difference between these bodies and other trade unions is that a special register body is a corporate body, while a trade union may not register under the Companies Acts. Special register bodies enjoy certain immunities granted to other trade unions in respect of tort, actions in tort and the doctrine of restraint of trade. Unlike other trade unions, they are not obliged to keep accounting records, to audit their accounts, or to submit annual returns.

——————————— Union rules ———————————

The rules of a trade union are set out in its rule book and constitute a binding contract between the union and its members. A member is therefore entitled to enforce a union's rules, and to sue the union's officials if they are in breach of the rules.

The courts have recognised the fact that the rules are not the only source of the agreement between the union and its members. It was stated in *Heaton's Transport v. TGWU* that 'it is not to be assumed that all the terms of the agreement are to be found in the rule book alone; particularly as respects the discretion conferred by the members upon committees or officials of the union as to the way in which they may act on the union's behalf' (per Lord Wilberforce).

In drafting its rules, a union is free to decide whom it will admit to membership, subject to certain limited exceptions. It may also impose any qualification it deems necessary for membership.

In *Boulting v. ACTAT*, a trade union sought to recover arrears of subscriptions from the plaintiffs, who had been members of the union, but had ceased to pay their subscriptions. The plaintiffs, who were managing directors of a film company, sought an injunction against the union as they contended that they were ineligible for membership in that they were directors and producers. It was held that they were eligible for membership as they exercised the functions of employees on the production floor.

Although the courts strictly interpret the rules relating to the procedural and substantive requirements for membership, a rule will not be regarded as invalid solely on the basis of its arbitrary character. In *Faramus v. Film Artistes Association*, a union rule provided that a person with a criminal record was ineligible for membership. The plaintiff at the age of 17 had been convicted of a criminal offence during the German occupation of the Channel Islands, but had not disclosed this fact. It was held that he was not a member of the union as he had never been eligible for membership. As more than four times as many people sought employment as film extras as there were jobs, 'the rules as to admission of membership must inevitably be in some degree arbitrary'.

A trade union is subject to the following Statutory limitations:

1 the rules must contain a term giving a member the right to terminate his membership on giving reasonable notice and complying with any reasonable conditions;
2 the rules must not discriminate against a person on the grounds of sex or race with regard to the terms on which a trade union is prepared to admit that person to membership, or by refusing or deliberately omitting to accept that person's application for membership;
3 the rules must not discriminate against a person on the grounds of being an EC national.

The question of reasonableness must be determined in accordance with equity and the substantial merits of the case. A union will not be regarded as having acted reasonably only if it has acted in accordance with its rules, or unreasonably if it has acted in contravention of its rules.

At common law, the courts have adopted a broad approach to the construction of a union's rules, looking to the intent and purpose of the rule, rather than seeking legal precision and clarity.

'Trade union rule books are not drafted by parliamentary draughts-men. Courts of law must resist the temptation to construe them as if they were; for that is not how they would be understood by the members who are the parties to the agreement of which the terms, or some of them, are set out in the rule book, or how they would be, and in fact were, understood by the experienced members of the Court' (Lord Wilberforce in *Heaton's Transport v. TGWU*).

The courts may therefore take into account the customs and practices of a union, as long as they do not conflict with a union rule. In the case of such a conflict, the rule will prevail. In *Heaton's Transport v. TGWU*, the court considered the scope and authority of a shop steward in the light of customary practice, as the union's rules were unclear on this matter.

The courts have always strictly scrutinised those rules which affect a member's livelihood, in particular those concerned with discipline and expulsion.

A trade union cannot exclude the courts as final arbitrators in questions of law. Although a union rule may provide that the internal remedies in the rules must be exhausted before a member can apply to the courts, the courts are not bound by such a provision. In this situation the member must show a reason why he should not initially exhaust the domestic remedies, as there is a presumption at common law that the internal procedures should be exhausted before a court intervenes in a grievance between a member and his union. If a question of law is involved, the courts may intervene at any stage of the proceedings.

Every member has the right to apply to the courts to pursue a grievance against the union (irrespective of any procedures laid down in the union's rules) at any time after six months from the date of his application to the union. The court must deal with the application, even though the member has not exhausted the internal procedures available under the union's rule book or the rule book states that the internal procedures must be followed before recourse is had to the courts (EA 88 s2).

If the court is satisfied that the delay in operating the internal procedures was due to the unreasonable conduct of the member, it may extend the six-month period (EA 88 s2).

Even if an application to a union to have the matter in dispute determined under the union's rule book is invalid, it will nevertheless be deemed valid for the purpose of exercising this right unless the union explains fully to the applicant within 28 days why his application was invalid (EA 88 s3).

The common law presumption against intervention before exhausting internal procedures still applies if a member seeks the aid of the court before the six-month limit.

The courts may intervene before the commencement of disciplinary proceedings, if it can be shown that no reasonable tribunal, acting in good faith, could uphold the complaint. In *Esterman v. NALGO*, a member disobeyed a union order not to volunteer to assist in certain local government elections. She obtained an injunction to prevent her branch committee from considering whether her conduct was such as to render her unfit for membership, as the court considered that, on the facts, it would be impossible to convict a member of such a charge.

Discipline

A trade union, in exercising a disciplinary function, is acting in a quasi-judicial capacity. It must therefore abide by the rules of *natural justice* and a failure to observe these rules will render any disciplinary actions void.

1   A member must be given *notice of the charges* levelled against him, of the rule which it is alleged that he has broken, and of the penalties which could be applied if the charge is proven. He must also be allowed sufficient time to prepare a defence.

In *Lawlor v. Union of Post Office Workers*, a plaintiff and other members of a district council of the union refused to give an assurance to the general secretary of the union that they would discontinue advocating a policy which was in contradiction of official union policy. The executive council of the union followed the general secretary's recommendation and expelled Lawlor and his colleagues from the union. The expulsion was set aside, for although the executive council were given a power of expulsion, Lawlor and his colleagues had not been informed in advance that disciplinary action against them was pending and so had not been given an opportunity to present their case to the executive council.

If during the proceedings the union wish to vary the charges or bring fresh charges against a member, the process must recommence. In

Annamunthodo v. Oilfield Workers' Union, the appellant was charged with four offences in breach of the union rules. None of the rules gave power to expel the appellant. He attended the initial hearing of the union's general council and denied the charges. The hearing was adjourned, but he did not attend the adjourned hearing. He was later notified that he had been convicted of all charges and had been expelled under another rule to which no reference had been made in the original charges. It was held that to proceed under an additional rule at the adjourned hearing, without adjourning to give the appellant notice, was contrary to natural justice and the expulsion was invalid.

2   A member must be given the opportunity to be heard by the committee making the decision and must be given a reasonable opportunity of answering the charges (*Annamunthodo v. Oilfield Workers' Trade Union*). The hearing must be fairly conducted, and the union officials must act in good faith and must not pre-judge the issues before the hearing.

In *Roebuck v. National Union of Mine Workers,* the plaintiff was disciplined by the union for allegedly misleading the union's solicitors in a case involving the Yorkshire area president. The disciplinary proceedings were chaired by the area president, who had initiated the proceedings and had earlier expressed a view concerning the member's guilt. It was held that the disciplinary proceedings were void.

In *Taylor v. National Union of Seamen,* the plaintiff was dismissed by the union's general secretary for insubordination. He appealed against the dismissal to the executive council. The general secretary chaired the meeting, and after the plaintiff had withdrawn, the meeting was treated to various statements which were not the subject of the charge, but were prejudicial to the plaintiff. It was held that as the plaintiff had no opportunity of rebutting these statements, the hearing was in breach of the rules of natural justice.

Unjustified disciplinary action

A union member has a general right not to be unjustifiably disciplined by the union. Disciplinary action in respect of the following would not be justified:

1   failure by a member to participate in or support any strike or industrial action, whether by members of that union or by others, or indicating opposition to or lack of support for any such action;

2   failure by a member to contravene, in connection with a strike or other industrial action, any requirement imposed on a union member by a contract of employment or by any other agreement made with his employer;

3   making an allegation that the union or a union official or representative or trustee of the union's property has contravened or is proposing to contravene the union's rules or otherwise act unlawfully, including bringing legal proceedings against the union;

4   encouraging or assisting any other person to:
    (a) perform an obligation imposed on him by a contract of employment;
    (b) make the kind of allegation mentioned in 3;

5   approaching the Commissioner for the Rights of Trade Union Members or the certification officer for advice or assistance on any matter or consulting any other person about an actual or contemplated allegation against the union or its officers;

6   contravening any requirement imposed by a determination of the union which amounts to an infringement of the member's rights, e.g. refusing to pay a fine imposed in 'unjustifiable' disciplinary proceedings;

7   proposing or preparing to engage in conduct outlined in 1 to 6 above.

However, a member will *not* be unjustifiably disciplined:

(a)   if the union disciplines him for an action, omission or statement, irrespective of whether it is in connection with the conduct set out in 1 to 7 above, e.g. a union may discipline a member for refusing to pay union dues (a separate breach of rules) at a time when he is disobeying an instruction to take industrial action;

(b)   if the reason for the disciplinary action is that a false allegation has been made under 3 above and that the member knew that it was false or otherwise acted in bad faith.

Disciplinary action includes the following actions carried out under the union's rules by a union official or by a number of persons including an official:

1   expelling an individual from the union (or branch or section);
2   the payment of fines and other financial penalties by an individual;
3   diverting an individual's union subscriptions or treating them as unpaid;
4   depriving an individual of access to benefits, services or facilities that would normally be available through union membership;
5   encouraging or advising another trade union (or any of its branches or sections) not to accept that individual as a member;
6   subjecting that individual to any other detriment (EA 88 s3).

A complaint by a member that he has been unjustifiably disciplined may be presented to an industrial tribunal. The application must be made within three months of the alleged infringement unless the industrial tribunal was satisfied that:

(a)   it was not reasonably practicable to present the complaint within that time;
(b)   the reason for the delay was that the member was making a reasonable attempt to pursue an appeal against the decision or to have it reconsidered or reviewed.

If the tribunal finds that the applicant has been unjustifiably disciplined it must make a declaration to that effect. There is a right of appeal to the EAT on a question of law.

An individual will not be able to make a complaint of unjustifiable discipline when he has an alternative remedy under section 4 of EA 80 in cases of unreasonable expulsion or exclusion from union membership where there is a closed shop in operation. If the expulsion or exclusion is for any of the reasons set out in section 3 (above), e.g., the complainant has failed to support industrial action, it is deemed to be unreasonable for the purposes of section 4 of EA 1980.

The applicant may also seek compensation in addition to a declaration. A separate application must be made to the tribunal or to the EAT, no earlier than four weeks, or later than six months, from the date of the tribunal's declaration.

(a)   If the union has revoked its decision or taken the necessary steps to reverse its disciplinary measures, the application is made to the tribunal.
(b)   If the union has not done so, the application must be made to the EAT.

In either case the tribunal or the EAT may award such compensation as appears just and equitable in the circumstances.

An award of compensation may be reduced either as a result of contributory fault on the part of the applicant or as a result of his failure to mitigate against loss.

The maximum compensation that may be awarded by a tribunal is 30 times one week's pay (maximum £198 per week = £5,940); and the maximum compensation award for unfair dismissal cases is £10,000.

If an application is made to the EAT these figures apply and there is also a statutory minimum figure of £2,650. This sum must be awarded even if the unjustified disciplinary action amounted to a small fine (EA 88 ss4, 5).

Expulsion

The power to expel a member must be expressly reserved in a union rule book, as such a right cannot be implied in the rules.

In *Spring v. National Amalgamated Stevedores & Dockers Society*, a union had admitted to membership members of the Transport and General Workers Union in breach of the 'Bridlington Agreement' relating to the 'poaching' of members of another union. The TUC ordered the union to expel the members, and it complied with the TUC ruling. The expulsion was invalid, as the union's rules did not provide for expulsion and such a power could not be implied into the rules.

The rules may confer on the union a general power of expulsion, e.g. for acting contrary to the interests of the union; or particular powers of expulsion which specify the circumstances in which the power can be invoked, e.g. failing to pay the union subscriptions.

Acting contrary to the interests of the union   Such a phrase is ambiguous and validity of an expulsion on these grounds has been challenged in the courts on numerous occasions. In *Kelly v. NATSOPA*, a union was given the power by its rules to expel a member for 'conduct detrimental to the interests of the union'. A union member was expelled under this rule, as he worked part-time in the day as a porter, in addition to his full-time employment at night as a printer. The union felt that his full-time work would be adversely affected and that fatigue might make him a danger to his fellow workers. It was held that his expulsion was invalid, as his conduct was not considered by the court to be detrimental. In *Evans v. NUPBPW,* an applicant was accepted for membership of a union on condition that he worked as a casual jobbing hand for a firm of printers. After periods of absence the firm gave his job to a non-unionist. Despite being told by the union that he must do the work, he refused to do so. It was held that his expulsion was lawful as he had acted to the union's detriment.

However, the power of expulsion must be exercised in strict compliance with the provisions of the union's rules. In *Bonsor v. Musicians Union,* a union rule provided that a member could be expelled by a branch committee if his subscriptions were 26 weeks in arrears. Bonsor, whose subscriptions were 52 weeks in arrears, was expelled by his branch secretary. It was held that his expulsion was void as the power of expulsion could only be exercised by the branch committee, and he was awarded damages against the union.

In *Blackall v. National Union of Foundry Workers,* a union member was fined for working overtime, contrary to a union instruction. He refused to pay the fine, and his subscription, and was expelled for non-payment of his subscription two days before the final date for payment. It was held that the expulsion was two days premature and therefore void.

Where a rule is found to be ambiguous, the courts will interpret such a rule in favour of the weaker party, i.e. the union member. In *Lee v. Showmen's Guild of Great Britain,* a member was expelled after a dispute over a pitch at Bradford fair. He was fined for indulging 'in unfair competition' under the rules of the Guild and was expelled when he refused to pay the fine. It was held that as the Guild had misconstrued the meaning of the term 'unfair competition', Lee's expulsion was void.

Every trade union member who is employed by or seeks employment with an employer where a union membership agreement (closed shop) is in operation, has the right not to be unreasonably expelled from the trade union specified in the union membership agreement (EA 1980 s4).

Remedies for wrongful expulsion

As an action for wrongful expulsion is technically an action for breach of contract, an expelled member may seek the appropriate remedy from the courts.

Injunction

A member may seek an injunction ordering union officials not to proceed with the wrongful expulsion, or not to bar his reinstatement, as may be the case.

Damages

A member may seek damages, in addition to the other remedies, to compensate him for any loss sustained as a result of wrongful expulsion. In *Edwards v. SOGAT*, a printer worked for a firm which operated a 'closed shop' and had a 'check off' arrangement with SOGAT. Due to an administrative error the union failed to arrange that his subscription was deducted from his wages, as had been agreed between Edwards and his employer. He fell into arrears, and under a rule which provided that he should automatically cease to be a member if his subscriptions were six weeks in arrear, he ceased to be a member and was dismissed by his employer. SOGAT conceded that he had been wrongfully expelled and he was awarded damages of £3,500 (1971).

Declaration

A declaration declares the position of the parties in law. Although it is of moral value only, it is nevertheless observed by the parties. In *Silvester v. National Union of Printers*, a union fined a member for refusing to work overtime. He refused to pay the fine and was subsequently expelled. He obtained a declaration from the courts that the union had misconstructed its own rules, and that his expulsion was *ultra vires* and void.

A member who is unreasonably expelled from a union, or a person who is unreasonably refused membership of a union, where employment is conditional on membership of that union (a closed shop), may make a complaint to a tribunal within six months of the date of expulsion or refusal of membership. An appeal may be made on a question of law or fact to the EAT.

If a tribunal finds the complaint to be well founded, it must make a declaration to that effect, and may also make an award of compensation. The amount of compensation is 'such as the tribunal considers appropriate for the purpose of compensating the applicant for the loss sustained by him in consequence of the refusal or expulsion which was the subject of the complaint'. The maximum award is 30 weeks' pay, plus the maximum compensatory award for unfair dismissal (£15,940). If the union refuses to abide by the tribunal's decision, the complainant may seek redress from the EAT, which may make an award of up to a maximum of 52 weeks' pay plus the maximum award of an industrial tribunal (£26,236).

Unlawful use of property by a union's trustees

A member may apply for a High Court order if he considers that the union's trustees have permitted an unlawful application of the union's property, or are planning to do so, or are proposing it follows an unlawful direction given to them under the union's rules.

If the court finds the application well founded it may make such order as it considers appropriate, including:

1   requiring the trustees to take steps to protect or recover the union's property;
2   appointing a receiver;
3   removing one or more of the trustees.

If the trustees act, or propose to act, in contravention of a court order, the court must remove all the trustees, unless a trustee can satisfy the court that there is a good reason for allowing him to remain as trustee.

Assistance may be available to a member bringing legal proceedings against the trustees from the Commissioner for Rights of Trade Union Members (EA 88 s9).

Indemnifying unlawful conduct

It is unlawful to use any of the union's property to indemnify an individual in respect of any penalty imposed on him for a criminal offence or for contempt of court. Any payment made to an individual is recoverable by the union and an individual is liable to account to the union for the value of any property applied for this purpose.

If the union unreasonably fails to take steps to recover such property from an individual, any member may apply to the High Court. If the court is satisfied that the union's failure is unreasonable it may authorise the member to continue proceedings on the union's behalf and at the union's expense.

These provisions apply to criminal offences only, and a union may lawfully indemnify an individual in respect of damages following a *civil* action, e.g. a libel action.

Assistance may be available to a union member, from the Commissioner for Rights of Trade Union Members, in such proceedings (EA 88 s8).

Inter-union disputes

The Trade Union Congress (TUC), at its conference in Bridlington in 1939, drew up a series of rules, known as the Bridlington Agreement, to deal with inter-union disputes. These were amended and extended in 1969 by the Croydon recommendations. In particular these rules deal with the poaching by one union of the members of another union and the extension of a union's sphere of influence. A union must not accept a member of another union whose contributions are outstanding, or who is 'under discipline or penalty'. Neither may a union commence organising activities at any 'establishment or undertaking in respect of any grade of workers in which another union has the majority of workers employed and negotiates wages and conditions unless by arrangement with that union'.

As a result of *Spring v. National Amalgamated Stevedores and Dockers Society*, the TUC drew up a model rule designed to overrule the decision, and enabling a union to expel a member in order to comply with a TUC ruling. It invited all affiliated unions to incorporate this model rule in their rule books.

The effect of one of these rules was considered in *Rothwell v. APEX*. APEX had affected a merger under the Trade Union (Amalgamation) Act 1964 with a staff association (SAGA) in the insurance industry. Another union, ASTMS, objected to the merger and the TUC Disputes Committee upheld the objection on the grounds that APEX had recruited the members of the smaller union from the area where ASTMS was the appropriate union. In consequence of this ruling, APEX expelled all those members of SAGA who had joined it as a result of the merger. It was held that the expulsion was invalid as ASTMS had never had anything near to

50 per cent membership of the company concerned (as required by the Bridlington Agreement). The decision of the disputes committee was therefore *ultra vires* and void. It was also unlawful for the union to attempt to undo a merger which had been properly carried out according to statute.

The decision in *Cheall v. APEX* also upholds the TUC disputes machinery. APEX admitted to membership a member of ACTSS without making inquiries of his former union. ACTSS complained to the disputes committee, which ordered APEX to terminate the plaintiff's membership. When APEX complied, the plaintiff brought an action for wrongful expulsion. It was held that his expulsion was valid and was not contrary to the rules of natural justice, as the parties to the dispute were unions. The House of Lords also held that the Bridlington Agreement was not contrary to public policy.

An employer who is caught in the middle of an inter-union dispute may seek the assistance of ACAS.

———————— The political fund ————————

The majority of trade unions engage in political activities and set aside funds to further these activities. The Trade Union Act 1913 stipulates that payments for political purpose can only be made from the union's political fund, which must be kept separate from the general fund. A majority of the membership must approve the establishment of a political fund.

A resolution to establish a political fund must be passed every 10 years by balloting all the union's members. If approved, a union may establish a separate political fund. Any resolutions passed before March 31 1986 lapse if they have not been renewed by that date. The ballot must be conducted in a manner approved of by the certification officer, who must be satisfied that all the members are accorded equal entitlement to vote, without interference or constraint by the union, its members, officials or employees and, as far as is reasonably practical, without incurring any direct cost to himself. As far as is reasonably practicable, every member who is entitled to vote must have the opportunity to vote either at his place of work (or other convenient place) or by post. The voting must be in secret, and the votes must be fairly and accurately counted (Trade Union Act 1913 s4 as amended by TUA 84).

Any member who does not wish to contribute to the fund must be free to contract out, and must not be placed at any disadvantage if he does so, other than in relation to the control or management of the political fund. However, a non-contributor may hold office partly concerned with the management of the political fund. In *Birch v. NUR*, the rules of the union provided that a non-contributor should be 'ineligible to occupy any office or representative position involving any such control or management'. The plaintiff was elected a branch chairman, but the union's national executive declared his election invalid as the union's political fund was controlled by a committee of all branch chairmen. It was held that the national executive's actions amounted to unlawful discrimination, as the plaintiff's office was only partly concerned with the management of the fund.

Members must be informed of their right not to contribute and those members who do not wish to contribute may give written notice which must take effect by the following January 1. If union dues are deducted from pay under a check-off agreement an employer may not deduct any sum equivalent to the political fund payment after notification, in writing, by the employee that he is no longer contributing to the political fund.

A member who complains that a ballot held on the political fund has not conformed, or that a ballot or proposed ballot does not conform, to the rules approved by the certification officer may apply to the certification officer or to the court for a declaration. The application must be made within 12 months of the announcement of the result of the ballot. The court may make an enforcement order requiring the union either to remedy the defect or hold an appropriate ballot (EA 88 s16).

A political fund may be used for the following purposes:

1 contributing to the funds of a political party or the payment of its expenses;
2 providing any service or property for use by or on behalf of any political party;
3 registration of electors, the candidature of any person, the selection of any candidate or holding any ballot by the union in connection with any election to a political office;
4 maintenance of any holder of a political office;
5 holding any conference or meeting connected with a political party;

6 producing, publishing or distributing any written, filmed or recorded material persuading people to vote for or against a political party or candidate (Trade Union Act 1913 s3 as amended by TUA 84).

If a political fund is established it must consist only of sums contributed to the fund by the members or any other person and property accruing to the fund in the course of administering its assets. No liability of the fund may be discharged out of any of the union's other funds. If at any time there is no resolution in force establishing the political fund, property may not be added to the fund other than that which accrues to the fund in the course of its administration, and no union rule may require any member to contribute to the fund. The union may, however, transfer the whole or any part of the fund to any other fund of the union. Where a political fund resolution lapses the union may nevertheless make political payments out of the fund for six months, but in so doing must not put the fund in deficit. The union must, however, take the necessary steps to ensure that the collection of contributions to the fund is discontinued as soon as is reasonably practicable. A member may apply for a refund of his contributions collected since the lapse of the resolution.

An individual member may apply to the court for a declaration that the rules have been broken and for an order for compliance. If the court finds the case proved against the union it may make an order specifying the steps to be taken by the union and time limits for compliance with the order.

Cessation of deductions of subscriptions

Where an employee certifies to his employer that he has resigned from a trade union or that he has given notice that his membership will terminate on a certain date, the employer must stop deductions of union subscriptions from the employee's pay from that date.

Any further deduction from the employee's pay is deemed to contravene section 1(1) of the Wages Act, if the right to make the deduction is contained in the employee's contract of employment or has been agreed in writing. An employee can apply to an industrial tribunal for an order for his employer to repay the amount unlawfully deducted (EA 88 s7).

Right to inspect accounting records

Every trade union and employers' association must keep proper accounting records and submit audited returns annually to the certification officer (TULRA ss10, 11). It must also keep accounting records available for inspection by its members for six years from January 1 following the period covered by the records. Any member has the right of access to the records in respect of any period when he was a member, even if the member was not a member of the branch or section to which the records relate. The member has the right of inspection within 28 days of making his request, to be accompanied by an accountant and to take or be supplied with such copies or extracts of the accounting records as he may require. The inspection must take place at a reasonable hour and the union may charge 'reasonable administrative expenses' for complying with the request.

If the trade union refuses to comply with the request for inspection of the accounting records the member may apply to the High Court, which can order the union to comply with the statutory provisions.

Register of members

Every trade union must compile and maintain a register of the names and addresses of its members and ensure that, as far as is reasonably practicable, the entries in the register are accurate and are kept up to date. The register may be kept by means of a computer (Trade Union Act 1984 s4).

These provisions are necessary if postal ballots are the primary method of holding elections.

—————— Union secret ballots ——————

The certification officer is empowered to provide financial assistance towards the expenditure incurred by independent trade unions in holding secret ballots for the following purposes:

1   calling or ending a strike or other industrial action;

2   carrying out elections provided for by the rules of a trade union or elections to the national executive as required by TUA 84;

3   electing a worker who is a member of a trade union to be a workplace representative;

4   amending the rules of the union;

5   continuation of the political fund;

6   obtaining a decision on a resolution to approve a transfer or an amalgamation;

7   accepting or rejecting an employer's proposal relating to remuneration, hours of work, level of performance, holidays or pensions;

8   any other purpose as may be specified by the Secretary of State (EA 80 s1 as amended by TUA 84).

At present the scheme covers postal ballot only. Payments may be made towards the postal costs of a ballot, the stationery and printing costs of the voting papers together with any explanatory literature enclosed with the voting papers.

An employer of more than 20 workers must comply with a request of an independent trade union to allow his premises to be used by employees who are members of that union to vote in a secret ballot. The question on the ballot must relate to any of the above purposes (EA 80 s2).

Ballot before industrial action

A trade union must hold a ballot and secure majority support before authorising or endorsing industrial action. A union forfeits the immunity granted to it under section 13 of TULRA if it authorises or endorses a strike or other form of industrial action without obtaining the prior approval of its members in a ballot. It must ballot all those members who it is reasonable to believe will take part in a strike or other industrial action.

If a union does not do so, employers and other affected parties can seek an injunction or damages against the union. Any member may apply to the court for an order requiring the union to stop authorising or endorsing industrial action not supported by a ballot. The court has no power to order a union to hold a ballot but only to refrain from instigating action which is not supported by ballot.

If a member is denied the right to vote in a ballot and is subsequently induced to take part in the action, the union will lose its immunity. Voting is by marking a ballot paper, which must contain a question, however framed, which requires the person voting to answer 'yes' or 'no' as to whether he is prepared to take part or continue to take part in a strike or other industrial action. The ballot paper must also contain the following words, which must not be qualified or commented upon by any other statement on the paper: *'If you take part in a strike or other industrial action you may be in breach of your contract of employment.'*

The strike or other industrial action must commence or be endorsed within four weeks of the date of the ballot. After that time it will be unlawful to initiate industrial action without obtaining the mandate of a fresh ballot. If legal proceedings are commenced against the union during the four-week period, e.g. an injunction prohibiting industrial action or an undertaking given to the court, and if the injunction or the undertaking lapses or is set aside, the union may apply to the court for an order that the time in which industrial action was prohibited will not count towards the four-week period. The application must be made within eight weeks of the original ballot date.

The court may not make an order if it appears that:

(a)   the result of the ballot no longer represents the views of the members;
(b)   an event is likely to occur as a result of which a fresh ballot would result in a vote against industrial action.

The voting paper must specify the name of the person authorised to call on the members to take industrial action when there is a vote in favour. If the call for industrial action comes from another person it will be regarded as unlawful and unsupported by the ballot. No industrial action must have been called, authorised or endorsed before the date of the ballot and any industrial action called by the specified person must take place within the specified time. These provisions are aimed at preventing individual union officials from calling industrial action while negotiations are in progress, unless they have been given specific authority by their unions.

A union must call a separate ballot for each place of work and it is unlawful for a union to organise industrial action at a particular workplace unless a majority have voted in favour at that workplace.

These requirements are relaxed in two situations where a union is allowed to hold an aggregate ballot of its members at different work-places:

(a)   where a union reasonably believes at the time of the ballot that all the members entitled to vote have the same workplace;
(b)   where a union believes that each member who is entitled to vote has a common factor, relating to the terms and conditions of employment, with the other members entitled to vote, which he does not have in common with other members employed by the same employer who are not entitled to vote. If a union ballots some members who have a factor in common, it must ballot all the members who have the same common factor, e.g. if the factor is being an hourly-paid worker, it must ballot all the employer's hourly-paid workers. A common factor must not be the fact that the employees have the same workplace, but a union may always ballot all its members who work for a particular employer as each member is bound to have some factor in common with one or more of the other members balloted (TUA s11(1B)).

The ballot paper must be supplied to each member or be made available to him before, during or immediately after his working hours, at his place of work or at a place which is more convenient for him. Each member must be given an opportunity to vote by post or before, during or immediately after his working hours or at a place which is more convenient for him.

The union must, as soon as is reasonably practical, inform all the members entitled to vote of the number of votes cast, the number of spoilt papers and the number of individuals voting 'yes' and 'no'.

Union elections

A ballot must be held every five years for all the members of a union's principal executive committee. This applies to voting and non-voting members as well as to the union's president and general secretary (or the nearest equivalent position). A non-voting member is defined as one who, under the rules or practice of the union, may attend and speak at a meeting of the principal executive committee, other than in a purely informatory or advisory capacity.

These provisions do not apply to:

1   a principal executive committee member, who is a full-time employee, employed for more than 10 years, and who is within two years of retiring age;

2   a president or general secretary of the union, who is not an employee of the union nor a voting member of the principal executive committee and who has been in office for less than 13 months.

A member elected to the principal executive committee may continue as a member or official for such a period (not exceeding six months) as is necessary to give effect to an election result.

A ballot for electing the union's principal executive committee or for approving a political fund must be a postal ballot.

All members of the union are entitled to vote except:

(a)   members in arrears;
(b)   unemployed members;
(c)   student members, trainee members, apprentices or new members;
(d)   members excluded by the rules from voting.

A union may also incorporate in its rules restrictions as to voting determined by reference to trade or occupation, geographical area, sections of the union, or a combination of these factors.

Voting is by marking the ballot paper by the voter, and every person entitled to vote must be allowed to do so without any interference or constraint imposed by the union or any of its members, employers or officials. So far as is reasonably practicable, the person voting must be able to cast his vote without incurring any direct cost.

Election addresses

A candidate in a union election has the right to prepare an election address which must be distributed with the ballot paper. A union may not impose a limit of less than 100 words on an election address and may not edit or modify an election address without the candidate's consent. The union must ensure, as far as is practical, that the same facilities and restrictions are accorded to each candidate.

Any civil or criminal liability arising from the publication of a candidate's election address is the candidate's sole responsibility, e.g. libel. The union will not be liable in respect of any defamatory material it circulates as part of an address.

Independent scrutineer

A trade union must appoint a qualified independent person as a scrutineer before holding elections for its executive committee or a ballot for the approval of a political fund. The scrutineer's name must be stated on the voting papers.

The union must also send a separate notice to each of its members, or take such other steps to inform them as is customary when matters of general interest are brought to their attention, notifying them of the scrutineer's name, before he begins to carry out his functions. Union members, including the candidates in a union election, are given an opportunity of objecting to the appointment if they have doubts as to the scrutineer's impartiality.

The scrutineer must supervise the production and distribution of all ballot papers. He must act as returning officer and retain custody of all returned ballot papers for one year, or longer if the result is challenged by the court or the certification officer.

He must make a written report on the conduct and result of the ballot to the union stating:

1 the number of voting papers distributed and returned;
2 the number of invalid votes returned;
3 the number of valid votes cast for each candidate or proposition;
4 whether he was satisfied that there was no contravention of any legal requirements and that the arrangements for the ballot or election minimised the risk or any unfairness or malpractice and that he was able to carry out his functions without interference or anyone questioning his independence.

Within three months of receiving the report the union must either send a copy to every union member, or take such other steps to inform them as is customary when matters of general interest are brought to their attention. The union must offer to supply any of its members with a copy of the report, on request, either free or on payment of a reasonable fee (EA 88 s15 as amended by EA 90 s9).

Commissioner for the Rights of Trade Union Members

The Secretary of State may appoint a commissioner for the Rights of Trade Union Members who is to assist union members in taking legal action against their trade union whenever their rights as trade unionists are in jeopardy. Neither the commissioner nor any member of his staff will be Crown servants (EA 88 s19).

The commissioner's function is to provide assistance to union members taking, or contemplating taking, legal action against their union in respect of the following matters:

1 failure to hold a ballot before authorising or endorsing industrial action;
2 a member's right to inspect accounting records;
3 the unlawful use of union property by trustees;
4 the unlawful application of union funds for political purposes;
5 failure to conduct a political fund ballot in accordance with the certification officer's rules;
6 failure to comply with the provisions of the Trade Union Act 1984 in respect of union elections (see page 224).

The Employment Act 1990 extends the power of the commissioner to provide assistance to union members in proceedings arising out of an alleged breach or threatened breach of the union's rules relating to any of the following:

(a)   the appointment or election to, or removal of a person from, any office in the union;
(b)   disciplinary proceedings by the union including expulsion from the union;
(c)   authorising or endorsing industrial action;
(d)   balloting members of the union;
(e)   the application of the union's funds or property;
(f)   the imposition, collection or distribution of any levy for the purposes of industrial action;
(g)   the constitution or proccedings of any union committee, conference or other body (EA 90 s10).

The commissioner may only provide assistance in proceedings falling within the above areas and the person applying for assistance must be an actual or prospective party to those proceedings. He may only act where he receives a request from a union member and may not act on his own initiative. He must, as soon as reasonably practicable after receiving the application, consider it and decide whether and to what extent to grant it. If he decides to provide assistance he must notify the applicant of his decision and the extent of the assistance to be provided. The matters to which the commissioner must have regard, include:

- whether the case raises a question of principle;
- whether it would be unreasonable, having regard to the complexity of the case, to expect the applicant to deal with it unaided;
- whether the case involves a matter of substantial public interest.

If the assistance sought is in connection with an application to the court over union elections or political fund ballots and the certification officer has made a declaration, the commissioner must grant assistance if he thinks the applicant has a reasonable prospect of success.

The assistance which the commissioner may give includes:

(a)   making arrangements to provide legal advice or assistance from a solicitor or counsel;
(b)   making arrangements for the representation of the applicant;
(c)   paying the applicant's costs;
(d)   arrangements for or paying the applicant's costs in a compromise of proceedings (EA 88 s20).

Any expenses incurred by the commissioner in providing assistance will be a first charge on any costs or expenses payable to the applicant, whether by virtue of a court judgment or order or under any compromise or settlement arrived at, to avoid or bring to an end any proceedings (EA 88 s21).

The commissioner may only provide assistance in these matters if it appears to him:

1   that the breach of the rules in question affect, or may affect, members of the union rather than the applicant;
2   that similar breaches have been or may be committed in relation to other members of the union.

The commissioner's powers under section 10 are similar to those laid down in section 20 of the Employment Act 1980 and apply to proceedings in the High Court, but not to applications made to the certification officer (EA 88 s21).

Where a person is receiving assistance from the commissioner in relation to court proceedings, he may, if he so wishes, add after his name in the title of the proceedings 'assisted by the commissioner for the Rights of Trade Union Members'.

14

THE LAW
——— RELATING TO ———
INDUSTRIAL ACTION

Virtually every form of industrial action involves, at common law, the commission of a tort or a breach of contract, e.g. an employee who goes on strike is invariably in breach of his contract of employment. The freedom to take industrial action, without incurring any liability in tort, is strictly limited to those acts which are done 'in contemplation or furtherance of a trade dispute'.

——————— Trade dispute ———————

A *trade dispute* is defined by section 29 of TULRA (as amended by the EA 1982) as a dispute between workers and their employers which relates wholly or mainly to one or more of the following:

1 terms and conditions of employment, or the physical conditions in which any workers are required to work;
2 the engagement or non-engagement or termination or suspension of employment or the duties of employment of one or more workers;
3 the allocation of work or the duties of employment between workers or groups of workers;

4 matters of discipline;

5 membership or non-membership of a trade union on the part of a worker;

6 facilities for officials of trade unions;

7 machinery for negotiation or consultation, and other matters relating to the foregoing matters including the recognition by employers or employers' associations of the right of a trade union to represent workers in any such negotiations or consultation or in the carrying out of such procedures.

A lawful trade dispute exists only when workers are in dispute with their own employer, and the dispute is wholly or mainly concerned with employment, pay or conditions of work. A dispute which is connected with these matters rather than wholly or mainly concerned with them is excluded from the definition.

A dispute between a trade union and an employer who is not in dispute is not within the definition of the Act, nor is a dispute between trade unions or groups of workers where no employer is involved. Immunity is granted to a trade dispute which relates to matters occurring outside Great Britain only in so far as the terms and conditions of British workers are affected by the outcome of the dispute.

In *Hadmor Productions Ltd v. Hamilton*, ACTT members employed at Thames Television took a decision to black a series of programmes made by a facility company with freelance ACTT members. The facility company was in the process of selling the programmes to Thames Television. It was held that a trade dispute existed in that it arose out of fears among the technicians at Thames Television for job security in a period of high unemployment.

A strike called for political motives, which has no bearing on employment, is not a trade dispute and therefore has no immunity. In *BBC v. Hearn*, the Association of Broadcasting Staff threatened to take action to prevent transmission of the Cup Final to South Africa, as they opposed racial policies in that country. South Africa was one of a number of countries served by satellite transmission and such action would have blacked out transmission to those other countries. As there was no trade dispute, the BBC was granted an injunction to restrain the union from inducing their members to act in breach of their contracts.

In *Mercury Communications Ltd v. The Post Office Engineering Union*, Mercury was granted a licence to run a telecommunications system in competition with British Telecommunications (BT). The Government also proposed to privatise BT. The Post Office Engineering Union opposed the liberalisation of BT and instructed its members not to connect the Mercury system to the BT system. Mercury applied for an injunction to restrain the union from calling industrial action to prevent the connection of the systems. The Court of Appeal granted an injunction as it was unlikely that the union would be able to establish, at the trial, that the dispute was a trade dispute related to the risk of losing jobs. The union's objections were political as the union was opposed to the breaking of the monopoly of the industry and to privatisation.

In *Express Newspapers v. Keys*, the general secretaries of four print unions instructed their members to withdraw their labour as part of the TUC 'Day of Action' in protest against Government policies. An injunction was granted restraining the unions from inducing their members to act in breach of their contracts, in what was clearly a political strike. The employer was in no position to concede to the demands of those who took part in the industrial action.

A dispute which aims to effect a change in government policy is not necessarily a political dispute. In *Duport Steel v. Sirs*, a trade union, in the course of a prolonged strike with the British Steel Corporation over a wage dispute, called out its members in privately owned steel firms in order to make the strike more effective. Although there was no dispute with the private sector it was held that the union's action was in furtherance of a trade dispute as the union's primary purpose was to persuade the Government, as the paymaster of a nationalised industry, to provide the additional funds to meet a wage claim. This motive did not invalidate the dispute.

'In contemplation of'

Lord Loreburn stated in *Conway v. Wade* that 'either a dispute is imminent and the act is done in expectation of and with a view to it, or that the dispute is already existing and the act is done in support of one side to it'.

In *Bents Brewery Co. Ltd v. Hogan*, a trade union official asked the managers of public houses to disclose information relating to sales and income in these public houses. It was held that the union official was inducing a breach of contract (i.e. disclosure of confidential information by an employee), for although his intention was to obtain information which would help in formulating a claim, there was no dispute in contemplation at that particular time.

A wider interpretation was given to the phrase in 1980 in *Health Computing Ltd v. Meek*. A private company supplying computer systems sought an injunction against NALGO which had instructed its members in the National Health Service not to co-operate with independent computer contractors. NALGO successfully contended that a dispute was contemplated as likely to arise, even though the union had made no demand to management.

'In furtherance of'

The test as to whether an act is 'in furtherance' of a trade dispute is subjective. Immunity will be given if the person who does the act honestly believes at the time he does it that it may help his side to the trade dispute achieve its objectives and he does it for that reason (*Duport Steel Ltd v. Sirs*; *Express Newspapers Ltd v. McShane*).

In *Express Newspapers v. McShane*, the National Union of Journalists was in dispute with the owners of provincial newspapers. In order to make the strike more effective it called upon its members employed by national newspapers to refuse copy from the Press Association which supplied stories to newspapers. The *Daily Express*, which was not a party to the dispute, sought an injunction to restrain the NUJ's action. It was held that the union's action was in furtherance of a trade dispute.

The act in question must further a trade dispute. An act which is motivated by other considerations may not be regarded as relating to a trade dispute.

In *Torquay Hotels Ltd v. Cousins*, a union blacked the plaintiff's hotel after the hotel's managing director had criticised the union's conduct in an existing dispute involving another Torquay hotel. It was held that there was no trade dispute, and hence no immunity, as the dispute between the union and the managing director or his company was a personal dispute.

An act which is initially in furtherance of a trade dispute may be outside the protected formula if the character of the act later changes because of other extraneous factors. In *Huntley v. Thornton*, the plaintiff's union called a one-day strike, but the plaintiff refused to comply with the union instruction and went to work on that day. The district committee of the union recommended that he be expelled from the union, but the union's executive council declined to take action. Nevertheless the local union officials prevented him from obtaining work locally and hounded him out of any job which he succeeded in obtaining. It was held that the local union officials had committed the tort of conspiracy as their acts had become more and more in the nature of a personal vendetta as the matter progressed.

An act may be too remote from the dispute to be in furtherance of that dispute. In *Beaverbrook Newspapers Ltd v. Keys*, the *Daily Mirror* was not published because of a trade dispute. The *Daily Express* decided to publish additional copies to cater for the demand in the market. The general secretary of SOGAT instructed his members at the *Daily Express* not to handle these extra copies, as it would weaken the union's dispute with the *Daily Mirror*. The *Daily Express* sought an injunction to restrain the union from inducing their employees to break their contracts. An injunction was granted: the union's action was not in furtherance of a trade dispute, as its action was 'too remote to be protected by statute'.

———— Secondary action ————

A trade union in dispute with an employer (the primary employer) may take action against other employers (secondary employers), who are not parties to the dispute, in order to exert pressure on the primary employer. This secondary action may consist of calling a strike or threatening a strike or other industrial action by employees of the secondary employers, e.g. inducing the employees of the secondary employer to suspend the supply of goods or services to the primary employer.

Such action is unlawful (EA 1980 s17 as amended by EA 1990 s4) and the only permitted secondary action is peaceful picketing at the primary employer's place of work.

Section 7 of the Employment Act 1990 extends the definition of secondary action. Under section 17 of the Employment Act 1980 (now repealed) liability for secondary action was limited to situations where the action resulted in a breach of commercial contract, i.e. a contract other than an employment contract. Liability now arises for inducing the employees of the secondary employer to break or interfere with their contracts of employment (or threatening to do so), whether or not this results in a breach of commercial contract.

A contract of employment now includes the contract of a self-employed person who contracts personally to work or perform services for another. This nullifies the decision in *Shipping Co. v. International Transport Workers' Federation* where a union had threatened to black a ship by inducing pilots not to pilot the ship out of the harbour. It was held that this was not secondary action as the pilots were self-employed.

Where more than one employer is in dispute with his employees, the dispute between each employer and his employees must be treated as a separate dispute, e.g. a nationwide campaign for an increase in pay in a certain industry, or for a shorter working week.

Action which is primary action in relation to one dispute may not be regarded as secondary action in relation to another dispute, e.g. if there are strikes arising out of trade disputes at two different companies and, as a result, one company fails to deliver goods to the other in breach of contract, the failure to deliver does not amount to secondary action by the organisers of the strike at the first company.

Liability at common law

It is necessary to examine the possible areas of tortious liability which encompass an industrial dispute. The torts in question are:

1 inducing a breach of contract;
2 procuring a breach of contract;
3 conspiracy;
4 intimidation.

1 Inducing a breach of contract

The tort of inducing a breach of contract occurs when a third party unjustifiably induces a breach of contract between an employer and an employee which results in damage to the party concerned. An early example is *Lumley v. Gye*, when Gye was sued for inducing an opera singer named Joanna Wagner to break her contract with the plaintiff, in order to sing at the defendant's theatre.

In order to succeed in an action the plaintiff must prove: the existence of a contract; a breach of that contract; and that the defendant had knowledge of the contract and had induced the breach. It is therefore not unlawful to induce a person not to enter into employment with a certain employer or to induce an employee to terminate his contract by lawful means, e.g. by giving proper notice.

A union official who calls a strike or who takes a significant part in organising a strike may be liable for inducing a breach of contract (as could the trade union). The inducement may take the form of persuasion, instruction, direction, threat, order or communication. Its effect must be to induce a breach of contract.

Liability may also arise if a trade union official induces an employer to dismiss an employee in breach of contract. This form of pressure may be achieved by threats or otherwise. If an employer dismisses an employee as a result of such pressure, but gives the employee the appropriate notice or wages in lieu of notice, no tort is committed.

In contrast to the direct inducement cited above, a trade union may incur liability when it boycotts or blacks a commercial contract and thereby indirectly induces a breach of contract. In *Torquay Hotels Ltd v. Cousins*, a trade union which was in dispute with the plaintiff's hotel company (after criticism of the union's dispute with other hotels in the area), contacted Esso Ltd's drivers who supplied oil to the plaintiff and instructed them not to deliver the fuel. An injunction was granted restraining the union from procuring a breach of the contract by Esso Ltd to supply the hotel with oil, by inducing Esso Ltd's employees to breach their contracts of employment.

Defence

Section 13.1 of TULRA (as amended) provides a defence to this tort. It states: 'An act done by a person in contemplation of furtherance of a trade dispute shall not be actionable in tort on the ground only:

(a)   that it induces another person to break a contract or interferes or induces any other person to interfere with its performance; or

(b)   that it consists in his threatening that a contract (whether one to which he is a party or not) will be broken or its performance interfered with, or that he will induce another person to break a contract or interfere with its performance.'

This section gives protection to a person who, in contemplation or furtherance of a trade union dispute, induces or procures a breach of contract. It covers both employment and commercial contracts.

2 Procuring a breach of contract

The tort of procuring a breach of contract occurs where a defendant induces a third party to act in an unlawful way so as to lead to a breach of or interference with a contract to which the plaintiff is a party. The plaintiff must show that a contract exists; that the defendant induced, persuaded or procured employees to breach their contracts of employment; and that the necessary consequence of the employees' breach of contract is the breach of the contract forming the subject matter of the action.

In *Stratford v. Lindley*, the plaintiff was the chairman of two companies. The holding company employed 48 lightermen, of whom 45 belonged to the Transport and General Workers Union (TGWU) and three to the Watermen's Union (WU). The plaintiff eventually recognised the TGWU for negotiating purposes. The WU, in order to bring pressure on Stratford to make him recognise that union, put an embargo on the barges hired out and repaired by the subsidiary company. As a result the barges were not returned to the company's moorings when the hiring contracts ended, causing a loss to the company of £1,000 a week. The WU were liable for indirectly procuring a breach of contract between the company and the hirers, who under the hiring contract were to return the barges to the company's moorings.

Another aspect of the tort is illustrated by *Daily Mirror Newspapers Ltd v. Gardner*, where the publishers of the *Daily Mirror* notified the wholesalers of a price increase in the paper and of a reduction in the discount allowed to wholesalers. The newspaper retailers, whose profit margin depended on the number of copies sold and the wholesalers' discount, attempted to bring pressure to bear on the company by proposing a week's boycott on the sale of the paper. The company obtained an injunction restraining the officials of the newspaper retailers' association from procuring a breach of the contract between the newspaper company and the wholesalers.

Defence

Section 13.1 of TULRA (as amended) adopts a similar approach to this tort as it does to the tort of inducing a breach of contract, and affords protection against the tort of procuring breach of a commercial contract.

3 Conspiracy

This tort occurs when two or more persons combine to do an act, which although lawful in itself, causes damage to a third party's trade or interests. There is no conspiracy if the real and predominant purpose of the defendants is to advance their legitimate interests. In *Mogul Steamship Co. v. McGregor, Gow and Co.*, the plaintiff alleged that the defendants, who were an associated body of traders in China tea, had caused him loss by threatening certain merchants in China that unless they ceased to act as his agent, the association's agency would be withdrawn from them. It was held that such action could be justified on the grounds of legitimate self-protection.

Another form of conspiracy exists when two or more persons combine to injure a third party by unlawful means. In *Quinn v. Leatham*, a butcher employed non-union labour. He refused to heed a union's request to dismiss the men, but offered to pay their subscription arrears if they were admitted to the union. The trade union officials refused as they wanted to teach the non-unionists a lesson and make them 'walk the streets for 12 months'. The union then persuaded his chief customer to cease dealing with him by threatening to call a strike of that customer's workmen. The customer did so and it was held that the union was liable for conspiracy as its legitimate activities could have been achieved by accepting Leatham's initial offer.

However, certain forms of collective pressures are permissible and lawful. In *Crofter Hand-Woven Harris Tweed Co. v. Veitch*, the TGWU wished to obtain 100 per cent membership in a company manufacturing Harris Tweed on the Isle of Lewis. It therefore instructed the dockers (who were union members) at the port of Stornaway to cease handling yarn imported by the plaintiff company and the finished cloth manufactured from that yarn. The plaintiff company were importing the yarn at a cheaper price than the yarn spun on the island. It was held that as the

TGWU believed in good faith that its action was in the best interests of the Harris Tweed industry, there was no conspiracy.

The House of Lords thus effectively reversed *Quinn v. Leatham* by recognising that establishing a 'closed shop' was a legitimated trade union activity.

Defence

Section 13.4 of TULRA (as amended) provides a defence to this tort. It states: 'An agreement or combination by two or more persons to do or procure the doing of any act in contemplation or furtherance of a trade dispute shall not be actionable in tort if the act is one which, if done without any such agreement or combination, would not be actionable in tort'.

This means that an act which is not actionable if done in contemplation or furtherance of a trade dispute by one individual does not become actionable on the grounds of conspiracy if done by a group of individuals. It is not unlawful for an employee to threaten strike action, and it is not a conspiracy for a group of employees to threaten such action.

4   Intimidation

The tort of intimidation consists of a threat to commit an unlawful act which results in damage to the plaintiff. The case of *Rookes v. Barnard* resurrected this ancient tort in 1964. The Association of Engineering and Shipbuilding Draughtsmen threatened to call a strike at London Airport (in order to preserve an informal closed shop) unless the plaintiff, a non-union member, was dismissed. This action constituted the tort of intimidation. The threat to strike was in breach of contract as a no-strike clause had been incorporated into the contract of every individual employee.

Defence

Section 13.1(b) of TULRA (as amended) gives protection against the tort of intimidation. It states: 'An act done by a person *in contemplation or furtherance of a trade dispute* shall not be actionable in tort on the ground only that it consists in his threatening that a contract (whether one to which he is a party or not) will be broken or its performance interfered with, or that he will induce another person to break a contract or interfere with its performance'.

This section gives protection against a threat to break a contract of employment, and against a threat to induce a breach of contract, or to interfere with its performance.

__ Union membership or recognition __ requirements in contract

Any term or condition in a contract for the supply of goods or services which requires a person to use only union labour, or non-union labour, is void.

It is also unlawful for a person, on the grounds of union membership or non-membership to:

1 exclude a particular person's name from a list of approved suppliers of goods or services;
2 terminate a contract for the supply of goods or services;
3 exclude a particular person from tendering for the supply of goods or services;
4 fail to permit a particular person to submit a tender; or
5 otherwise determine not to enter into a contract with a particular person for the supply of goods or services (EA 1982 s12).

A person who is adversely affected by any of these acts may bring an action in respect of a breach of statutory duty, and so recover damages.

Any term or condition of a contract for the supply of goods or services is void in so far as it purports to require any party to the contract to:

1 recognise one or more trade unions; or
2 negotiate or consult with any official of one or more trade unions (EA 1982 s13).

A breach of this section will entitle an injured party to bring an action for damages.

Section 14 of the EA 1982 provides that any industrial action to induce a person to contravene sections 12 and 13 of the Act (above) is unlawful and is not given the trade dispute immunity of section 13 of TULRA.

Section 14 also provides that any industrial action or threat or industrial action which interferes with the supply of goods and services is unlawful if the reason for taking such action is:

(a)   that work done or to be done in connection with the supply of goods or services has been or is likely to be done by non-union labour or by members of a particular trade union; or

(b)   the supplier of the goods does not employ union labour, or does not recognise, negotiate or consult with a trade union.

These provisions, designed to protect non-union companies, also protect unionised companies against discrimination as they employ union members.

———— Trade union immunity ————

A union's liability in respect of actions for inducing or threatening to induce a breach of contract or for conspiracy is limited to those acts which are authorised or endorsed by a responsible person.
    A responsible person is defined as:

1   the principal executive committee;
2   any other person who is empowered by the union's rules to authorise or endorse such actions;
3   the president or general secretary;
4   any official of the union, whether or not employed by the union, e.g. shop steward;
5   any union committee, i.e. any group of persons constituted in accordance with the union's rules.

An act will not be taken as having been authorised or endorsed by the union if the act was repudiated by the principal executive committee or by the president or general secretary. The repudiation must be made as soon as is reasonably practicable after the purported authorisation or endorsement of the act has come to the knowledge of the principal executive committee, or the president, or the general secretary, who must not behave in a manner which is inconsistent with the purported repudiation. The person who purported to authorise or endorse the act must be notified in writing and without delay of its repudiation, and the union, without delay, must give individual written notice of the fact and date of repudiation to every member of the union who the union has reason to believe is taking part, or might take part in industrial action as a result of the act which is being repudiated and to the employer of every such member.

The notice to members must contain the following statement: 'Your union has repudiated the call (or calls) for industrial action to which this notice relates and will give no support to unofficial industrial action taken in response to it (or them). If you are dismissed while taking unofficial industrial action, you will have no right to complain of unfair dismissal'.

An act will not be treated as repudiated by the principal executive committee, the president or the secretary if they do not immediately confirm the repudiation in writing if so requested, within three months of purported repudiation, by a party to a commercial contract that has been or may be interfered with as a result of the act in question and who has not already been given written notice of the repudiation. (A commercial contract is any contract other than a contract of employment, apprenticeship or for personal services.)

A court, in injunction proceedings against a union, may require the union to take steps to ensure that there is no, or no further, inducement of persons to take part in industrial action and that no person takes part or continues to take part in the industrial action to which the injunction relates.

A trade union which is unable to claim immunity for its actions may be sued for an injunction and damages in tort. The amount which may be awarded as damages against a union is limited, and is determined by the size of the union's membership.

The amounts are as follows:

- £10,000 if the membership is less than 5,000;
- £50,000 if the membership exceeds 5,000 but is less than 25,000;
- £125,000 if the membership exceeds 25,000 but is less than 100,000;
- £250,000 if the membership exceeds 100,000.

Any damages, costs or expenses awarded in an action against a trade union cannot be recovered from protected property of the union. Protected property is defined as:

(a)   property belonging to the trustees, other than in their capacity as trustees;

(b) property belonging to any member, other than property owned jointly with other members;

(c) property belonging to any union official;

(d) property comprised in a political fund or a provident benefit fund.

Strikes

An employee who takes strike action withdraws his labour and is therefore in breach of his contract of employment. An employer may, if he so wishes, treat the contract as terminated.

In *Simmons v. Hoover Ltd*, an employee on strike was dismissed by his employer. It was held that although the real reason for the dismissal was redundancy, the employee was not entitled to a redundancy payment as he had repudiated his contract of employment by taking strike action.

Most employers regard a strike as a suspension of the contract. Many factors dictate this course of action, e.g. industrial relations, the cost of training a new work-force.

This view is also taken by the legislature, as strike action is not regarded as breaking continuity of employment in calculating an employee's length of service when claiming a redundancy payment, compensation for unfair dismissal, or entitlement to maternity leave and pay. The period during which an employee was on strike is subtracted from his total length of service.

An employee who takes strike action without giving his employer adequate notice of his intentions runs a risk of being sued by his employer for damages for breach of contract. In *Ebbw Vale Steel, Iron & Co. v. Tew*, the defendant was held liable in damages for refusing to work a shift in a mine. The measure of the damages was the value of the coal he would have dug, less the expenses incurred in obtaining it. (See also *NCB v. Galley.*)

The view held by the Donovan Commission was that an employee who gives notice of strike action cannot be regarded as acting in breach of contract, as he has terminated his employment by giving notice to his employer. The employer may nevertheless treat the contract as terminated.

An employer has several options open to him in these circumstances. He may, as most employers do, ignore the legal implications and treat the contract as subsisting, or he may reinstate or re-engage the employee. An employee who is reinstated will be treated as if his employment after the strike ran on without a break from his employment prior to the strike. An employee who is re-engaged will begin a new period of employment from the time he commences work.

An employee who takes strike action, despite having entered into a no-strike agreement (i.e. until an agreed disputes procedure has been followed), is acting in breach of contract, and may not only be dismissed, but also sued for damages for breach of contract. The measure of damages recoverable will be the loss actually suffered by the employer.

Industrial action short of strike action may nevertheless amount to a repudiation of the contract. A work-to-rule (*Secretary of State for Employment v. ASLEF*), or a refusal to deliver goods to a destination 'blacked' by the union, amounts to a breach of the contract and its repudiation by an employee. Notice by an employee that he intends such action is an anticipatory breach of the contract and an employer is entitled to sue for breach of contract on receipt of such notice. The employer can treat the contract as repudiated when the employee's action commences.

Picketing

Picketing is a means by which certain forms of industrial action, especially strikes, can be made more effective. The term is used to describe the actions of a group of workers attempting to:

1 persuade other workers to join a strike or not to deliver goods and services to their employer;
2 prevent 'blacklegs', i.e. substitute labour, from taking the jobs of those workers on strike or those workers who have been dismissed.

The law provides immunity for pickets if the picketing is within the provisions of section 15 of TULRA (as amended by EA 80 s16). This provides that it is lawful for a person in contemplation or furtherance of a trade dispute to attend:

(a) at or near his own place of work; or
(b) if he is a trade union official, at or near the place of work of a member of that union whom he is accompanying and whom he represents, for the

purpose *only* of peacefully obtaining or communicating information, or peacefully persuading any persons to work or abstain from working.

If a person works or normally works at more than one place, or at a place where it is impracticable to picket, his place of work will be any of his employer's premises from which he works, or from which his work is administered. A worker whose employment is terminated in connection with a trade dispute is permitted to picket at his former place of work, but only for as long as he remains unemployed.

A trade union official who has been elected or appointed to represent some members of the union will be regarded as representing only those members. Otherwise a trade union official will be regarded as representing all its members.

Any other form of picketing may render a picket liable to civil or criminal liability.

Civil liability

A picket may be liable for the tort of private nuisance, where he interferes with another's use or enjoyment of land, e.g. blocking an access; or for the tort of trespass to the highway if he uses the highway for any other purpose 'otherwise than reasonably for passage and repassage and . . . any other purpose reasonably incidental thereto' (*Hickman v. Maisey*).

Criminal liability

A picket may commit any of the following offences.

(a) *Obstructing the highway*　An offence is committed if a person without lawful authority or excuse wilfully obstructs free passage along the highway (Highways Act 1980 s137).

In *Broome v. DPP*, a trade union official, having failed to persuade a lorry driver not to deliver goods to a factory where a dispute was in progress, stood in front of the lorry to prevent its progress. He was told by a policeman to move, but refused and was later convicted of obstructing the highway.

(b) *Breach of the peace*　A picket may be found guilty of a breach of the peace if he obstructs a police constable in the execution of his duty. In *Piddington v. Bates*, several pickets arrived outside a factory where a dispute was in progress. Two pickets were stationed at the front gate, and four at the back gate. A police constable asked two of the pickets on the back gate to leave, as he reasonably apprehended a breach of the peace, and they did so. One returned and tried to rejoin the picket line, pushing past the constable, and was arrested. It was held that a policeman may 'take such steps as he thinks proper', and that this includes limiting the number of pickets.

(c) *The Conspiracy and Protection of Property Act 1875* Section 7 provides that a criminal offence is committed if a person wilfully and without legal authority:

(i) uses violence towards or intimidates another person, his wife or children or injures his property;

(ii) persistently follows that person from place to place;

(iii) hides any tools, clothes or other property of such person, or deprives him of their use or hinders their use;

(iv) watches or besets any house where that person resides, or the approach to such house;

(v) follows that person in the street with two or more persons in a disorderly manner.

(d) *Public nuisance* A picket may be guilty of a public nuisance if he obstructs the highway and prevents the public from exercising their lawful right of free passage.

In *Tynan v. Balmer*, the leader of a strike led 40 pickets in an orderly manner in a circle on the road in front of the factory's main gate and effectively prevented traffic from entering the factory. He was asked by a police constable to stop the pickets from circling, and on refusing to do so was arrested. It was held that there was an obstruction of the highway and the pickets had committed a public nuisance.

(e) *Public Order Act 1986*

The Public Order Act 1986 created five new statutory offences which may be invoked during the course of an industrial dispute, should the dispute get out of hand.

(i) *Riot* (s1), where 12 or more people use or threaten to use violence for a common purpose which would cause a person of reasonable firmness to fear for his personal safety.

(ii)   *Violent disorder* (s2), where three or more people use or threaten to use violence for a common purpose which would cause a person of reasonable firmness to fear for his personal safety.

(iii)   *Affray* (s3), where a person uses or threatens unlawful violence towards another and his conduct is such as would cause a person of reasonable firmness present at the scene to fear for his personal safety.

(iv)   *Causing fear or provocation of violence* (s4), by using threatening, abusive or insulting words or behaviour, or distributing or displaying any visual representation which is threatening, abusive or insulting, where the act is intended to make a person fear immediate violence, or is likely to provoke immediate violence.

(v)   *Causing harassment, alarm or distress* (s5), by using threatening, abusive or insulting words or behaviour or displaying any writing, sign or other visual interpretation which is threatening, abusive or insulting within the sight or hearing of a person who is thereby likely to be caused harassment, alarm or distress.

The Act also gives new powers to control marches, processions, demonstrations and public assemblies and to ban marches.

A picket has no right to stop vehicles. He may persuade a driver to stop, but he has no right to make him stop and listen (*Broome v. DPP*).

'One is familiar with persons at the side of the road signalling to a driver requesting him to stop. It is then for the driver to decide whether he will stop or not. That, in my view, a picket is entitled to do. If the driver stops, the picket can talk to him, but only for as long as the driver is willing to listen' (per Lord Reid in *Broome v. DPP*).

Draft Revised Code of Practice on Picketing

The Secretary of State has recently published a draft revised Code of Practice on Picketing. The new Code reflects the changes in the law since the introduction of the previous Code in 1980. It also contains several new recommendations on picketing.

1   Where picketing takes place at a place of work shared by more than one employer, care should be taken not to involve calls for a breach of or interference with the performance of contracts by employees of the other employer(s) not involved in the dispute.

2 Where there is a choice of locations 'at or near the place of work', picketing should be confined to those locations that are as near as practicable to the place of work.

3 A picket should not be designated as 'official', unless it is organised by the trade union and union authority, and support should not be claimed by the pickets if the union has repudiated the action.

4 A new section outlines other torts, apart from the normal trade dispute torts, which may be committed during the course of picketing, e.g. private nuisance to the area's residents, defamation from placards, unlawful harassment.

5 It makes no recommendation as to the maximum number of pickets at any entrance to any workplace, which remains at six.

Secondary picketing

Secondary picketing, i.e. picketing other than at one's place of work is unlawful. Such a picket is generally liable in tort for the consequences of his actions, e.g. he can be sued in tort if he induces workers to break their contracts of employment.

However, peaceful picketing by pickets at their own workplace or former workplace is permitted if they are employees or ex-employees of the employer who is a party to the dispute, unless they are union officials who are accompanying their members.

Abbreviations

See Appendix 1 on page 250

AC	Appeal Cases
A11ER	All England Reports
CA	Court of Appeal
Ch	Chancery
ICR	Industrial Courts Reports
IRLR	Industrial Relations Law Reports
KB	Kings Bench
KIR	Knights Industrial Reports
QB	Queens Bench
WLR	Weekly Law Reports

Appendix 1

TABLE OF CASES

Page references are given in bold type

Appendix 2
MODEL QUESTIONS AND ANSWERS

Question 1

Tom has been employed for six months by a firm, but has not received any details of the terms of his employment. Advise him.

An employer is required to provide an employee with a written statement of the basic terms of employment, within 13 weeks of the commencement of the employment. The statement must give particulars as to the general terms of the employment contract, including hours of work, pay, entitlement to sickness pay, notice etc, and information as to disciplinary matters. The statement does not form part of the contract of employment but is evidence of its terms.

If an employer is unable or unwilling to provide the written statement or certain particulars which should be contained in a written statement, an employee may apply to an Industrial Tribunal which may determine these particulars.

An employer must also provide an itemised pay statement with each payment of wages or salary.

Express terms relating to the contract may also be found in an employer's works' rules. These may be found in a book of rules given to each employee, or a rule book located in the works' office, or they may simply consist of a number of rules relating in the main to disciplinary matters which are pinned to the works' notice board.

The terms of a collective agreement may well provide the express terms of Tom's contract of employment. Although a collective agreement is made between an employer and a trade union its terms may have been expressly or by implication incorporated into employers' contracts of employment (*National Coal Board v. Galley*).

Tom is also entitled to the minimum periods of notice, which are laid down in EPCA s49. An employer must give one week's notice to an employee who is employed for one month but less than two years, and one week for each year of employment up to a maximum of 12 weeks for 12 years.

Question 2

On what principles does the law decide whether an individual is an employee of another?

There are certain tests which have been formulated to help determine whether the employer/employee relationship exists.

The 'control' test rests on the premise that an employer controls what the employee does, the way in which the work is done and where the work should be done. It remains a useful test for certain types of employment, e.g. sales representatives, but is inadequate for modern employment relationships. The greater the degree of control exercised by the employer, the more likely an indication of a contract of service.

The 'organisational' test was formulated to remedy the limitations of the control test. The criterion of this test is whether a worker and his work are an integral part of an organisation. It has proved suitable for cases involving professional employers, e.g. local authorities and health authorities for whose employees the control test was inappropriate, such as nurses and doctors (*Cassidy v. Ministry of Health*).

The organisational test has been largely abandoned in favour of the 'economic reality' or 'multiple' test which relies on practical criteria to establish whether an employment relationship exists or whether the worker is performing services as a person in business on his own account. The test was originally adopted by McKenna J. in *Ready Mixed Concrete (SE) Ltd v. Minister of Pensions and National Insurance*, where he posed three questions.

1 Did the worker provide his own work and skills in return for remuneration?
2 Was there a sufficient degree of control for an employment relationship to exist?
3 Were the other factors consistent with a contract of employment?

Each case will depend on its own particular set of facts, but the following have been considered relevant.

(a) The concept of personal service and control (*Ready Mixed Concrete (SE) Ltd v. Minister of Pensions*).

(b)   The intentions of the parties (*Massey v. Crown Life Insurance Co.*).

(c)   Financial considerations, including the payment of a regular wage or salary. The payment of a regular wage and the provision of sick pay and holiday pay indications are of an employment contract, as is the deduction of income tax on a PAYE basis.

(d)   The delegation of work to others.

(e)   The power of dismissal.

(f)   The hours of work.

(g)   The custom or practice of a particular trade or industry.

Question 3

Consider XYZ's liability for the actions of the following employees.

(a)   William, who is known to be a fast driver, is warned to drive carefully. In the course of a journey he drives too fast and hits a pedestrian.

(b)   Tom, a lorry driver, decides to change his route and makes a detour of 30 miles in order to see his girlfriend. In the course of the detour he collides with a cyclist.

(c)   Albert, a storeman, sees some boys stealing material from the firm's yard. He hits a young boy across the ear, which results in the boy receiving hospital treatment.

There are circumstances where vicarious liability, i.e. substituted liability, is imposed on an employer in respect of torts committed by an employee during the course of his employment.

In order for a third party to recover damages from an employer in respect of the torts of the employee, three conditions must be fulfilled.

1   The wrongful act, i.e. the tort, was committed by the worker.

2   The worker is an employee.

3   The tort occurred during the course of his employment.

The employment status of the worker is determined by applying the various tests formulated to establish the employee relationship.

The act must be committed in the course of employment, i.e. an employee is doing what the employer has authorised him to do even if he chooses a wrongful way of doing it, or the act is not what he is strictly employed to do. In *Limpus v. London General Omnibus Co.* an employee who was racing in a horse-drawn bus committed a wrongful act which had been expressly forbidden. In *Century Insurance v. Northern Ireland Road Transport Board* a lorry driver was negligent when he smoked while transferring petrol from his lorry. In *Lloyd v. Grace Smith* an employee committed a criminal offence, forging documents, while dealing with conveyancing matters relating to a client.

As William is acting within the scope of his employment, although driving fast and negligently, XYZ is liable for the injury to the pedestrian.

If an employee diverts from his job to attend to personal matters that are not within the scope of his employment, the employer is not liable for any damage caused by the employee, i.e. the employee is on a frolic of his own. In *Storey v. Ashton*, two employees on an errand in a cart took a diversion on the return journey and drove in the opposite direction on private business. In the course of that journey they injured a pedestrian. It was held that the employees were driving away from their duty and the employer was not liable.

Tom's deviation from his journey takes him outside the course of employment and therefore XYZ Ltd are not liable to the injured cyclist.

An employee may be acting within the course of his employment if he commits an assault, even though it may amount to a criminal act, if his actions are in furtherance of, or in protection of, his employer's interests. An employee has an implied authority to protect his employer's property in an emergency. In *Poland v. John Parr* a carter hit a boy whom he believed was attempting to steal sugar from the cart. The boy was injured when he fell under the cart and the employer was held liable. An act of personal hostility or retribution on the employee's part will take the act out of the scope of employment, as in *Warren v. Henlys Ltd*, where a petrol pump attendant assaulted a motorist.

Albert's actions in assaulting the boy would most certainly be considered an act to protect XYZ Ltd's property and would be considered to be within the scope of his employment.

Question 4

Spanner plc owns a chain of garages. Consider the legal position relating to the actions of the following employees.

(a) David, a representative, parks his car in a public car park overnight and does not deposit expensive equipment in the car boot, but leaves it on the back seat.

(b) Jack, a mechanic, carries out repairs at cut-price rates in his spare time.

(c) Edward, a car salesman, is given a personal cheque of £50 by a grateful customer after a part-exchange transaction.

(d) Penny, a petrol pump attendant, complains that tax and deductions for stoppages have left her with less than half of her gross pay this month.

(a) An employee is under a duty to take good care of his employer's property that is entrusted to him. In *Superlux v. Plaidsted* an employee parked his van overnight under a street light where its contents of 14 vacuum cleaners was clearly visible. They were stolen and the employee was held liable to re-imburse his employer. David is therefore liable for the theft of the equipment.

(b) An employee is under a general duty to serve his employer loyally and not to undertake any work which would harm his employer's interests. Working for a rival company or competing with one's employer in one's spare time is a breach of this duty. In *Hivac v. Park Royal* employees of a firm who worked in their spare time for a rival competitor were restrained by injunction. A person may, however, work in another capacity for another employer.

Jack could be prevented from carrying out these repairs as he is taking work which might otherwise be given to his employer.

(c)   Employees are under a duty to show good faith to their employers and not to make a secret profit from their employment. In *Boston Deep Sea Fishing Co. v. Ansell* a managing director took a secret commission from a company supplying ships to the Boston Deep Sea Fishing Co. Spanner plc would be able to recover the £50 from Edward and would be entitled to dismiss him without notice. The company would also be entitled to repudiate the contract.

(d)   Section 2 of the Wages Act 1986 stipulates that it is permissible to make a deduction from an employee's wages in respect of cash shortages or stock deficiencies in retail employment, subject to two conditions. Firstly, there must be a contractual agreement for the deduction to be made; and secondly, the deduction must not exceed 10 per cent of the gross wages payable on the day in question. Assuming that there is a clause in Penny's contract of employment allowing deductions to be made, Spanner plc is in breach of the Wages Act in respect of a deduction in excess of 10 per cent of her gross wages. She may complain, within three months, to an industrial tribunal, who may order Spanner plc to reimburse Penny with the amount of the unauthorised deduction.

Question 5

Agnes works as Ted's personal secretary. Ted informs her that she will not be getting a pay rise this year. When she asks the reason, Ted tells her in front of Mary, another secretary, that she is 'bloody incompetent, can't type and doesn't deserve a pay rise'. A week later Agnes hands in her notice, claiming that she has been dismissed. Advise her.

An employee is treated as having been dismissed by an employer if the employee terminates the contract, with or without notice, because of the employer's conduct. This is known as constructive dismissal.

In order to succeed in a claim for constructive dismissal an employee must show that the employer is in fundamental breach of contract which goes to the root of the contract, or no longer intends to be bound by the essential terms of the contract. The point at issue is whether Ted's conduct justifies Agnes tendering her resignation.

The fact that Agnes has not been given a pay rise does not amount to a repudiation of the contract of employment, unless there is an express term in the contract stipulating an annual pay rise, although in *Gardner v. Beresford*, it was stated that an employer should not treat employees arbitrarily, capriciously or inequitably with regard to pay increases.

An employer must treat his staff with dignity and not use foul language. In *Isle of Wight Tourist Board v. Coombes* a director said of his secretary to another employee, 'She is an intolerable bitch on a Monday morning'. The secretary was present at the time. It was held that this destroyed the confidential relationship and she was entitled to resign and claim constructive dismissal.

In *Courtaulds Northern Textiles v. Andrews* an overseer was able to claim constructive dismissal when he was told by an assistant manager that he could not 'do the bloody job anyway'.

The statement made to Agnes would therefore entitle her to treat the contract as repudiated.

It was stated by Lord Denning MR in *Western Excavating Ltd v. Sharp* that in those circumstances an employee may leave immediately or give notice and leave at the end of the notice. He must make up his mind soon after the offending conduct. If he continues for any length of time without leaving he will be regarded as having affirmed the conduct.

Agnes' delay in giving notice would not in these circumstances be taken as an affirmation of the contract and she would be entitled to claim constructive dismissal.

Question 6

Is an employer obliged to provide work for an employee?

As a general rule an employer is not under an obligation to provide work for an employee as long as he continues to pay him the agreed wages. As Asquith J. stated in *Collier v. Sunday Referee Publication Co.*, 'Provided I pay my cook her wages regularly she cannot complain if I choose to take any or all of my meals out'.

There are, however, exceptions to the rule, which recognises that employees are entitled to opportunities to enhance their career prospects or financial prospects in certain types of employment.

In *Collier v. Sunday Referee*, the plaintiff entered into a contract to work as editor for the defendant's newspaper for a fixed period. The paper was subsequently transferred to another newspaper group, who paid Collier his salary but did not provide work. It was held that, as Collier had not been given the opportunity to develop his editorial skills and establish a reputation which might well enhance his future prospects, he was entitled to damages.

In *Clayton & Waller Ltd v. Oliver* an actor who had been promised a leading role in a West End musical was awarded damages for loss of publicity when the offer was withdrawn, although he was to be paid the previously negotiated salary.

It would appear that a claim for the provision of work, as well as the payment of wages, could be established by employees in occupations which are subject to technological skills which can only be maintained with a reasonable amount of work, e.g. a chief engineer (*Breach v. Epsylon Industries Ltd*); a chartered accountant (*Provident Financial Group plc v. Hayward*).

When an employee's remuneration depends on the volume of work provided, e.g. a sales commission, an employer is obliged to provide the work to enable the remuneration to be earned. In *Turner v. Goldsmith* a commercial traveller was employed on a five-year contract and was to be paid on a commission basis. Two years later the employer's factory burned down. It was held that he was entitled to damages on the basis of the amount of commission he would have earned in the remaining three years.

In *Devonald v. Rosser* an employee's wages depended on the number of items he completed. The employers closed down the works where he was employed. It was held that his employer was under a duty to provide him with work during the period of notice.

The modern-day piece worker is often governed by a collective agreement which gives a right to minimum earnings.

Question 7

What is summary dismissal?

Summary dismissal occurs when an employee is dismissed without being given the proper period of notice to which he is entitled under the contract of employment. If there is no justification for the employer's action, such a dismissal is wrongful and an employee may bring an action, at common law, for wrongful dismissal, i.e. for breach of a major term of the employment contract. The measure of damages would be the loss of wages that ought to have been paid during the period of notice.

Whether a summary dismissal can be justified depends on the circumstances of the case, the employee's position and whether the conduct is such 'as to show the servant to have disregarded the essential conditions of the contract of service' (*Laws v. London Chronicle Ltd*). The following cases illustrate situations where summary dismissal was justified.

Sinclair v. Neighbour – where a betting shop manager borrowed money from the till for his own use.
Pepper v. Webb – where a gardener refused to obey a lawful order and was very abusive.
Boston Deep Sea Fishing Co. v. Ansell – where a company's managing director accepted a secret commission.

Turner v. Mason – where a domestic servant asked for, and was refused, permission to visit her dying mother. The servant ignored the prohibition and was dismissed.

A summary dismissal may also be an unfair dismissal within the meaning of EPCA s5, but an employee may not bring an action under both headings.

The importance of the power of summary dismissal has declined in the light of employment legislation and the Code of Practice which lay down the procedures to be followed in dismissal cases. Nevertheless, in certain cases, especially involving theft, an employer may use the ultimate sanction of summary dismissal.

Question 8

ABC Ltd decides to shut down a production line in order to install new machinery as part of a modernisation programme. As the work will take 12 weeks to complete, the employees who work on the production line are laid off, but are told that work will be available when the production line re-opens. Henry, the engineer in charge of production, is offered a post as assistant engineer in another department of ABC Ltd. Consider the rights of Henry and the other employees to a redundancy payment.

The employees appear to have been made redundant by virtue of EPCA s81, which provides that a dismissal is due to redundancy if an employer has ceased to carry on business for the purposes for which the employee was employed. In *Gemmell v. Darngivel Brickworks Ltd* employees were entitled to a redundancy payment even though they were only dismissed from the brickworks for 13 weeks when the factory closed down for repairs to be made to machinery. A temporary cessation of business can therefore amount to a redundancy situation and redundancy payments would be available to those workers. The temporary closure would also amount to a lay-off, which might well give rise to a redundancy payment entitlement, as a lay-off lasting for four consecutive weeks out of the last eight weeks, or any six weeks of the last thirteen, entitles an employee to give notice to the employer of his intention to claim a redundancy payment.

Henry has been made redundant as the employer has ceased to carry on the business for which Henry was employed (EPCA s81), even though the cessation may be of a temporary nature. Henry has, however, been offered alternative employment. If such an offer is deemed suitable and is unreasonably refused by him, he would forfeit his right to a redundancy payment. Consideration will be given to all the aspects of the new employment, including the hours of work, domestic circumstances, remuneration and the status of the new post. Although the remuneration is similar to that of the old post it is doubtful whether it is suitable due to the down grading and the consequent loss of status.

In *Taylor v. Kent County Council*, a redundant headmaster who was offered a post as a supply teacher at the same salary was held to be justified in refusing the post due to the loss of status and authority.

The renewal of employment on different terms also allows an employee a trial period of at least four weeks to decide whether the employment offered is suitable.

Question 9

What rights has an employer in respect of an invention of an employee?

The rights of an employer to an invention made by an employee are governed by the provisions of the Patent Act 1977. According to section 39 of this Act, an invention made by an employee belongs to the employer if it was made during the course of the employee's normal duties which might reasonably be expected to produce an invention; or the employee's responsibilities are such that he is obliged to further the employer's interests. Any other invention made by an employee belongs to him and can be disposed of as he wishes, notwithstanding any term to the contrary in his contract of employment.

In *Reiss Engineering Co. Ltd v. Harris* a manager of a valve department was not employed to design or invent and had no special obligation to further his employer's interests. He invented a new valve. It was held that the invention belonged to him.

Even if the invention belongs to the employer an employee may apply to a court or to the Comptroller of Patents for an award of compensation on the grounds that the patent is of 'outstanding benefit' to the employer and the employee should be compensated for his efforts and entitled to a 'fair share having regard to all the circumstances of the benefit which the employer has derived, or may reasonably be expected to derive, from the patent'.

If an invention belongs to an employee and he assigns his interest to his employer he may nevertheless apply for additional compensation if he can show that he has not been given an adequate financial return in relation to the benefit derived from the patent by the employer.

Question 10

A claim for unfair dismissal will fail if the dismissal is held to be fair. What reasons may an employer put forward to justify a dismissal?

An employer may justify a dismissal on the grounds that he acted reasonably in dismissing an employee for any one of the following reasons.

1   The capability or qualifications of the employee.
2   The conduct of the employee.
3   The employee was redundant.
4   The continued employment of the employee would be in contravention of statute.
5   Some other substantial reason.

When examining a dismissal on the grounds of capability or conduct it is important to consider whether the employee has had time or the opportunity to improve and whether the employer offered re-training or alternative employment. Capability is assessed by reference to skill, aptitude, health or any other physical or mental quality. Qualifications refer to any degree, diploma, or other academic, technical or professional qualification relevant to the position which the employee held.

A sales director who did not achieve the standard of sales expected by the company was fairly dismissed (*Winterhalter Gastronom v. Webb*). An airline pilot whose landing was hazardous and incompetent was fairly dismissed (*Taylor v. Alidair*). An employee with 20 years' service whose work was of poor quality on a single occasion was unfairly dismissed (*Tiptools v. Curtis*). A manager offered re-training at a different location and who refused the offer was held to be fairly dismissed (*Coward v. John Menzies Ltd*).

A dismissal for misconduct not only has regard to conduct in the workplace but also conduct outside working hours. Conduct which has been held to justify dismissal includes dishonesty (*Parker v. Dunn Ltd*); suspected dishonesty (*Whitbread plc v. Thomas*); disobedience (*Kingston and Richmond Health Authority v. Kaur*); sexual misconduct (*Gardiner v. Newport County Borough Council*) etc.

A dismissal for redundancy is a fair dismissal as long as proper procedures are followed and there is no unfair discrimination. If an employer does not follow a set procedure or breaches a customary procedure, the dismissal may be considered unfair (*Williams v. Compair Maxam Ltd*).

An employee may be dismissed if his continued employment contravenes a statutory restriction, e.g. a driving licence requirement when an employee is disqualified from driving (*Appleyard v. Smith (Hull) Ltd*); contravention of food regulations (*Gill v. Walls Meat Co. Ltd*).

'Some other substantial reason' is a general residuary category covering situations which are difficult to catalogue or envisage in standard legislation, e.g. a refusal by an employee to agree to the insertion of a non-solicitation clause in his contract in respect of his employer's clients (*R. S. Components v. Irwin*); a failure to disclose a long history of mental illness in a job application (*O'Brien v. Prudential Assurance Co. Ltd*).

INDEX

OTHER TITLES AVAILABLE
IN TEACH YOURSELF

☐ 0 340 49429 8 **Company Law** £8.99
Colin Thomas

All these books are available at your local bookshop or newsagent, or can be ordered direct from the publisher. Just tick the titles you want and fill in the form below.

Prices and availability subject to change without notice.

HODDER AND STOUGHTON PAPERBACKS, P.O. Box 11, Falmouth, Cornwall.

Please send cheque or postal order for the value of the book, and add the following for postage and packing:

UK including BFPO – £1.00 for one book, plus 50p for the second book, and 30p for each additional book ordered up to a £3.00 maximum.

OVERSEAS, INCLUDING EIRE – £2.00 for the first book, plus £1.00 for the second book, and 50p for each additional book ordered. OR Please debit this amount from my Access/Visa Card (delete as appropriate).

Card Number ☐☐☐☐☐☐☐☐☐☐☐☐☐☐☐☐

AMOUNT £..........................

EXPIRY DATE ....

SIGNED ....

NAME ....

ADDRESS ....

....